Embodying the Way of Jesus

Embodying the Way of Jesus
Anabaptist Convictions for the Twenty-First Century

TED GRIMSRUD

Wipf & Stock
PUBLISHERS
Eugene, Oregon

EMBODYING THE WAY OF JESUS
Anabaptist Convictions for the Twenty-First Century

Copyright © 2007 Ted Grimsrud. All rights reserved. Except for brief quotations in critical publications or reviews, no part of this book may be reproduced in any manner without prior written permission from the publisher. Write: Permissions, Wipf & Stock, 199 W. 8th Ave., Eugene, OR 97401.

ISBN 10: 1-59752-987-7
ISBN 13: 978-1-59752-987-7

Manufactured in the U.S.A.

For Kathleen

Contents

Introduction / 1

PART ONE: Getting Oriented / 7

1. Anabaptism for the Twenty-First Century / 9
2. Whither Contemporary Anabaptist Theology? / 23
3. Constructing an Anabaptist Theology in a Congregational Setting / 37
4. Is God Nonviolent? / 47

PART TWO: Bible / 55

5. Biblical Interpretation: Anabaptist Theology and Recent Hermeneutics / 57
6. The Core Message of the Bible: God's Healing Strategy / 73

PART THREE: Tradition / 89

7. From Sixteenth-Century Anabaptists to Mennonite Church U.S.A. / 91
8. Practice-Centered Convictions: Some Central Themes / 109

PART FOUR: Experience / 125

9. The Significance of Civilian Public Service
for Anabaptist Pacifism / 127
10. Anabaptist Faith and American Democracy / 141
11. Who is Part of the Conversation?
"Neo-Mennonites" and Anabaptist Theology / 161

PART FIVE: Vision / 177

12. Why Are We Here?
Two Meditations on an Ethical Eschatology / 179
13. Theological Basics:
A Contemporary Anabaptist Proposal / 191

PART SIX: Church / 241

14. Rethinking the "Church-Sect" Typology / 215
15. Anabaptist Theologians as Members
of the Community of Faith / 235

Bibliography / 241
Index / 249

Introduction

I STARTED WRITING this book, I suppose, during the summer of 1976—even before I knew anything about Anabaptists or Mennonites. A new graduate from the University of Oregon with a B.S. degree in Journalism, late that June I set off in my Volkswagen bug to see as much of North America as I could in two months.

My senior year in college I had become enamored with the gospel. Having read Dietrich Bonhoeffer's *The Cost of Discipleship* with mounting excitement, I sought to learn as much as I could about the simple but oh so challenging command of Jesus: Take up your cross and follow me.

My initial impetus as a teen-ager to become a Christian had been a deep-seated desire to know truth, genuinely to understand the world and my place in it. I became convinced that committing myself to Jesus would serve that quest for understanding. In college, I had found a small, independent congregation, Orchard Street Church, that gave me a home for this quest. At Orchard, we sought to be a radical Christian community—sharing deeply in all areas of life and witnessing to our wider society. Some of us even decided to join together to buy a house, expecting to "share all things in common" and live out the rest of our lives together.

At this same time, I came to a pacifist commitment. The year I turned 19 (1973), the Draft ended. The Vietnam War wound down by 1975, but discussions about war and military involvement continued. I don't remember many particulars; as far as I know, at the time I was not aware of such a thing as Christian pacifism and knew none who called themselves pacifists. One night, though, I realized I was a *pacifist*—I utterly rejected using violence. This rather mystical awareness stuck—from that moment on, my pacifist commitment became a matter of faith continually seeking understanding.

I had learned of Reba Place Fellowship from a book on Christian communities, and figured a week there would be great preparation for moving into our community household. My visit to Reba Place exceeded my expectations. For the first time, I learned of the Anabaptist tradition and its most numerous present-day representatives, the Mennonites. Reba Place began as a Mennonite fellowship and still drew most of its members from the

Mennonite world. While at Reba Place, I read essays giving a theological basis for Christian community, including a couple from a man I was told was a particularly important Mennonite theologian, John Howard Yoder. I also learned that Mennonites were pacifists and that Yoder was their most prolific writer on pacifism.

When I first learned of the Anabaptist tradition, I was a spiritually energized evangelical Christian, a newly convinced pacifist, and a seeker of close-knit Christian community. My first impression was that here was a living tradition that sought to embody close-knit community and live out a profound commitment to the way of peace. I could not wait to learn more.

Well, after all these years I am still learning! For better and for worse, I have learned that Reba Place Fellowship and John Howard Yoder did not represent all Mennonites, or even necessarily the mainstream of Mennonites. I have learned both that it is not a simple, easy, or automatic thing simply to throw one's lot in with Mennonites and that the impressive ideals of close-knit community and pacifism even themselves have shadow sides.

My adult life and that of my wife Kathleen Temple (whose partnership was the best outcome for me of what proved to be a rather short-lived attempt to form our intentional community in 1976) have been defined by our involvement with Mennonites.

First, we read and discussed Anabaptist theology. We discovered a small (wonderful!) Mennonite congregation in Eugene that eventually became our church home. We next attended Associated Mennonite Biblical Seminary in Elkhart, Indiana (where Yoder was teaching) and while there decided for sure that we wanted to be Mennonites. I served a couple of interim pastorates before we moved on to Berkeley, California, for graduate studies in theology. In the ecumenical environment of the Graduate Theological Union, I reveled in often being the spokesperson for the Anabaptist perspective.

After Berkeley, I spent nine years as a Mennonite pastor, seven of them back in our "home" congregation in Eugene, the others in a shared pastorate with Kathleen in a large, rural congregation in the Mennonite-thick community of Freeman, South Dakota. In 1996, I joined the Bible and Religion faculty of Eastern Mennonite University in Harrisonburg, Virginia.

Graduate school research, congregational teaching and preaching, teaching in an undergraduate liberal arts program, and participation in numerous academic conferences have all provided contexts for reflecting on Anabaptist convictions. Two of the following chapters (five and four-

Introduction

teen) originated as papers in my doctoral program, and one (chapter nine) is drawn from my dissertation. Two others (chapters seven and eight) are adapted from various classes on Anabaptist and Mennonite history and theology I taught in each of the congregations where I pastored. Two chapters (three and eleven) were originally written near the end of two of my pastorates as reflections on my work as a pastor/theologian. The other chapters have been written since I joined EMU's faculty (chapters one and two were written specifically for this book).

All the chapters reflect their original settings to some extent, but most have been significantly rewritten to reflect more my current thinking and to fit more coherently into to the larger book (though in many cases I have been unable to update the research).

I find myself wanting to speak especially to two distinct but increasingly overlapping audiences. One audience would be those involved in Anabaptist communities—most obviously (though not exclusively) Mennonites. These communities do not have a thick tradition of self-conscious theological writing, which was not earlier needed, at least in part due to the sustaining power of close-knit, relatively distinct common life. However, those close-knit ethnic enclaves are increasingly entities of the past. Increased mobility, young people leaving home and not returning, non-Mennonites moving in, the penetration into the communities of outside influences through the media, education, and other forms of acculturation all make the self-conscious articulation of Anabaptist convictions more vital for the sustenance of those convictions.

A second audience would be those from outside the Anabaptist tradition who would like to know more about it. The other side of the acculturation dynamic—the first side being the exposure of Mennonites to non-Mennonite influences just mentioned—has been greater awareness of Mennonites by people on the "outside."

Briefly, I want to define a few key terms and mention a few of my most important intellectual mentors. Probably the most important term is "Anabaptist." I will devote all of chapter one to unpacking what I mean by this word. Here I will just say that by "Anabaptist" I especially have in mind the most relevant theological ideals associated with Christian communities that emerged in the context of the Protestant Reformation of the sixteenth century—ideals that flowed directly from their reading of the story of Jesus.

The most obvious ideal, linked with the practice of adult baptism (from which the label "Anabaptist," or, "re-baptizer," came) was rejecting infant baptism and its link with universal membership in the state church.

These Anabaptists believed baptism and church membership should be free from state control. Probably the most relevant Anabaptist ideal for today, in my view, is the peace position held by many, though not all, in the various communities in the movement—the view that followers of Jesus may not take up arms and use death-dealing violence.

I have already referred to my first and still most important mentor in Anabaptist convictions, John Howard Yoder. Yoder wrote many important books. His central text remains *The Politics of Jesus*, a book I first read in 1975 and that I continue to read annually with great profit. Yoder's *Politics* presents the case that Jesus' message is a message for *this* world, normative for our *social* ethics as Christians, and relevant for *all* cultures and contexts. And this message is at its heart one of active, self-sacrificial, nonviolent love.

As a mentor in Anabaptism, I need also to mention my first Mennonite pastor, Harold Hochstetler, who took me under his wing in the late 1970s. Harold introduced me to key Anabaptist writings and always patiently and perceptively responded to my many questions.

I must also mention my various Mennonite communities as mentors in Anabaptism, especially the various Sunday School classes and study groups in Eugene (Oregon) Mennonite Church, Trinity Mennonite Church (Glendale, Arizona), Salem Mennonite Church (Freeman, South Dakota), Park View Mennonite Church (Harrisonburg, Virginia), and Shalom Mennonite Congregation (Harrisonburg, Virginia), where most of the ideas discussed in this book were first tested.

I self-consciously use the term "convictions" in my sub-title—not "beliefs," "theology," "ideas," "doctrines," or other similar terms that could have been used. I owe this term to another of my teachers, Jim McClendon. McClendon's weighty trilogy, *Systematic Theology: Ethics, Doctrine, Witness*, was completed in 2000 and is becoming known as a unique contribution in doctrinal theology—an approach consistently in a "baptist" mode. McClendon, himself from Southern Baptist background, understood "baptist" to be a rough synonym with "Anabaptist," though more broad and inclusive.

McClendon thought carefully about language (he was deeply influenced by Ludwig Wittgenstein) and has taught me a great deal about the importance of precision and the *practical* meaning of the words we use. In his book *Convictions*, McClendon uses "conviction" as the term for fundamental beliefs. "A conviction means a persistent belief such that if X (a person or community) has a conviction, it will not easily be relinquished and it cannot be relinquished without making X a significantly different person (or community) than before."[1]

So, when I write about "Anabaptist convictions," I will be considering those key theological commitments that make Anabaptists Anabaptists, the relinquishment of which would significantly alter the nature of Anabaptist communities.

By speaking of the twenty-first century in my subtitle, I seek to underscore my concern for the *present* relevance of these convictions as well as to situate my own voice as that of a theologian, ethicist, and pastor rather than historian or social scientist. My concern is how the Anabaptist tradition speaks today, how this tradition may inform *our* convictions.

I will mention two mentors in relation to this point. From Gordon Kaufman, I have been challenged to recognize that *all* theological language is human language, human beings reflecting on ultimate reality, that *we* must take responsibility for *our* convictions *today* regardless of what our forebears said and did in the past, and that the most important criterion for good theology is whether our convictions serve human well-being or not.

And by Walter Wink, I have been challenged to take very seriously our worldviews and to work hard appropriating biblical themes that help illumine the challenges we face as people living amidst the power delusions of the world's one superpower. Wink has profoundly illumined the relevance of Jesus' domination-free way for life in our present.

Both Kaufman and Wink have modeled for me ways theologians might do our work explicitly integrating theological reflection with ethical commitment. Both, in particular, model the application of an overt commitment to nonviolence to constructive theological reflection.

My experience of being part of Anabaptist faith communities has been a creative mixture of walking with numerous Anabaptist/Mennonite friends from the very beginning and bringing my own unique personal (and non-birthright-Mennonite!) individuality into the mix.

My reflections in this book are quite personal; they emerge from *my* experiences, *my* thinking, *my* research. They are articulated in *my* voice. I accept full responsibility for what is included here. But I have *not*, ever, been alone. So I will name a few of my companions—not in order to deflect responsibility but simply in order to express appreciation.

First and last comes Kathleen Temple, my life partner since 1976. She is my best friend and my continual conversation partner. I dedicate this book to her.

---

[1] McClendon and Smith, *Convictions*, 5.

Harold Hochstetler was our first Mennonite mentor. Of the many wonderful other people who graced the fellowship of Eugene Mennonite Church, Mark ("Amos") Keim and Henry Dizney probably helped me learn the most about the ideas articulated in this book. Willard Swartley and John Howard Yoder were two Associated Mennonite Biblical Seminary professors who especially influenced me. David Myers was my fellow AMBS student who had the deepest impact on me. Paul Keim has been the friend with whom I have had the longest sustained conversation, now well more than twenty years and counting. Ray Gingerich, Earl Zimmerman, Howard Zehr, and Christian Early have been my closest colleagues since I have been teaching at Eastern Mennonite University. Finally, our son, Johan Grimsrud and his brilliant wife, Jill Humphrey, with their son Elias, continually keep me honest and continually remind me why seeking to live peaceably and justly in *this* world matters.

PART ONE: Getting Oriented

Our first task will be to get a sense of what we are considering when we reflect on *Anabaptist* convictions. What do we mean by "Anabaptist?" How will we approach the distinctive theology of this type of Christian faith? In Part One, I will explain why I believe the Anabaptist tradition presents an attractive perspective on Christian faith and flesh out my theological method in relation to an embodied peace theology.

Chapter one, "Anabaptism for the Twenty-First Century," proposes that the Anabaptist tradition, with its strong message of dissent in relation to the linking of Christian faith with warfare and power politics so prevalent in contemporary America, might have a special contribution to make to our culture. With Anabaptism, we have a nearly five-century-long tradition of understanding Jesus' message to be one of peace, of separation from the politics of empire, and of upside-down notions of power and economics. This tradition offers a source of encouragement for all Christians who desire a peace-oriented faith.

Chapter two, "Whither Contemporary Anabaptist Theology?," interacts with the recent book by Anabaptist theologian Thomas N. Finger, *A Contemporary Anabaptist Theology: Biblical, Historical, Constructive*. This chapter proposes an approach to Anabaptist theology that emphasizes engagement with real-life issues of the present world.

Chapters three, "Constructing Anabaptist Theology in a Congregational Setting," and four, "Is God Nonviolent?," outline and illustrate outline and illustrate a theological method that understands Anabaptist theology to be a conversation among biblical, historical, and present-day themes that gains its ultimate direction from the faith community's vision of the world to which God calls us. The elements of this method—Bible, history, present experience, and vision—provide the outline for the next four sections of this book.

This Anabaptist-oriented theological method provides a basis for self-consciously articulating a vision for Christian convictions centered on embodying the way of Jesus. My approach is based on my understanding of the core elements of Anabaptism that promise to speak to the twenty-first century. However, I will be going further than most earlier Anabaptists in explicitly describing theological convictions. In doing so, I intend to help readers from outside Anabaptist communities better to understand core Anabaptist convictions. And I intend to help readers from within Anabaptist communities better to articulate their own convictions for the sake of fostering faithful discipleship in our contemporary world that has not shown itself particularly friendly to the traditional ethos of such communities.

CHAPTER ONE

Anabaptism for the Twenty-First Century[1]

Anabaptist Christianity faces opportunities in North America today that may be unprecedented in its nearly five hundred year history. Its core convictions stand in tension with the dominant understandings of Christianity held by people with power and wealth. Especially, the Anabaptist belief and practice of pacifism offers a reading of Christianity that provides an alternative to traditional Christian comfort with militarism and violence. Such beliefs and practices will be attractive to many who believe the needs of our day are for closer adherence to Jesus' way of peace.

In contemporary American culture, religious labels have become increasingly imprecise. Our dominant religion remains Christianity, but what does "Christian" mean?

Until very recently, many modern observers of America have spoken of moving into a *post*-Christian era. However, clearly we have not yet arrived at such a state. Currently, we are in the midst of a revival (of sorts) of the public expression of overt Christian religiosity. High-profile politicians use explicitly Christian language as much as, if not more than, ever.[2] Evangelical and fundamentalist Christians such as James Dobson exercise extraordinary influence over public policy makers.[3]

For those Christians who find their faith calling them to Jesus' way of peace,[4] of resistance to injustice, of exercising strong support for addressing

---

[1] This article is adapted from "Anabaptist Faith for the Twenty-First Century," *Mennonite Quarterly Review* 80.3 (July 2006). Used with permission.

[2] For example, see the evangelical faith of various U.S. governmental leaders described in laudatory articles in the prominent evangelical magazine, *Christianity Today*, including: Blunt, "Condi Rice"; Carnes, "Bush Doctrine"; and Carnes, "Defining Moment."

[3] Crowley, "James Dobson" and MacQuarrie, "Dobson's spiritual."

[4] This essay depends heavily upon John Howard Yoder's articulation of a modern Anabaptist understanding of the message of Jesus and its normative relevance for Christian social ethics. When in the paragraphs that follow, I used terms such as "Jesus-oriented" what I have mind is "Jesus-oriented" along the lines Yoder defines in *Politics of Jesus*. Yoder asserted at the beginning of his classic text that he intended to pursue "the hypothesis that the ministry

the needs of vulnerable people, of a desire for more mercy and less retribution, the current scene is profoundly challenging. Such Christians see the very basis for their core convictions—the Bible (which they read as centered on Jesus' message)—being associated in the public eye with policies and rhetoric and values that they abhor.

What is presented as the "biblical" or "Christian" view, by common popular agreement among people who both agree and disagree with it, seems to include support for the wars and militarism of the United States[5] and for capital punishment and a harshly retributive criminal justice system.[6]

So, what do Jesus-oriented Christians in America do? If they cede Christianity to those who are pro-military and pro-death penalty, they cut themselves off from the taproot of their own meaning system and spiritual empowerment. If they explicitly affirm their Christian convictions, they run the risk of being lumped in the public eye with these prominent expressions of "Christianity" that so contradict their reading of the gospel message.

The Relevance of Anabaptism

Our time of anxiety, uncertainty, and contention concerning the viability of Jesus-oriented Christian faith actually may provide heirs of the sixteenth-century Anabaptists[7] an important opportunity. The time may be right to present Anabaptism as an important resource for articulating an alternative style of Christianity in a culture that too-often associates Christian faith with domination.[8]

---

and the claims of Jesus are best understood as presenting to hearers and readers not the avoidance of political options, but one particular social-political-ethical option" (11). In a nutshell, Yoder characterized the option Jesus presented as "an ethic marked by the cross, a cross identified as the punishment of a man who threatens society by creating a new kind of community leading a radically new kind of life" (53).

[5] For a pro-militarist America critique of pacifism see Pavlischek, "Vital Center" and Skillen and Pavlischek, "Political Responsibility."

[6] See Ballard, "Death Penalty."

[7] See below, chapter seven, for more historical description of the original Anabaptist movement and its immediate descendants.

[8] See Gish, *New Left*, for a perceptive attempt to link the Anabaptist tradition with the countercultural politics of the 1960s. John Howard Yoder cited Gish approvingly in *The Politics of Jesus* (page one, footnote one), and I see my argument being somewhat parallel to Gish's perspective. However, as Yoder does, I too mostly seek to draw on the message of *Jesus* as the basis of my proposal—and Anabaptism as an important application of Jesus' message. That is, my concerns are not intended so much to be reduced to "leftist" partisan politics as to be an attempt to apply the *perennially* normative "politics of Jesus" to early twenty-first-

I want to reflect, as a theological ethicist and pastor, on how pacifist, Jesus-oriented Christians might best draw on the Anabaptist story for inspiration and guidance for their witness in our current highly militarized environment in twenty-first-century America—and especially in face of the association in the public eye of this militarism with Christianity.

What do I mean by "Anabaptist"? I will not equate the term "Anabaptist" with "Mennonite," though they are closely related. The Mennonite tradition evolved directly from the first Anabaptists of the sixteenth century and remains the most visible and widespread embodiment of the fruits of the Radical Reformation. However, "Mennonite" seems too narrow a term for a perspective that will help a wide range of pacifist, Jesus-oriented Christians to affirm and witness to their faith in *contrast* to imperial Christianity.

"Mennonite" refers to a specific denomination with limited relevance for those not part of that denomination. I seek a label with broader appeal that in some sense might be relevant to people with similar convictions from other traditions—be they near "relations" to Mennonites such as Church of the Brethren, more distant "cousins" such as Baptists or Disciples of Christ, or even more distant "cousins" such as Lutherans, Presbyterians, and Roman Catholics.

The term "Anabaptist" may be closely linked with a concrete embodiment (which is important for my purposes, showing how a set of convictions works on the ground) in the Mennonite tradition, yet also may speak more of vision and ideals and be freer from being reduced to denominational specificity than "Mennonite." "Anabaptist" may be seen as more amenable to being linked directly to the way of Jesus, having a sense of transcendent ideals *combined* with concrete embodiment.

So what is "Anabaptism" and how might it contribute to a renewal of peace-oriented Christianity in the twenty-first century? To answer this question, we will be helped by looking at the development of the modern use of the term.

Though the term "Anabaptist" (literally meaning "re-baptizer") dates back to the sixteenth century, only in the past sixty years has it gained wide currency as a *positive*, self-affirming label. Mennonite historian Harold Bender, in his famous 1943 presidential address to the American Society of Church History, entitled "The Anabaptist Vision," played a major role in transforming the term. Bender provides what is still a useful perspective on the term "Anabaptism."

Bender boiled the Anabaptist vision down to three basic convictions. "First and fundamental in the Anabaptist vision was the conception of

---

century North America.

the essence of Christianity as discipleship."[9] Anabaptists saw Christian faith as requiring outward expression, the response to God's grace with the "application of that grace to all human conduct and the consequent Christianization of all human relationships."[10] While this first point certainly reflected traditional Mennonite self-understandings, Bender's use of the rubric "discipleship" actually was new—he himself had previously used the term "holiness of life."[11] The language of "discipleship" added rhetorical force to the vision.

"A second major element in the Anabaptist vision [was] voluntary church membership based upon true conversion and involving a commitment to holy living and discipleship."[12] Bender saw the rejection of infant baptism that gave the movement its name as stemming from this view of the church. In the Anabaptist view, the church is to be made up of people self-consciously seeking to follow Jesus in *all* areas of life. The Anabaptists vision for transformed life at its heart was a vision for a new kind of church, in which all members lived lives of deeply committed discipleship.

"The third great element in the Anabaptist vision was the ethic of love and nonresistance as applied to all human relationships."[13] Bender supports this point with quotes from Anabaptist leaders representing Mennonite and Hutterite streams, and from all three geographical centers of early Anabaptism—Switzerland, Holland, and South Germany/Austria. He goes on to make what came in time to be a controversial assertion, that "Biblical pacifism . . . was thoroughly believed and resolutely practiced *by all* the original Anabaptist Brethren and their descendants throughout Europe from the beginning until the last century."[14]

So, "Anabaptism," as defined by Bender, included at its core seeing discipleship as central to Christian faith, basing church membership on true conversion and a commitment to follow Jesus in life, and seeking to shape the life of discipleship around pacifism. This basic definition remains useful, even if we must take care in how we use it.

---

[9] Bender, "Anabaptist," 42.
[10] Bender, "Anabaptist," 43.
[11] Keim, *Bender*, 326.
[12] Bender, "Anabaptist," 47.
[13] Bender, "Anabaptist," 51.
[14] Bender, "Anabaptist," 52 [emphasis added].

Particiating in the Anabaptist Tradition

The spirit of the sixteenth-century Anabaptist movement, following on the spirit of the first-century Jesus movement, inspires those who see themselves as Anabaptists today. Baptist theologian James McClendon provided a helpful perspective on what links these three moments (and many others). We have to do with *one* on-going story. When we participate now in the story of Jesus, in some sense we are present with him, "this is that," it is the same story (e.g., Jesus challenging the temple-merchants, the sixteenth-century Anabaptists refusing to take up arms against the Turk, our own resistance to widespread violence in twenty-first-century America).[15] So we cannot, *should not want to*, simply treat past expressions of the story as mere artifacts of the past.

Hence, present-day Anabaptists are in sync with the spirit of the sixteenth-century Anabaptist movement when they consider the movement as *participants* in the same story, recognizing that they do not stand outside of it as "neutral." The kinds of questions participants will ask of the story by definition will be at least somewhat different from non-participants' questions. And the questions asked will inevitably shape how the story is retold.

At the same time, present-day appropriation of the sixteenth-century Anabaptist story is not served by airbrushing objectionable elements out of the story.

Present-day Anabaptists seeking to witness to peace in our current context will want to avoid a narrow, ideological reading that mainly serves to reinforce their biases. They will also be wary of a neutral, objectivist reading that by blinding them to their own biases actually also serves to reinforce those biases. A third path may be found through the affirmation of a hermeneutical-circle type of approach. I will describe this third path with reference to the thought of German philosopher Hans-Georg Gadamer,[16] though various other ways of describing the participatory interpretive process would also be appropriate.

We may think of the sixteenth-century Anabaptist materials as one horizon, or one particular perspective with its own concerns and biases. A second horizon is ours in the present, our perspective with our own concerns and biases. We will only be able to access the voice of the distant horizon by bringing it into conversation with our own horizon. We will only be able to gain understanding from the sixteenth-century horizon by being

---

[15] McClendon, *Ethics*, 33. "The . . . 'is' in 'this is that' is . . . neither developmental nor successionist, but mystical and immediate."

[16] In particular, I draw on *Truth and Method*.

conscious of our own biases. We recognize that our questions—which are required in order to hear the other story at all—cannot help but reflect our biases, our agenda that arises out of our own particular life-setting.[17]

Gadamer insists, though, that to recognize and affirm our biases need not lead us down the path of only seeing that which reinforces those biases. The key is truly to be attentive to what the other is actually saying. When we genuinely listen, we will find ourselves revising our assumptions in light of what we hear. True understanding happens when we walk a fine line, use our particularity to provide access to the particularity of the other and then transcend our particularity to hear the other as other.[18]

Historical research, in uncovering and describing the materials that give us access to the Anabaptists, provides an absolutely necessary service for our contemporary appropriation and application of the sixteenth-century Anabaptist story. However, all historians too have biases (their own questions that guide their research) shaping which materials they describe and how they describe them. Sometimes historians' questions may be different than ours in pacifist, Jesus-oriented Anabaptist communities. Ultimately, present-day Anabaptists are not accountable to definitions of meaning and relevance from within the discipline of academic history nearly so much as to the needs and interests of present-day Anabaptist communities. At the same time, historical research does serve to help us avoid mistaking *our* biases for sixteenth-century Anabaptists' (even when these biases overlap a great deal).

We may forego Harold Bender's apparent desire to set up boundary lines for determining valid expressions of Anabaptism (past *and* present) while still valuing his summary of the vision. If we think of such a summary more as a basis for conversation, inspiration, and guidance, an aid for fostering clarity of self-identification, and a provisional definition for interested seekers, we may see value in trying to emulate his efforts.[19]

Bender's own three-point summary retains much that is commendable, and the suggestions I will make below overlap with his in significant ways. I propose that we are best suited to think of "Anabaptism" as a *herme-*

---

[17] To be clear about my own biases, *I* write as a committed pacifist who seeks to follow Jesus' model of resistance to the powers of death and violence. I read the Anabaptists to gain guidance and inspiration for this approach to life.

[18] For more on Gadamer, see chapter six below.

[19] See an example of such a useful presentation of the sixteenth-century Anabaptists in John Howard Yoder's chapter, "A Summary of the Anabaptist Vision," in Dyck, *Introduction*, 136–45.

neutic.[20] By "hermeneutic" here I mean an interpretive framework, a set of values and convictions that guide how we see our world.

The content of this framework, the source of these convictions, emerges initially and most formatively from the story of Jesus. The sixteenth-century Anabaptists and their successors sought to embody Jesus' way and certainly understood themselves to be subject to the Jesus story. Consequently, those who draw on the sixteenth-century Anabaptists appropriately value that from the sixteenth century most closely linked with the Jesus story.[21]

The category "Anabaptist" has in some sense *always* been a construct, a kind of heuristic device. From 1525 on, no concrete entity existed with the self-identity of "Anabaptist" and clear markers of who belonged to this entity "Anabaptist" or not. In fact, in many ways up until Bender's rehabilitation work, "Anabaptism" was a *negative* term for the Catholics' and mainstream Protestants' most hated enemies—and not a term Mennonites, Amish, or their close spiritual relatives commonly used of themselves.

Since 1943, as reflected in Bender's own essay and in myriads of *different* definitions of "Anabaptist" by historians and theologians, the term has been fluid. So, there is no historically objective entity "Anabaptist" that has ever existed as such. All there ever has been are various attempts to apply a modern definition to a variety of people with no formal over-arching unity. Hence, I am not claiming to have *the* Anabaptist Vision—just one perspective for the conversation, shaped by peace concerns.[22]

Because of the fluid nature of the category "Anabaptist," we are free to recognize that it *is* an appropriate term for phenomena that extend beyond the first half of the sixteenth century. It is an ideal type, a creation of the

---

[20] In this statement I am following John Howard Yoder in his essay, "Anabaptist Vision and Mennonite Reality." He wrote, "what is meant here by the label 'Anabaptist' is not a century but a hermeneutic. It is represented for certain types of discussion by the sixteenth-century movement, but it can be valid apart from that particular period" (in Yoder, "Anabaptist," 5).

[21] For instance, on the issue of pacifism, present-day Anabaptists are not bound by "loyalty" to historical objectivity to argue that Anabaptism was not pacifist due to the existence of scattered non-pacifist sixteenth-century Anabaptists. To a large (and, given the context, quite impressive) extent, the Anabaptist movement as a whole in its early years did embody Jesus' way of peace. The affirmation of pacifism as central to Anabaptism, then, is a synthesis of evaluating the Anabaptists in light of the Jesus story, recognizing the impressive (though not universal) embodiment of pacifism in those early years, and a conviction that both in the years since 1540 and in our present, pacifism stands as an extraordinarily high priority. See Yoder, *Christian*, chapter 10, "Anabaptism in the Continental Reformation."

[22] For more on these concerns, see chapter ten below and Grimsrud, "Negotiating Democracy."

interpreter meant to foster understanding. We seek to correlate our "type" as closely as possible to the actual events of history, but recognize that we must always hold it lightly, guarding constantly against the tendency to reify the type and mistake it for actual reality. The ideal type is meant to serve understanding, to aid in interpretation, not to define actual reality.

Thinking of Anabaptism as a hermeneutic, shaped by the sixteenth-century story but dynamically and continually applicable to present reality, for the purpose of perceiving and practicing how to live in the context of the *on-going* story of Jesus' way of peace, fits with how the term has actually always functioned.

Anabaptism for Twenty-First-Century Americans

What I will outline below is intended to reflect just *one* perspective on how to participate in the Anabaptist story. Hopefully, it may stimulate thoughts and conversations drawing on *other* perspectives.

As we work at articulating an Anabaptist vision applicable for early twentieth-first-century Americans, we start with reflections on *our* situation. What kinds of guidance do we need? What issues shape the questions we ask of the Anabaptist tradition? To ask what is relevant for us from the Anabaptist tradition is to ask: what resources might we find in the tradition to help us face creatively and faithfully the challenges, even crises, of our day?

We certainly have plenty of crises demanding our attention. The following examples are not suggested with the assumption that Anabaptism promises to solve them. Nor should we think that Anabaptism should be seen primarily as a tool for determine public policy in secular nations such as the United States and Canada. It is in the spirit of the biblical prophets that we may see Anabaptist convictions as providing bases for critiquing social currents that contradict God's intentions for shalom-shaped human living.

The world's ecological balance has been profoundly upset, as seen in problems such as global warming, air and water pollution, toxic wastes, extinction of ever-increasing numbers of species, depletion of wildlife populations. Millions upon millions of people are living in abject poverty in a world increasingly becoming a "planet of slums" as neo-liberal economics continues to drive formerly subsistence farm families off the land.[23]

The United States expands its militarism as the world's only superpower, reaching the point of spending roughly as much on the military

---

[23] See Davis, *Planet*.

as the whole rest of the world combined—a shocking outcome following "victory" in the Cold War and the elimination of any major military rivals. Such militarism requires expression, and the United States' in the winter of 2005–6 is centered on the invasion and occupation of Iraq—an excursion that surely has reached the "quagmire" state.[24]

Within the United States, we have in recent years seen the myth of secularism shattered with the stunning emergence of right-wing Christianity as a major political and cultural force. Many Anabaptist Christians (and Christians of various other stripes) worry that right-wing Christianity is dealing the Christian faith a serious body blow in its linking of Christianity so closely with what seem to be anti-democratic public policies and governmental policies.

As traced in Thomas Frank's book, *What's the Matter with Kansas? How Conservatives Won the Heart of America*, politicians beholden to the powers of wealth and militarism have exploited the vulnerability of right-wing Christians to be manipulated based on their religiously based views. Such politicians use issues such as abortion and homosexuality to gain support from conservative, working-class Christians, and then proceed to enact policies that undermine the livelihoods and communities of these same Christians.

What kinds of questions for the Anabaptist tradition emerge from our present context? How may these crises I have mentioned, and others unmentioned, shape our appropriation of the resources of our faith story?

Modern-day American Anabaptists should see themselves as, to some degree at least, sharing the sixteenth-century Anabaptists' sense both (1) of separating themselves from many of the basic values of the wider society, especially those that under gird violence and domination and are underwritten by Christian rhetoric, and (2) of witnessing *against* that violence and domination, making known as widely as possible the peaceable message of Jesus.[25]

In sharing such a sense of separation and call to witness, modern-day Anabaptists might focus first of all on the elements of the early Anabaptist movement that led to their getting in trouble with the established churches and governments of Western Europe. Such a starting point is not an anachronistic imposing of a twenty-first-century agenda onto a sixteenth-century

---

[24] See several examples from across the political spectrum: from a former member of the United States foreign policy establishment, Johnson, *Sorrows*; from a long-time critic of U.S. foreign policy, Chomsky, *Hegemony*; and from a self-described conservative Republican, Bacevich, *Militarism*.

[25] See Gingerich, "Mission Impulse," for a presentation of this passion for such witness on the part of the first Anabaptists.

context. In fact, perhaps the main commonality of the various groups of Anabaptists, with all their differences, beyond practicing adult baptism was that they almost all got into trouble, almost all were persecuted, almost all faced the genuine possibility of martyrdom.

This tendency to get into trouble for their faith was one of the main "this-is-that" elements of their own self-perception. By getting into trouble they linked back with Jesus. Scholars today are recognizing that one of our keys to understanding Jesus and his ministry is to ask what it was that he did to get into so much trouble.[26] Consequently, in considering the Anabaptists as continuing in the story of Jesus, we will understand that this is a logical question to ask of them as well. If we consider what kinds of things got the Anabaptists in trouble we might actually find both important elements of commonality among the groups of the sixteenth century *and* direction concerning their relevance for us today.

Many present-day American Mennonites and other Anabaptists have gained a level of comfort and prosperity heretofore uncommon in the Anabaptist tradition. Is it possible that our present social location may contribute to a reluctance to risk "getting into trouble"? Present-day Anabaptists face a challenge of discernment. Are we reluctant to risk prophetic critique and engagement because of a legitimate concern about the need to provide a biblically faithful alternative to polarizing "partisan politics"? Or is our reluctance more due to a desire to avoid the precise kinds of risks biblical prophets and sixteenth-century Anabaptists took in confronting the powers-that-be in their day? [27]

Four central characteristics of the sixteenth-century Anabaptists may be seen as directly linked to their being attacked by the powers-that-be and as potentially constituting the core of an Anabaptist Vision for twenty-first-century America. These four characteristics overlap a great deal with Bender's three core characteristics from 1943.[28]

---

[26] See Wright, *Jesus,* and Herzog, *Jesus.*

[27] See Roth, "Called," along with the various responses, for stimulating reflections on these issues.

[28] For a similar summary, see Klaassen, "Who," 6. The sixteenth-century Anabaptists "challenged virtually everything their Christian culture took for granted. They rejected all religious coercion and insisted that governments had no role in the internal life of the church. They rejected the emerging capitalist economic system primarily because it discriminated against the poor and defenseless. They refused to accept any justification for the use of force and killing in defense of the gospel. They paid an extremely high price for the baptism of believing adults, because it was against the law and often carried the death penalty. If we in North America are going to call ourselves Anabaptists, it would seem we ought to resemble them in some way."

(1) The Anabaptists established themselves as a church *free* from state control and from the dominance of the state churches. In the debates that led to the first Anabaptist baptisms in January 1525, the issue was framed as one of whether they would accept the state's demand that they limit their push for reform by continuing to baptize infants. The Anabaptists saw infant baptism linked with the lifelong membership of all citizens in the state church, signaling to them the subordination of the faith community to the political structures. Such subordination would, in their view, compete with their highest priority on following Jesus' way.

By breaking with the state-church and refusing to submit to the state's domination expressed through infant baptism, Anabaptists were not simply guilty of heresy; they committed sedition, *rebellion*, a capital offense. They were executed by both Catholics and Protestants; to all of Western Europe they were rebels.

(2) A second and closely related reason the Anabaptists got into trouble was their refusal to participate in or even support the state's wars—especially in the sixteenth century, wars with the Muslim Turks invading from the south. For the first fifteen years or so following 1525, the Anabaptists were not universally pacifist.[29] However, though the debates continue in our day among historians, the evidence does point to strong support for pacifism among most Anabaptists following the Schleitheim Confession's explicit rejection of the sword in 1527 and the martyrdom of the one overtly non-pacifist Anabaptist leader, Balthasar Hubmaier, in 1528.[30]

The other main context for Anabaptists using violence was the infamous incident in the city of Münster in 1534–35. The devolution of the Anabaptist rule of that city following their nonviolent gaining of power, when in the face of a brutal siege from Catholic forces the desperate and increasingly deranged people in the city resorted to violent self-defense, stood as an unique event in the entire Anabaptist movement. The events at Münster actually served to push the movement as a whole even more in the direction of pacifism. On the heals of Münster, a former Catholic priest named Menno Simons ascended to leadership among the Dutch Anabaptists and overtly guided them in pacifist directions.

A common complaint against the Anabaptists was that they were refusing to take up arms to defend their nations—especially to defend Christian Europe from the Turks. In doing so, they threatened the security and well

---

[29] As documented by Stayer, *Anabaptists and the Sword*.

[30] See Yoder, *Christian*, chapter 10.

being of their societies. As Walter Klaassen writes, "Refusal to fight meant that one was ready to let the infidel conquer Christian Europe."[31]

(3) A third characteristic indicative of a counter-cultural sensibility that posed a threat to the cultural consensus was the Anabaptists' upside-down sense of social power and hierarchy.

German Mennonite historian Hans-Jürgen Goertz argues that the main commonality for the various Anabaptist groups was their anticlericalism, their rejection of church hierarchies and top-down leadership.[32] This stance of deep suspicion towards established power dynamics was a source of conflict between the Anabaptists and their society. Though, before long, Anabaptists established their own internal hierarchies and suffered under authoritarian leadership (witness the "banning wars" in mid-sixteenth-century Holland), they remained suspicious toward the powers-that-be in the state-church and government.

(4) A fourth characteristic is the alternative economics that characterized Anabaptist communities. They valued economic *sharing*, supporting people in need in their communities rather than the accumulating of wealth that at the same time was driving nascent capitalism and the emergence of European empire building with the "discovery" of the New World.

While only the Hutterites self-consciously instituted thoroughgoing community of goods, all Anabaptist groups worked at mutual aid and wide-ranging sharing of wealth.[33] These practices ran against the grain of the broader society and occasioned much scorn and criticism from those outside the Anabaptist movement.

All four of these core characteristics remain of great relevance for the articulation of an Anabaptist Vision for today's American Anabaptists. In what follows, my intention is mainly to speak to the calling of pacifist, Jesus-oriented Christians to witness to the way of restorative justice and transformative peace and to resist the dehumanizing dynamics of the "spirit of our age" in twenty-first-century North America. I am not advocating an attempt to impose Christian values from the top down on an unbelieving society. I write in a spirit meant to reflect A.J. Muste's response to being questioned about whether he undertook his political protests because he truly thought he could change governmental policies. He said he protested not so much because he expected to change those policies but because he did not want those policies to change him.[34]

---

[31] Klaassen, *Anabaptism*, 2d ed., 50.

[32] Goertz, *Anabaptists*.

[33] Stayer, *German*.

[34] See McNair, "War."

In a time of trumpet-blowing nationalism that underwrites imperialism as a "Christian" duty, for Anabaptists to insist on a reading of the Jesus story that names nationalism as *idolatry* certainly might lead to trouble. When this trumpet-blowing nationalism rallies behind the invasion and violent occupation of another nation (in our present case, Iraq), outspoken witness to a faith that *rejects* warfare might well seem seditious.[35]

In face of a national political culture that through absolutist assertions of power by leaders, closely-guarded secrecy of policy deliberations, strong efforts to institute one-party rule, and seeking to intimidate and thereby silent media scrutiny,[36] moves ever closer to authoritarianism, to insist that genuine power flows from the bottom up goes strongly against the grain.

As our economic system continues to extract wealth from the world's poor that flows into the hands of the wealthy and powerful in the name of "free trade," and "privatization," and to empower corporations to seek the lowest possible labor costs, for Anabaptist Christians to reiterate their convictions concerning economic sharing, simplicity, and accumulating wealth is to witness against some of the most tenaciously "religious" beliefs in our culture.[37]

These examples illustrate that the core Anabaptist convictions maintain an undiminished relevance. Communities seeking to embody this vision may also face at least some of the same kinds of hostility from the dominant culture that sixteenth-century Anabaptists did. Hence, to consider following this path also requires taking seriously the need to cultivate various sources of encouragement, solidarity, and hopefulness. These sources certainly include at their heart a critical mass of similarly committed people to stand with one another.

The calling to live in the Anabaptist tradition is a rigorous calling. If "Anabaptism" is linked with Anabaptists of sixteenth-century history, it will never be used simply to evoke some vague positive feelings. The historical specificity of actual Anabaptism is a specificity of genuine commitments that generally required a self-conscious counting the costs of living out convictions seen as heretical and treasonous by the people with power to arrest, to injure, even to execute.

---

[35] Witness the inflammatory post-9/11 statement by Washington *Post* columnist Michael Kelly that pacifism is "objectively evil," "Pacifist."
[36] On the media, see Alterman, *What*.
[37] See Loy, "Religion" and Cox, "Market."

The Contemporary Challenge

Many different kinds of Christians may draw guidance, inspiration, and hope from the witness of the Anabaptist tradition. In the sixteenth century, as in the first century, various political, cultural, and religious dynamics coalesced creatively to say "no!" to religion linked with political authoritarianism. In both settings, courageous and far-sighted peaceable communities emerged—amidst great suffering—to witness to an alternative to domination and power politics.

The early years of the twenty-first century call for nothing less. American Anabaptists have a responsibility not only to witness to Jesus' gospel of peace to the wider "secular" world, but also to their fellow Christians. Such a witness may both challenge easy generalizations that link Christianity with U.S. imperialism and retributive justice *and* provide a rallying point of encouragement for other Christians who share Anabaptists' convictions concerning peace, freedom from state domination, and upside-down views of power and economics.

In drawing overtly on Anabaptism, present-day Jesus-oriented Christians may bring together both a set of ideals clearly connected with prophetic biblical faith (especially as taught and lived by Jesus) and an actual embodied tradition that has sought to live in the real world based on those ideals.

Certainly, the living out of Anabaptist convictions since the sixteenth century in Mennonite, Hutterite, and Amish communities (and those of related groups) has reflected some faithfulness and some unfaithfulness to gospel ideals. Those ideals are not negated by the unfaithfulness of actual Anabaptists. The ideals remain a living challenge—always calling those who profess them to greater faithfulness. Nonetheless, that these ideals *are* livable (if only partially) is borne out by the many examples of faithfulness across the generations.

The twenty-first-century American heirs of sixteenth-century Anabaptism face great opportunities and responsibilities. A creative, living relationship with their tradition remains necessary to their calling.

CHAPTER TWO

Whither Contemporary Anabaptist Theology?

During the last half of the twentieth century and now into the twenty-first, North American Anabaptists have sought to address the need for more self-conscious articulation of their distinctive convictions as a means of sustaining their tradition. Perhaps for the first time in the now nearly five hundred years since the first Anabaptists, we have an abundance of intellectually-rigorous, overtly-expressed doctrinal theology being written by Anabaptists.

Among many factors that have stimulated this production, certainly a key one follows from a sense that with modernity leading into postmodernity, we have seen a weakening of the tradition-sustaining communal environments that made it possible for Anabaptist convictions to survive without much more sophisticated, self-consciously constructed doctrinal theology.

However, the question of how best to articulate theological convictions that reflect the core commitments of Anabaptists remains vital and contested. One of the central players in the writing of contemporary theology in an Anabaptist perspective, Thomas N. Finger, in 2004 published a massive contribution to this conversation. In the context of interacting with Finger's thought in this chapter, I will make a proposal for an Anabaptist approach to doctrinal theology that seeks to reflect the intellectual implications of distinctive characteristics of Anabaptist Christianity.

I understand these central characteristics to be centered in an integration of theological convictions with ethical practices. The ethical commitments of the sixteenth-century Anabaptists such as their pacifism, their emphasis on economic sharing, and their rejection of the subordination of the church to nation-states, reflected a *distinctive theology* that placed central importance on commitment to the way of Jesus in costly discipleship.

Finger helps us a great deal in understanding the central characteristics of Anabaptist theology. However, I will suggest that in his decision to frame his theological proposal within the general approach of mainstream Christian theology (which has *not*, as a rule, placed ethical faithfulness to the way of Jesus at the center of theological reflection), he risks minimizing the theological convictions that may be the most important contribution Anabaptists have to make the Christian existence in twenty-first-century North America.

Finger joins with others who have sought to construct Anabaptist theology in ways that stress commonalities with mainstream Christian theology and place major importance on drawing on the post-biblical (and, maybe even more so, the post-fourth century) dogmatic theological tradition and on centering more on the internal rituals of Christian communities. These emphases may threaten to diminish the potential of theology in the Anabaptist tradition to recover the core ethos of the biblical portrayal of the life of faith.

Tom Finger's Project

A longtime professor at Eastern Mennonite Seminary, an ordained Mennonite pastor, one of the most prolific serious Mennonite theologians of his generation, active participant as a Mennonite representative in various ecumenical endeavors (including serving as an official observer to the World Council of Churches), Tom Finger has made distinguished contributions to the theological life of the Mennonite tradition throughout the course of his career.

Finger's book, *A Contemporary Anabaptist Theology: Biblical, Historical, Constructive*, provides what will surely be a widely referenced approach to Anabaptist theology, both of the sixteenth century and in our contemporary North American setting. Certainly Finger has made an important contribution to theological work within the Anabaptist community with this book, but he also has offered to the wider Christian community an entrée into Anabaptist thought.

Few contemporary theologians have read the sixteenth-century sources as widely. Finger investigated for himself what the sixteenth-century Anabaptists actually said. And few have read as widely in twentieth and twenty-first-century Anabaptist/Mennonite theology. Finger's work is a pioneering effort to try to provide an analysis of the contemporary ferment.

Finger stands with feet firmly planted both in the Anabaptist and the broader ecumenical worlds. An adult convert to the Mennonite faith, he brings wide ecumenical connections to the task. Yet he has also been deeply immersed in Anabaptist communities for several decades.

Finger also cares deeply for peace and justice as a committed pacifist, committed to ecological healing,[1] and committed to following Jesus' way and doing theology in light of that commitment. However, these commitments do not becloud Finger's ability to listen respectfully to and learn from the whole spectrum of Christian theological frameworks.

The book begins with a brief summary of key aspects of the sixteenth-century Anabaptist movement based on up-to-date scholarship, followed by a summary of currents in recent historiography. Next comes a groundbreaking description of what Finger calls "Contemporary Approaches to Theology in Anabaptist Perspective."

In sketching the present scene, Finger's concerns are *theological*. He states, "since I am mainly concerned with comprehensive theologizing, I will chiefly consider authors who have completed at least one work of this kind or who often addressed this task otherwise."[2] He focuses on formal doctrines, understandings of personal salvation, and church rituals.

The heart of the book contains in-depth discussions of six themes that presumably constitute what Finger sees as Christianity's core convictions. These are: (1) the personal dimension (personal salvation and justification theology), (2) the communal dimension (the community of faith especially focused on baptism, the Lord's Supper, church discipline, and economic sharing), (3) the missional dimension (evangelism and responses to the world), (4) Jesus and divine reality (doctrines of the person and work of Jesus Christ and the Trinity), (5) human nature (theological anthropology), and (6) the last things (eschatology).

Finger follows the same outline for each theme. He begins by summarizing sixteenth-century Anabaptist views, then he describes and critiques contemporary Anabaptist discussions of his themes. He concludes each chapter by articulating his own constructive proposal.

Finger understands one of the central elements of *Anabaptist* theologizing to be a concern with integrating belief and practice, not simply focusing on disembodied ideas. Finger expresses this concern by suggesting at that since Anabaptist theology emerged among people on the margins of their societies, it might have special relevance today for reflecting theologically about present-day situations of marginalization.

---

[1] Finger, *Self, Earth, and Society*.

[2] Finger, *Contemporary*, 57.

Appreciation and Critique

A Contemporary Anabaptist Theology usefully brings together a wide range of conversation partners. Finger both introduces his readers to many significant perspectives from the sixteenth century and today and models a style of respectful, constructively critical exchange of perspectives.

Finger provides access to sixteenth-century materials rarely presented in an overtly theological context—reflecting an up-to-date awareness of historical scholarship and, most importantly, an eye to the present-day theological relevance of these materials. Side-by-side with this effort of historical retrieval, Finger gives us a fascinating portrayal of theological ferment among current Anabaptist theologians. He helps us to see the wide diversity in our dynamic community of scholars. Finger also helps us to see how those within this diverse community of thinkers are nonetheless united in their deep concerns for peace and for the integration of belief and practice.

However, Finger's method of jumping directly from the sixteenth century to our current scene in discussing Anabaptist theology raises concerns. To do otherwise would have surely thickened even more an already overthick book. Yet, a very important part of the tradition is thereby left out, rendering Finger's account more along the lines of reporting ahistorical theological ideas than giving an account of a living, evolving, in-history tradition.

Of all theological traditions, it would seem the Anabaptist tradition, with its central emphasis on lived-out beliefs, must be understood in terms of its concrete expressions. Surely, taking into account the four centuries between 1550 and 1950 would greatly complicate an account of Anabaptist theology, but can anything less do adequate justice to the tradition?

Though Finger is obviously concerned with ethics, and with how theology translates into practice, as a rule this concern is evinced mostly in statements that he has this concern more than in the clear content of the theological analysis. That is, Finger in practice still seems to treat theology more as *ideas* and *disembodied beliefs* than as always-embodied convictions that reflect political and socio-cultural interests and cannot truly be understood apart from those interests. For Finger, ethics seems more like an add-on to pure theology than something that is inextricably a part of *all* theological reflection.

Finally, Finger is by far the strongest on description. He carefully and cautiously describes, then proposes. This descriptive element of his work greatly overshadows the sharper prophetic critique and ethical exhortation that seems to have been at the *center* of sixteenth-century Anabaptist faith.

The irenic tone of *A Contemporary Anabaptist Theology* will insure that it will not alienate and drive away readers from other traditions. Finger will likely get a respectful, considered hearing from such readers, which is all to the good.

At the same time, this means that Finger does not share the conflictual dynamics characteristic of his Anabaptist forebears that followed from their directly challenging status quo religion. Given that probably the most universal characteristic shared across the diversities of sixteenth-century Anabaptism was how their convictions and practices got them into serious trouble, one wonders whether there might be somewhat of a tension with latter-day theologies that want to call themselves Anabaptist and yet end up being quite safe and comfortable.

What *Should* Contemporary Anabaptist Theology be Like?

Because of his admirable (in my mind) boldness in claiming the label "Anabaptist" for his theology, Finger challenges others in his theological community to reflect on how we, in turn, would construct a contemporary Anabaptist theology. He presents one perspective. In what follows, I will present a somewhat different one. I have no intention of challenging Finger's right to use "Anabaptist" for his theology, but I do want to suggest a somewhat different take on what I think an Anabaptist theology might look like.

Finger's book could not be timelier. More than ever before, North American Anabaptists are challenged to become self-conscious about articulating our theological convictions. Our tradition has been sustained for many generations more by the strength of family and cultural ties than by clearly, overtly stated common convictions. However, in North America's ever-more transient culture, into which Anabaptists are increasingly being acculturated, those old ties are weakening. The future viability of our tradition cannot be taken for granted. We need, more than before, to be self-conscious about why we want to be Anabaptist Christians. So, theology becomes much more important—and Finger's work speaks directly to this need.

I read Finger as making an important contribution in uncovering and helping to make more coherent important theological resources from the sixteenth century *and* familiarizing his readers with contemporary options. Certainly his constructive proposals are well considered, and useful for contemporary Anabaptists (and all other Christians for that matter).

However, my take on what questions contemporary *Anabaptists* might be asking is different. I am not convinced that theologizing as Finger has done, focusing mostly on doctrinal formulations, the internal debates of theological discourse, and the sacramental practices within the church—theologizing that will likely not get him into trouble with anyone—is the best reflection of the spirit of sixteenth-century Anabaptist theology or the best kind of contribution pacifist Christians might make to theology seeking to engage our present historical context.

As Finger shows us, we in the Anabaptist tradition need continually to be reflecting on what our theology is and should be. For one reason, as pacifist Christians, we have a call to witness to Jesus' way in the face of *whatever* forces in our present world are hurting, violating, oppressing, and dominating the human beings God loves.

I support Finger's use of "Anabaptist" as a rubric for the kind of theology we need to be producing. This rubric both anchors us in a particular tradition, the spiritual descendants of the Radical Reformers, and allows us to be open in engaging the entire Christian tradition and to seek to be relevant in the catholic Christian community.[3]

A Proposal: "Radical Pacifist Anabaptist" Theology

I propose an Anabaptist theology that reads Anabaptist history (sixteenth century *and* the years since) similarly to how we say that we read the Bible. We today are part of the same, on-going story as the biblical people, especially Jesus, and as the Anabaptists of the sixteenth century and since. We do not critically distance ourselves from the story, but we also recognize that we need to read the story truthfully, to allow it to challenge us and not simply say what we want it to say.

We consider the entire story, trying to listen to it on its own terms. However, in approaching the Bible, Anabaptists say we use a reading strategy that privileges themes in the broader story that (1) most accurately support Jesus' own summary of the Law and Prophets (that is, his Commandment to love God and neighbor) and that (2) most helpfully support our calling today to apply Jesus' Commandment to our context.

So, I suggest that reading both the Bible and the Anabaptist stories in the light of Jesus' life and teaching underscores that both stories at their

---

[3] I mean here to echo Anabaptist theologian John Howard Yoder's sentiment at the beginning of his book, *Priestly Kingdom*: "The vision of discipleship projected in this collection is founded in Scripture and catholic tradition, and is pertinent today as a call for all Christian believers" (8).

cores integrate belief and practice. The stuff of biblical theology and the stuff of Anabaptist theology are made up primarily of real life, concrete moral practices, efforts to live faithfully. This kind of theology does not place abstract doctrines or what other theologians have said about theology at the center—either in theory or in practice.

The sixteenth-century Anabaptists wrote little formal theology. Most early leaders had little formal education and the few more highly educated ones ended up dying early (e.g., the one leader with a doctorate in theology, Balthasar Hubmaier, was executed in 1528, three years after the movement began). Few of their spiritual descendants have written formal theology either until recently; this relative silence has led to debates about how much we should assume they share with the mainstream of orthodox Christian theology.

Do the Anabaptists' mostly positive allusions to commonly held Christian doctrines (trinitarianism, creedal formulations, et al) imply that they are best seen as theologically orthodox Christians who added on some distinctive ethical practices such as pacifism? Or does their basic lack of interest in formal dogmatic theology imply an alternative orientation to Christian faith that privileges right practice over right belief in ways that actually, if spelled out, may lead to an entirely different type of theology, root and branch?

I lean towards the latter inclination in relation to Anabaptist theology.[4] I believe one way of doing theology *after* the Anabaptists (meaning, following their path even while going beyond what they directly said) may end up being a distinctive kind of theology in relation to most theology from the mainstream Christian tradition. As a rule, in the sixteenth century and since, Anabaptists would seem to have resisted the systematizing and formalizing of theology into doctrinal formulations and insider language games. Their approach to faith has been more concrete and practical.

If we in North American Anabaptist communities are in a new era, where the times require more self-consciously articulating our theological convictions (since we may no longer so easily depend upon family and cultural ties to sustain our tradition), is our best strategy to link more closely with traditions with a longer history of formal theology, simply adding our ethical distinctives to the already-formulated "classical" theologies? Or is the best strategy to think through the entire theological enterprise anew in light of core Anabaptist convictions?

---

[4] I have been influenced by J. Denny Weaver's work on this point. See especially *Anabaptist Theology*. See also Weaver's critique of Finger's book, "Parsing."

This latter approach, which I endorse, would emphasize that, e.g., a *pacifist* doctrine of God[5] might be different than doctrines of God formulated by theologians in, say, Augustinian, Thomistic, Lutheran, or Calvinist traditions that have explicitly approved of Christians fighting wars.

To be clear on this point I could call the type of Anabaptist theology I advocate "radical pacifist Anabaptist theology." Since such a term, in my mind, would actually be redundant, I will not seriously propose to use it. But when I say that my "Anabaptist theology" should be seen as, by definition, meaning "radically pacifist Anabaptist theology" I am asserting that the core of "Anabaptist theology" as I approach it is pacifism.

I believe that theology drawing on the Anabaptist stream of Christianity should see its root or foundational theological conviction being Jesus' love command. Hence, it is "radical pacifist theology," "radical" in that sense that at its root pacifism affirms love as the core truth. By "pacifist" I mean understanding loving God and each human being as the core conviction that exceeds all others. For pacifism, no other value, truth, conviction, or commitment can be important enough to take priority over the love command—that is, no value is worth committing violence for.

I want to emphasize (in a way not clearly seen in our tradition until quite recently) that the "peace" Jesus embodied was the "peace" described in the Old Testament with a cluster of socially oriented terms such as *shalom* ("peace"), *mishpat* and *sedeqah* ("justice") and *chesed* ("mercy"). This is a broad, positive, active, life-affirming, world-transforming, and injustice-resisting concept. "Peace" as presented by Jesus includes direct involvement in resisting evil (nonviolently), in seeking to bring healing to the world's brokenness through fostering genuinely restorative social justice.[6]

For my approach, reading the Anabaptist convictions that matter most as "radical pacifist convictions" captures the authentic core of tradition as read through the lens of Jesus' message. This is not to say that Anabaptists have always embodied this message so much as to say that insofar as they *have* done so, at that point what matters most about the tradition is at the forefront.

For "Radical pacifist Anabaptist theology" (from now on, just "Anabaptist theology"), the stuff of theology is the message of love, its em-

---

[5] See chapter four below, "Is God Nonviolent?" and other contributions to the symposium of which it was part, *Conrad Grebel Review* 21.1 (Winter 2003).

[6] For a description of "restorative justice" see Zehr, *Changing Lenses*, and Marshall, *Beyond Retribution*. For a portrayal of Jesus' vision being one of active nonviolence, see Yoder, *Politics*; Wink, *Engaging*; and Gingerich and Grimsrud, eds., *Transforming*. See also Driedger and Kraybill, *Mennonite*, for an account of the evolution of Mennonite understandings of their peace position.

bodiment in actual life, the need for it in our broken world, and theological reflection in light of this message, embodiment, and need. The doctrines, formal traditions, creeds, technical theological language, only have value for Anabaptist theology as I construe it insofar as they illumine the message of love; they are not valued as ends in themselves.

Practice-Oriented Theology

Contemporary Anabaptist theology as I approach it may thus be conceptualized as directly connected to social life and concrete ethics. It seeks to follow the biblical mode of focusing on people's actual lives and applying theological convictions directly to practices that sustain a people's faithfulness to their vocation as agents of God's shalom. It sees as its model Jesus' style of communicating his convictions concerning God and truth—life-oriented, practical, accessible, embodied in life, directly in service of the love command.

This practice-oriented theology sees its central concern as theological reflection on the stuff of actual life. It may be contrasted with other types of theology that focus their reflection more overtly on doctrines and creeds, past and current theological formulations, and insider rituals as the stuff of theology. This more doctrine- and ritual-oriented theology primarily refers to its own internal set of concerns.

To see contemporary Anabaptist theology as practice-oriented theology points toward theological reflection that *directly* applies the biblical story to life in the world such as the problems of violence and poverty, the quest for meaning in a consumerist society that dominates the world economically and militarily, and the future of life in face of environmental degradation. This focus contrasts with theological reflection that focuses first of all on theological formulations in various forms and only turns to life in the world as a second level concern.

This Anabaptist theology will see the life and teaching of Jesus as the most fundamental contribution the Bible makes to present-day theology. Rather than focusing much energy on the formulation of doctrines of scripture's authority, it will focus on drawing on the story of Jesus for interpretive clues for engaging with the crucial issues of present-day life.

These are some of the questions contemporary such an Anabaptist theology might engage:

•Why does so much theology support violence? Why are American Christians more likely to support capital punishment and the Iraq War than non-Christians? How might we think theologically in ways that overcome this problem?[7] How do we challenge what Walter Wink calls the "myth of redemptive violence" so widespread in American society?

• How does Christian theology respond to its rival, the "faith" of capitalism[8] that currently is transforming our world into a "planet of slums"?[9]

• What are the religious beliefs that underwrite the commodification and accompanying destructive exploitation of our natural environment?

• How do we reflect theologically on the ways many Christians have lifted the alleged sins of gay and lesbian Christians as bases for unprecedented levels of intra-church conflict all out of proportion with the weight these "sins" are given in the Bible?

We may contrast these questions with other types of questions and concerns expressed in more doctrinally oriented theology, both from the evangelical side and from the mainstream side.

The kinds of concerns focused on by evangelical theology may be illustrated by issues raised by Roger Olson in the final section, entitled "Issues in Evangelical Theology," in his recent handbook on evangelical theology.[10]

• How do we understand the baptism and gifts of the Holy Spirit? Do we think in terms of a "second blessing" or second definite work of grace that lifts the Christian to a new level of faith-experience or more in terms of one completed baptism of the Spirit at the point of conversion?

• What beliefs are acceptable for one who wants to be identified as an "evangelical Christian"? What are the boundary lines to acceptable belief?

• How does one know the truth status of truth claims about God? Is true knowledge of God based only on special revelation and faith in God's Word? Can the existence of God and the resurrection of Jesus Christ be rationally proven?

• Which view about the End Times is most persuasive—premillennialism, amillennialism, or postmillennialism?

• Is the Bible perfect—historically accurate and internally consistent—in every detail or is it more that it is trustworthy in what it teaches concerning salvation while also reflecting human fallibility in some of its historical accounts?

We may illustrate the concerns of mainstream theology by noting a randomly chosen (June 14, 2005) issue of *The Christian Century* that de-

---

[7] For reflection on these issues, see Grimsrud and Zehr, "Rethinking," and Grimsrud, "Violence."

[8] See Loy, "Religion" and Cox, "Market."

[9] See Davis, *Planet*.

[10] Olson, *Westminster*, 291–315.

voted its cover article to various contemporary views of the doctrine of justification by faith. The article examines recent writing on this doctrine, focusing on how theological ideas about justification are being debated. As it turns out, the article concludes with some sharp questions of these writers and their neglect of the social-ethical relevance of justification. Nonetheless, except for these questions at the end, the article focused on an internal doctrinal theme as an example worth extensive discussion illustrating what is currently seen as important in ecumenical theology.

Another example of the concerns of mainstream theology, concerns tending to be theological ideas more than actual life, may be seen with the table of contents from the most recent issue available to me (April 2005) of *Modern Theology*, probably the pre-eminent English-language journal devoted to academic theology. These are some of the article titles: "On the Meaning and Relevance of Baader's Theological Critique of Descartes," "Philosophy and Salvation: The Apophatic in the Thought of Arthur Schopenhauer," and "The Simplicity of the Living God: Aquinas, Barth, and Some Philosophers."

My point with these contrasting tendencies is not to critique more doctrinally-oriented theology but simply to suggest that Anabaptist theology might, at least as I seek to practice it, be seen as something very *different*.

Whither Contemporary Anabaptist Theology?

With this perspective on "practice-oriented" theology in mind, I want to return to *A Contemporary Anabaptist Theology*. I do believe Tom Finger has made a major contribution to the task of Anabaptist theology today. Yet I want to propose a contemporary Anabaptist theology that is pursued somewhat differently.[11]

---

[11] My concerns are paralleled by these comments from John Driver: "Members of radical faith movements frequently direct their lives according to the authority of scripture. They often attempt to translate scripture into living experience. Historically, that has contrasted with the established church's dependence on right doctrine, as defined in ecumenical councils, and on the church's institutional tradition, embodied in its clerical leadership and ecclesiastical polity. Clearly there exist notably different understandings of what constitutes a history of the Christian church. The history of established Christianity is traditionally told through church doctrines and institutions, with a focus on the influence of clerical leaders. Considerable attention is also given to the on-going development of doctrine and tradition. Radical movements tend to focus on the salvation story as told in the Old Testament and New Testament. The biblical history is central to the history told by radical movements because that story underpins their own life and mission. Radical movements generally bear a closer resemblance to the Messianic restoration movements of biblical history than do their established church counterparts" (*Radical*, 328).

Finger seeks to mediate between Anabaptist and mainstream theologies in a way that accommodates to the latter more than I want to. Two others who have also produced major theological works that could be seen as "contemporary Anabaptist theologies" (though neither uses that term for their work), James Reimer and James McClendon, reflect similar tendencies.

Reimer's massive collection of theological essays, *Mennonites and Classical Theology*, has the sub-title, "Dogmatic Foundations for Theological Ethics." In the introduction, Reimer explains that though often criticized for focusing too much on "dogmatics," he does indeed take ethics (which he defines as "the principles guiding human behavior") seriously. But he is convinced that "ethics, particularly Christian ethics (including the Mennonite concern for peace, justice, and nonviolent love) needs a ground outside itself"—what he calls a "foundation."[12]

Consequently, "there are few essays in this volume which deal specifically with ethical topics."[13] Indeed, beyond on occasion mentioning that he is concerned with ethics, Reimer's theological reflection rarely touches down in concrete reality—focusing almost exclusively on thinkers, thoughts, and traditions.

In doing theology that serves as a "foundation" for ethics while rarely directly touching on real life ethics—and, for that matter, in understanding "ethics" primarily as "principles" rather than concrete, embodied practices—Reimer situates himself much closer to the doctrinally-oriented than to practice-oriented theology. So, I see his approach, profound as it may be, as a quite different model for a contemporary *Anabaptist* theology than my approach.

McClendon completed his three volume systematic theology in 2000. Most of his life a Southern Baptist (he joined a Church of the Brethren congregation late in life), McClendon coined the term (lower-case "b") "baptist" to describe his theology. However, he did write that, under the influence of John Howard Yoder, he became, "though I still have no love for the term itself—an 'Anabaptist' Baptist."[14] McClendon wrote his trilogy in an attempt to provide an alternative to the mainstream Christian traditions. Rather than starting with the "foundations," he started with "ethics." Then came his "doctrine" followed only at that point by the more foundational third volume. And even that volume turned out to be "witness."

---

[12] Reimer, *Mennonites*, 15.
[13] Reimer, *Mennonites*, 16.
[14] McClendon, "Radical Road," 22.

So McClendon sought to give us what could certainly be termed "a contemporary Anabaptist theology." And it is a tremendous resource. However, his stimulating but always demanding volumes almost overwhelm with their detailed focus on other theological work more than on life itself—this is especially the case with volume two, *Doctrine*.

McClendon himself tells us why he took this approach. "I was determined to write every sentence in light of my new-gained radical convictions, and yet to write in such a way that standard-account people, those who shared my pre-Yoder standpoint, could make sense of it."[15]

Admirable as McClendon's strategy was—and profound as his influence on "standard-account theology" may be—what he produced may be better seen more as a doctrinally-oriented theology seeking to break free from and transform the problems of theology in that mode more than an actual practice-oriented theology. And, hence, McClendon's systematics also provides a different kind of model for contemporary *Anabaptist* theology than my approach.[16]

Finger follows a similar strategy—working within the mode of doctrinally-oriented theology but with the intent of moving it more toward practice-oriented theology, bringing core Anabaptist convictions (e.g., peace, close attention to Jesus' life and teaching, an integration of belief and practice) to bear on the theological enterprise in a way that "makes sense to standard-account people." Like I do with McClendon, I perceive that Finger also would hope to persuade the "standard account people" to regard Anabaptist convictions more positively.

However, theology done in the doctrinally oriented mode, even with overt delineation of Anabaptist convictions, is a different approach for contemporary Anabaptists than the thoroughgoing practice-focused theology I seek to articulate. I fear the doctrinally oriented mode may relativize these convictions so much that what we end up with may be less than "radically pacifist."

The construction of contemporary Anabaptist theology remains an always-open task. The ideal I am pointing toward *combines* serious engagement with the biblical story with careful analysis of contemporary social issues. It remains a point of debate whether Anabaptist theology may take the form of *systematic* theology and remain consistently Anabaptist. If such an articulation is possible, it must retain at its core a privileging of the biblical story understood as centered in Jesus' life and teaching as more central

---

[15] McClendon, "Radical Road," 22.

[16] For a summary of my attempt to model practice-oriented theological reflection see chapter eight below.

than later creedal formulations and internally-oriented rituals. Only in this way, I tend to think, will an Anabaptist systematic theology remain "radical pacifist" theology.

Conclusion

Self-consciousness about our theological convictions is more important for Anabaptist Christians in North America than ever before. Tom Finger deserves our gratitude for his valuable contribution to our common task of thinking carefully about and articulating those convictions.

In the approach I propose, though, the way we embody and apply Jesus' love command is our core Anabaptist conviction. Because of this belief, I seek to do *Anabaptist* theology that self-consciously focuses on practical social ethics as an intrinsic part of all our theologizing rather than seeing it as a second-level concern after working on "pure theology." That is, my theology from the start and throughout seeks to be practice-oriented more than doctrinal-oriented.

Pacifist theology, which by definition is concerned at its core with the embodiment of Jesus' love command, will always be practice-oriented. Anabaptist theology in my construal understands itself, above all else, based on the message of Jesus. This would seem to lead to Anabaptist theology always being pacifist theology. Such a theology may find itself at odds with non-pacifist theology in relation to its articulation of the core convictions of Christian faith.

Rather than trying to fit within the Western (non-pacifist!) theological tradition, accepting this tradition's basic theological articulations but *adding* on an ethical, even nonviolent, component, contemporary Anabaptist theology as I seek to practice it rethinks theology root and branch in light of its most fundamental conviction—that no other value or commitment takes precedent over the love command.

CHAPTER THREE

Constructing an Anabaptist Theology in a Congregational Setting[1]

ANABAPTIST THEOLOGY, the articulation of Anabaptist convictions today, best focuses on immediate, concrete life, reflecting a particular ethically-oriented reading of the message of Jesus, appropriately termed "radically pacifist Anabaptism"—more so than theological reflection focused on doctrines, abstract ideas, and the writings of theologians and philosophers.

What follows in this book are various chapters modeling such an approach. The next two short essays serve as a methodological overview to my approach. The four resources for theology that I discuss in these chapters—Bible, tradition and history, experience, and vision—will provide the organizing rubrics for most of this book.[2]

In the summer of 1996, I marked my tenth year as a pastor by making a career change. I left congregational ministry and joined the faculty of Eastern Mennonite University. I believe, though, that my experience as a pastor had a permanent effect on how I approach theology.

In this chapter, I want to reflect on how pastoring shaped my thinking about the task of Christian theology. The main lesson I learned is that the theology that matters most emerges from and directly addresses *historical* existence (that is, life in the here and now). Theology is for the *present*. A second lesson I learned is that theology has to do with an *integration* of

---

[1] This chapter is adapted from an article originally titled "Constructing a Mennonite Theology in a Congregational Setting," published in *Mennonite Life* 52.1 (Spring 1997), 30–35. The article was based on a presentation at the October 1996 conference at Bethel College, North Newton, Kansas, on the thought of Gordon Kaufman. Used with permission of Bethel College.

[2] I wrote this chapter as I moved from pastoral ministry to the professorate. I reflected then on how my theologizing had been shaped by my context as a pastor. I still believe now, a decade later, that my suggestions for doing theology remain valid, so I offer the essay here with only minor revisions. I include chapter four, "Is God Nonviolent?", as a concise application of the approach sketched in chapter three to a specific—and particularly vexing—theological question. I offer it here primarily as a methodological illustration.

beliefs and ethics. Theology is not only about beliefs, or even about "applying" beliefs to life. Theology is about life itself—emerging from experience, speaking to experience.

I came to my present understanding of theology as an *Anabaptist* pastor, seeking to think theologically in an Anabaptist context. I realize now that in those ten years pastoring I was working at constructing Anabaptist theology in a congregational setting.

In general, academic theologians (even Anabaptists) do not tend to take congregational life as their *starting point*. Consequently, the theology needs to be *translated* by pastors into more concrete terms. However, the work of translating academic theology into more concrete terms, integrating academic theology with congregational life, generally is not a very high priority for many pastors. So, what has resulted is a serious gap between academic theology and congregational ministry—even in the Anabaptist world.

Anabaptist theology has a message of peace and wholeness to offer a modern world continually plagued with inter-human violence, alienation between human beings and nature, and increasing loss of meaning and hopefulness in work and other parts of everyday life.

However, to grasp and communicate this message, Anabaptist theology must seek to bridge the gap between academic theology and congregational life. One way of bridging the gap between academic theology and congregational life is to take seriously the two lessons I mentioned—(1) that theology needs to emerge from and directly address historical existence, and (2) that theology has to do with the integration of belief and ethics.

I like the term "congregational theology" for the way I want to theologize. The term "congregational" situates this reflective and constructive activity in the present, concrete, historical lives of people in local communities. It situates the reflection in the historical lives of *particular* traditions and groups of churches.

By calling this reflective activity "theology" I am situating it within the tradition of normative, ordered thinking about the big issues of life in light of *God*. "Theology" is not simply description of religious beliefs. "Congregational theology" is not simply concerned with what people in congregations happen to believe. There is a normative aspect included as well. "Congregational theology" has the task of fostering faithful living within the community of faith. The fostering of such living provides criteria for evaluating beliefs—"good" congregational theology fosters faithful living.

In what follows, I want briefly to discuss four distinct sources for thought and reflection, what I call the four building blocks of congregational theology in an Anabaptist context. These include: (1) the Bible, (2) the history of the Christian tradition in general and, more specifically, our Anabaptist tradition, (3) the present-day lives of people in the congregation, and (4) our hope, our vision for the future.

As a pastor, I especially tried to shape these various sources into a coherent theological perspective through preaching. I sought to construct an imaginative synthesis out of these four sources. I sought always to speak to congregants' historical existence, focusing on meaning and hope and encouragement for the here and now.

Gordon Kaufman's reflections on theological method were enormously helpful for me in my ministry. In particular, his proposal that theology in practice is always an act of construction rather than "hermeneutics."[3] What theology does is *not* simply finding out from past doctrines what we are supposed to believe now. Theology is something *we construct*. We theologize in light of our historical existence—our present thought forms, our present needs. Our theology is an act of imaginative synthesis, an act of creativity, drawing on many sources and flowing out of our experience of life. Kaufman's discussion of theological construction encourages me to affirm what I did as a pastor. I was theologizing.

When I describe the four sources of congregational theology, I am not thinking of them as authorities to be prioritized and that I would seek merely faithfully to represent. I am not proposing a "scientific method" wherein my theological task is merely to interpret revealed truths. Rather, I am thinking of the sources as the raw materials out of which one fashions a vital and creative perspective meant to speak to our present, real-life world.

The Bible

Since the beginning of the movement, Anabaptists have defined themselves as biblical people. Anabaptists commonly assert that we believe what the Bible says and that determines our faith and practice. However, in my experience, the actual role the Bible plays in Anabaptist congregational life is more ambiguous. As a pastor, I became somewhat disillusioned about that practical authority of the Bible in the congregation.

For one thing, I found few people willing to do the work serious Bible study requires. When some difficult, conflictual issues arose in any of the

---

[3] Kaufman, "Mennonite," and *Essay*.

several congregations I pastored, it seemed that few people were interested in doing detailed Bible study as a means of discernment. There was at least one occasion, though, when people did engage in some serious Bible study. However, then a new set of problems arose.

In my first pastorate, our congregation struggled with a difficult moral issue. An individual from each of two sides presented detailed exegetical work to the congregation. Both used the Bible in careful ways and yet came to *opposite* conclusions. In response, most in the congregation threw up their hands in discouragement. They concluded that the Bible as supreme authority for specific decisions does not work because it lends itself to too many interpretations.

Nonetheless, in spite of these problems, I came to realize that the Bible *did* serve as an important resource for that congregation. Discussion of the moral issue quite often took place with the use of biblical metaphors, images, and stories. The point was not so much proving an argument as it was simply communication. The Bible offered a common language and store of images. It did not offer a lever for a final answer, but it did help people to converse together.

The Bible, amidst its diversity, does contain a central message: God loves the world and works to bring about healing and restoration to it. Agreement on this core motif helped our congregation to work redemptively with the dilemma it faced. The resolution was somewhat of a compromise that did not please everyone. However, the style with which the decision was made included everyone, and the congregation as a whole shared a commitment to the values of mercy, respect, and seeking wholeness for all people.

This experience helped me understand that the Bible's importance lay primarily in its message of God's healing love more than it serving as an answer book for each of our complex issues. Part of the reason why the Bible is such a crucial resource for congregational theology is that congregational theology is most of all concerned with the struggle we have to live faithfully in everyday life. The Bible is best understood as a record of past people doing precisely that same thing—struggling to live faithfully in everyday life. The Bible is useful more due to this commonality with our lives than due to its uniqueness as direct revelation of timeless truths that relieve us of the responsibility to seek faithfulness in new ways in our new contexts.

My experience with the Bible contributed significantly to my conviction that theology has most of all to do with historical existence (not abstract, timeless truths). The historicity of the Bible speaks powerfully to *our* historicity.

Anabaptist History

The history of our tradition provides the second source for Anabaptist congregational theology. By this I mean the Christian tradition in general—and especially self-consciousness about our particular Anabaptist tradition.

In the past sixty years, fueled by Harold Bender's landmark essay, "The Anabaptist Vision," a great deal of Anabaptist scholarly energy has gone into sixteenth-century Anabaptist studies. Not nearly as much energy has gone into the years since then. But the changes *after* the first-generation Anabaptists have formed present-day Anabaptist identity more than have the original Anabaptists. So I think this on-going history, more than simply sixteenth-century Anabaptist history, is important for present-day Anabaptist congregational theology.

I want to discuss one reason for this assertion—the transformation of early Anabaptist ideals due to persecution.

The early Anabaptists were extraordinarily creative and had an impact on the world in important ways. Some of the key values that were broadly characteristic of Anabaptists include: believers baptism, Lord's Supper as a memorial, church discipline, how salvation was understood, discipleship, mutual aid, and their ethic of love (pacifism).[4] These values do remain central to the Anabaptist tradition.

However, the past four hundred-plus years have seen many changes and adaptations. The effects of the intense persecution that the first generation of Anabaptists faced cannot be overstated. In response to the persecution, Anabaptists tried to remain faithful to their central values. After the first generation, their way of doing this was to exist largely as a migrating people. They sought tolerance and the possibility of practicing their faith with a minimum of resistance from the outside.

This era of harsh persecution and the resultant evolution of the group into a migrating people, who primarily sought tolerance and security, was a crucial defining moment for our tradition. What are some of the changes wrought by this era of persecution on the movement?

(1) *A change from adult baptism to baptizing children of the church.* The practice of baptizing adults who made a conscious choice to move from the world of darkness to the world of light characterized the first Anabaptists. Their practice changed as the movement evolved more toward ghetto-like communities. In time, baptism centered more on the integration of children of the church. Baptism became more of an initiation rite set at a

---

[4] This list is drawn from Weaver, *Becoming*, 1st ed., 113–41, and Snyder, *Anabaptist*, 365–78.

somewhat arbitrary age to mark the membership of children whose faith generally evolved gradually.

(2) *A change from aggressive evangelism to seeking toleration.* The first Anabaptists were zealous evangelists. In face of hostile reactions from their societies' powers-that-be, they soon became much more concerned with finding tolerant locales to quietly practice their faith within their isolated communities. Often, part of the agreements they made with estate owners included the promise *not* to evangelize.

(3) *A change from open membership to ethnicity.* The first Anabaptists came from the wider society in which the movement arose. They shared their neighbors' language and cultural practices. In time Anabaptist communities became distinct from surrounding culture. This led to the emergence of Anabaptist ethnicism, a development that perhaps marks the transition between sixteenth-century Anabaptism and later expressions. There were no "ethnic sixteenth-century Anabaptists."

These changes were not simply a case of later generations losing the zeal of the first generation believers. More so, these changes and others that followed resulted from the need to develop new understandings in new situations.

Present-day Anabaptist congregational theology certainly will gain much from an appreciation of the sixteenth-century Anabaptists. However, we also need a greater appreciation of developments in the years since. Partly, this is simply so we may better understand how we got to where we are. Also, however, throughout Anabaptist history, people have sought to respond faithfully to their own particular contexts. We may not always like how they responded, but we benefit from a sympathetic consideration of their part in our history.

Present-Day Life

My third source is present-day life. Early in my pastoral ministry, I recognized the importance of *listening* to parishioners. Two issues that I had to face almost immediately were divorce and homosexuality. I soon realized that my prescribed answers on these issues were actually of little interest to many of the people in my congregation. They were *not* looking to me for clear-cut absolute answers nearly so much as for respect, compassion, and a listening heart.

In face of my experiences, I gained a more *positive* view of human beings. I came to recognize that almost always people are doing the best they can in such difficult situations, and that usually these people are extraordinarily resourceful. The people with whom I worked did not need to be confronted with their sinfulness. They needed the church to be a healing environment, offering a place for worship and mutually respectful fellowship and support.

Martin Buber spoke directly to me in this context. His book *I and Thou* taught me that the core of life, of religion, of what God can mean to us, is found in relationality, being in loving relationships with other people and with God. Listening and caring are more important than winning arguments and developing irrefutable "answers."

Buber also taught me that we meet God in the concrete reality of this world, with its brokenness and pain. People in congregations are looking for God to be present for them in the here and now. If God is to be found, this world, this life, is where the finding will happen.

Understanding *present* life and the issues people face in struggling to live out their faith is absolutely essential for any theological construction that draws on materials from the Bible and tradition. Such understanding is necessary for our theology to be relevant and coherent.

Vision

The fourth source for congregational theology is *vision*. We might call this the eschatological component, in which our vision for the future enters our present life.

Hope for the future is closely connected with how we view life in the present. Hope and vision for the future have especially to do with identifying, cultivating, and ultimately trusting in the rightness, the truthfulness, of what we experience right now as life enhancing.

I learned a great deal about hope from my study of and preaching and teaching from the Book of Revelation. Revelation tells us, basically, that, in spite of present-day struggles and suffering, the fundamental reality of the universe *is* God's healing love. The reality of God's healing love is *present* reality, and (in mysterious ways), we can hope for God ultimately to bring about wholeness for all of creation.[5]

Revelation teaches that the mercy of God has already been established as the decisive force in the universe. There will be no *future* battle; the victory of God is already assured. God's faithfulness to the promise of healing has been expressed in the life, death, and resurrection of Jesus. Followers of the Lamb can be assured that healing is coming, and that faithfulness to Jesus' way is possible and is the best way to flourish. In the Christ-event, the

---

[5] Grimsrud, *Triumph*.

ultimate nature of reality is revealed: God's mercy and creativity are more fundamental to reality than are the violence, oppression, and seemingly overwhelming might of the powers of evil.

We may see that God's mercy and creativity define the ultimate nature of reality in the particular events of Jesus' life. We may also see this in the wider reconciling community that grew up in response to Jesus' ministry.[6] The message of hope contained in Revelation speaks to all communities that cling to the conviction that love and mercy are the central aspects of life—even in the face of many pressures and counter-examples that glorify power politics, material gratification, and narrow self-interest as ultimate.

Hope and vision for the future serve as sources for congregational theology by clarifying for us where we want to be going. As we see in Revelation, where we *want* to be going is determined by our awareness in the *present* of the abundance of God love and mercy. It is also determined by our awareness of God's promise that love and mercy are the goals toward which history is moving.

Conclusion

The "congregational theology" I advocate addresses several needs:

(1) We need explicit theological work that keeps the Anabaptist vision for Christian faith alive and vital—not in order simply that our tradition survives, but much more in order that the special insights of this tradition continue to be cultivated in order to serve God's purposes.

(2) We need a presentation of the Christian faith that emerges from and directly addresses historical existence. Life in our congregations is life in the "here and now." Our theology must be concrete, applicable, and relevant—theology that shapes "real life" in ways that glorify God and enhance human well-being.

(3) We need to be constructing theology that at every point integrates beliefs and ethics. When the early Anabaptists asserted that only in following Christ may we know him, they merely echoed Jesus' own teaching that love of God and neighbor *together* constitute the human calling. In our on-going Anabaptist tradition, we believe faithful theology must *always* be self-conscious about its ethical ramifications.

(4) We need theological work that bridges the gap between academic theology and congregational life. Congregations must seek to discern the signs of the times and the on-going relevance of the gospel for life in the contemporary world. Self-conscious theological reflection is a necessary

---

[6] See Gordon Kaufman's discussion of "a wider Christology," *Mystery*, chapter 25.

part of this discernment—and academically trained theologians are crucial resources for such reflection. At the same time, academic theology's life source is real life. Theology cannot survive as a living discipline without direct involvement in present day Christian existence. Academic theology and congregational life *need* each other.

CHAPTER FOUR

Is God Nonviolent?[1]

THE IMPORTANCE of self-conscious theological reflection for Christians in the Anabaptist tradition may be illustrated by considering an issue at the heart of Christian ethics, the moral acceptability (or not) of the use of violence. From its beginning in the sixteenth century, the Anabaptist movement has as a rule affirmed pacifism as the will of God. However, this affirmation has not generally stemmed from sustained theological reflection so much as from a more existential belief that Jesus' commands to love enemies apply in all circumstances. What has sustained this belief has generally been the on-going existence of pacifist communities that have claimed a loyalty from its members higher than the loyalty given to nation-states that might ask involvement in warfare of its citizens.[2]

However, in the twenty-first century, the close-knit, homogenous, rural communities that sustained Anabaptist pacifism in a way that did not require sustained theological reflection are disintegrating. If pacifism is to remain a central aspect of Anabaptist convictions, such theological reflection will become more important—including, at its heart, reflection on the character of God. In what follows, I address this theme of violence and the character of God, self-consciously working within the framework of the four sources for theology I discussed in chapter four: Bible, tradition, present experience, and vision.

In our day of heightening sensitivity to the role of religion in violent conflict—"terrorism," "wars on terrorism," retributive criminal justice practices, religious-supported nationalist movements—the question of how we understand God in relation to violence has never been more urgent.

---

[1] This chapter originated as a presentation to the Mennonite Scholars and Friends forum at the American Academy of Religion and Society of Biblical Literature annual convention, November 2001, Denver, Colorado. A shorter version was published in *The Conrad Grebel Review* 21.1 (Winter 2003), 13–17. Used with permission.

[2] See below, chapter nine, for an account of the sustenance of Anabaptist pacifist practices.

Certainly, not only pacifists have a stake in this question. And not only religious people have a stake. The urgency of the question stems not so much from the need to "get it right" about how God actually is (as if human beings could actually nail this down). Rather, the urgency stems from the reality that *our view of what God is like* greatly shapes our behavior. How people act in relation to their view of God affects us all.

The connection between our view of God and our behavior in relation to violence may be understood in four possible ways. Most people who believe in God believe God is violent and that human beings thus are also appropriately violent, at least in morally justifiable circumstances. As human existence grows ever more precarious, though, this simple assumption grows more problematic—violence, it becomes increasingly clear, leads to more violence. The spiral of violence more clearly all the time becomes a threat to the viability of human life itself.[3] And, of course, for Anabaptist Christians, the assumption that human violence is appropriate has always been questioned.

As a second logical possibility, one could presumably believe that *God* is nonviolent but that human beings need not be, though I am not aware of anyone taking this stance.

A third view would be that God is *not* nonviolent—but human beings should be. Some of those who believe human beings are called to nonviolence understand this calling to stem more directly from the specific teaching of Jesus, not God's own pacifism.[4] Perhaps based on the biblical portrayal of the "warrior God," perhaps based on the need to allow God freedom from anthropocentric moral restraints, perhaps based on the necessity of recognizing God's need to use violence in effecting final justice in relation to a rebellious creation, perhaps based on an awareness of nature itself as "red in tooth and claw"—many pacifist Christians answer our question, "Is God nonviolent?" with a clear "No, but *we* should be."

Other pacifist Christians hold a fourth view, that *God* is nonviolent (or, more precisely, that we should view God as nonviolent) *and* that human beings are called also to be nonviolent. In this view, human nonviolence is both what God through Jesus commands us to embody and what has become a necessity for the sake of our survival in the contemporary world. And, God's nonviolence is the necessary grounding for human non-

---

[3] For analyses of problematic connections between assumptions about God as violent and retributive criminal justice practices see Grimsrud and Zehr, "Rethinking" and Grimsrud, "Violence."

[4] See Reimer, "God is Love but Not a Pacifist," in *Mennonites*, 486–92, and Holland, "Gospel."

violence.[5] If nonviolence does not go with the grain of universe, if our deepest ethical imperative does not cohere with God's very character, we are in the end hopeless romantics to think that nonviolence is a realistic human possibility. And if nonviolence is not a realistic human possibility, pacifism is indeed parasitic idealism of the worst sort—calling us to live in ways that are impractical, irresponsible, counter-productive, needlessly guilt-inducing, and (ironically) conflict fostering.

Traditionally, Anabaptist pacifists have not concerned themselves with speculation of the sort implied by this question. They have not worried a great deal about the logical ramifications of their pacifism in terms either of theological coherence or of the applicability of nonviolence to the wider world.

Various factors have contributed to the transition from what Mennonite sociologists Leo Driedger and Donald Kraybill call "quietism" to "active peacemaking."[6] Some of these include (1) general acculturation that has pushed Anabaptist Christians to think more broadly, to identify more thoroughly with their wider culture and seek to apply their pacifist convictions as widely as possible; (2) increasing participation in social movements inspired by the transformative nonviolence of Mohandas Gandhi, with their optimism about the wide applicability of pacifism; and (3) growing engagement with philosophical and theological currents that may provide deeper intellectual grounding for a more positive view of human possibilities in the world (for example, Process thought, the I-Thou philosophy of Martin Buber, and liberation theology).

What follows is a sketch of an argument for the fourth option (God *and* human beings as nonviolent) following the theological method proposed above in chapter four.

Is God nonviolent? Yes, I *believe* God is. However, the evidence is ambiguous. People from opposing points of view cite data from every area of consideration to support their views. The debates continue without resolution. We get mixed messages about everywhere we look.

Let's think in terms of the standard sources for theology: scripture, history or tradition, and present experience.

Scripture. On the one hand, the Bible seems clearly to present God as directly involved in violent acts as well as commanding human beings to commit violence. The evidence is so well known and so massive that we really don't need to say much about it. If we draw our conclusions from the perspectives of the many specific biblical references, we have to say that

---

[5] For two examples, see Wink, *Engaging,* and Gingerich, "Theological Foundations."

[6] Driedger and Kraybill, *Mennonite.*

the God of the Bible is violent. If we go from the particular to the general, from individual stories of violence to general conclusions, and give equal weight to all these individual stories, then we have to conclude that the Bible clearly teaches that God is violent.

This is the God who brought the overwhelming flood down upon Noah's generation, who rained fire and brimstone upon Sodom and Gomorrah, who brought death to all of Egypt's young children, who massacred hundreds of Hebrews when they idolized golden calves, who ordered the massacre of every man, woman, and child in various areas of Canaan in the time of Joshua—and I could go on. If I were to do so it would likely become clear that I was proving too much. That is, this violence of God in the Bible becomes too much to believe.

We need to recognize that the biblical materials contain other evidence.[7] The God of the Genesis one creation account—in contrast to other gods—does not create in the context of violence but in peace. The God of the Hebrew people from the calling of Abraham and Sarah down through the exile and beyond is a God in many ways who barks more than bites. The God of the actual story is mostly characterized by patience and persevering love, a God whose saving intentions toward the Hebrews find expression, time after time, in acts of unearned love and mercy. The story gives the impression that God has determined to work *within* the framework of historical processes, bringing salvation ultimately through mercy, not through coercive power.

This is how God is shown in the life and teaching of Jesus and the first Christians: the merciful father of the wayward son in Jesus' parable, the one who brings rain on the just and unjust alike, that one who—in Paul's words—loves us even while we are God's enemies.

The ambiguity of the Bible's portrayal of God in relation to violence can be seen in a paradigmatic way in the Book of Revelation. One way of reading the book, focusing first of all on the specifics, concludes that Revelation portrays God as profoundly violent. Another way, focusing more on the overall message of the book, concludes that Revelation actually portrays a God who through persevering love ends up healing even God's enemies—the kings of the earth and the nations (Revelation 21).

Tradition. Christian tradition certainly continues this ambiguity. Augustine, Anselm, Aquinas, Luther, and Calvin portray God as having a dark, violent side. Not surprisingly, such theologians also accepted the

---

[7] See Grimsrud, *God's*, summarized in chapter six below, for an attempt to show that the overall message of the Bible supports nonviolence.

Constantinian accommodation with its assumption that Christians at times are called upon to imitate God's retributive style of justice.

Yet there have always been dissenters. Many of these voices have been silenced (often violently, "in the name of God"), labeled heretical, dismissed as irrelevant and worse. But they keep springing up, in large part because they can draw pretty directly on the life and teaching of Jesus as the basis of critiquing the pro-violence viewpoint.

If we see upper-case T Tradition as normative for our understanding of God, we probably would be bound to conclude that God is violent. But if we look at the *entire* tradition, we will recognize some diversity. If we look at the *consequences* of traditional beliefs about God, we will see ambiguity in the Christian legacy. Many Christians indeed have understood that God is violent, but that understanding has fostered behavior that has *undercut* the gospel of Jesus Christ.

Stephen Toulmin argues that we find in the sixteenth-century wars among Christians (fought in the name of a violent God) the roots of modern *atheism*.[8] Another consequence of the Christian tradition's portrayal of God as violent, according to Timothy Gorringe,[9] is that we can see a direct connection between traditional theologies of God and the soul-destroying criminal justice practices in present-day America.

So, history and tradition are also ambiguous, depending upon how one weighs the evidence. We have clear evidence of beliefs that God is violent and the dissent of a minority to those beliefs. We also see problematic consequences to belief in God as violent that have jeopardized witness to Jesus. These problematic consequences are not themselves evidence that God is nonviolent, but they at least challenge us to question the utility of the *belief* that God is violent.

Experience. Present-day experience also offers ambiguous evidence. If we include our perceptions of nature under this rubric, assuming that in some sense the natural order reflects the character of its Creator, we easily find evidence of this ambiguity. The sociobiology perspective of writers such as Edward O. Wilson[10] tends to assume that nature is inherently violent. Wilson is an atheist, but many Christians are sympathetic to the understandings of the sociobiologists and use their arguments as evidence for the creator also being violent.

---

[8] Toulmin. *Cosmopolis*.
[9] Gorringe, *God's*.
[10] See, for example, Wilson, *Consilience*.

On the other hand, anthropologist Ashley Montagu[11] argues that human beings and nature are not violent by nature. International scientists issued "The Seville Statement on Violence" in 1986 stating, it is scientifically incorrect to say "that we have inherited a tendency to make war from our animal ancestors . . . that war or any other violent behavior is genetically programmed into our human nature . . . that in the course of human evolution there has been a selection for aggressive behavior more than for other kinds of behavior . . . that humans have a violent brain."[12]

Criminal justice theorist Robert Q. Wilson argues that experience proves that human beings are innately violent; whereas James Gilligan, a long-time prison psychiatrist, argues that violence is something we are socialized for. Those who believe human begins are created in God's image could use Wilson's argument as support for seeing God as violent, or Gilligan's for the opposite conclusion.

It appears that we cannot draw decisive evidence from the realm of nature or of human experience to prove that God is violent or that God is not violent. This is true as well, as we have seen, of scripture and Christian tradition. We will never find resolution simply based on these three central sources of guidance. Nonetheless, we do not actually *live* as if all we have are uncertainty and ambiguity. We *do* make choices, and they are *theological* choices.

To use violence, I believe, is ultimately to assume that it is God's will that we do so. Or, truly to reject the use of violence is to make certain assumptions about the nature of the universe and, hence, about the nature of God.

Vision. So, which view of God should we affirm? I suggest that we need to add a fourth source along with scripture, tradition, and experience. This source I will call "vision." By "vision" I mean our convictions about both where we are going and about what we believe we are called to do. We must ask, what concept of God best fits with our vision for our lives? Where do we believe we are meant to go? What kind of concept of God will help get us there?

I believe, for the sake of the flourishing of human life, that we *need* to understand God as a God who seeks healing, not retribution, as a God who defeats evil not through redemptive violence but through persevering love. We *need* to understand God as a God who empowers us to respond to our enemies with love and not with hostility. These "needs" might be pipe-dreams if the universe *clearly* went the other way. These "needs" might

---

[11] Montagu, *Nature*.

[12] Cited in Kohn, *Brighter*.

be heretical if the Bible and tradition *clearly* went the other way. But they do not.

As Christians, we confess Jesus as our normative revelation of God. This confession apparently means different things to different people. Some theologians argue that our Trinitarian confession of three *distinct* members means we ought not move from the revelation of God in Jesus to drawing conclusions about "God the Creator."[13] However, following John Howard Yoder,[14] I believe that only by understanding Jesus as revelatory of God can we be protected from making God a projection of human power politics. Following Gordon Kaufman, I believe that what distinguishes Christian understandings of God is seeing Christ as paradigm for God. Kaufman writes, "To worship the God-revealed-in-Christ—the God defined and constructed with Jesus and the new order of human relationships surrounding him as the model—is to worship the true God."[15]

This is to say that, although even in the story of Jesus we find some ambiguity regarding God and nonviolence, Jesus ultimately pulls us toward a view of reality that reveals nonviolence to be with the grain of universe. We are not simply whistling in the dark when we say that we need a vision of a nonviolent God. This vision will best foster the flourishing of life. It is possible to understand such a vision as coherent with the vision we are given in the life and teaching of Jesus and in the community that arose around him.

To have the conviction that God is nonviolent is therefore not arbitrary, nor does it impose extra-biblical thinking onto the Bible. It simply affirms that we read Scripture and life through the lens of Jesus' life and teaching. With his way as central, the ambiguity of some of the biblical materials, of the message of the Christian tradition, and of present-day experience shrinks. Not that we do not still get mixed messages. Rather, we have an interpretive key allowing us to see the consistent nonviolence of God being expressed amidst these mixed signals of history and present experience. This key comes to us from Jesus, and it gains clarity when we realize that Jesus teaches us what it is that we are meant to be (and will become).

---

[13] See Reimer, *Mennonite*, 486–92.

[14] Stated most thoroughly in Yoder, *Politics*.

[15] Kaufman, *Mystery*, 388.

PART TWO: Bible

Our first theological source for articulating Anabaptist convictions is the Bible.

Close attention to the Bible has characterized the Anabaptist movement since its beginnings, when its founders broke with Reformer Ulrich Zwingli in Zurich, Switzerland. At the heart of the break lay Anabaptist convictions concerning biblical teaching, especially concerning baptism and concerning the priority of faithfulness to Jesus' way over acceptance of state dominance over the community of faith. For the Anabaptist tradition, the centrality of the Bible has generally not meant simply proof-texting, and certainly has not meant a "flat-Bible" approach that, for example, would give equal weight to various Old Testament treatments of warfare in comparison with Jesus' life and teaching. The two chapters in Part Two each reflect the Anabaptist concern with reading the Bible as a resource for faithful living in the present.

Chapter five, "Biblical Interpretation: Anabaptist Theology and Recent Hermeneutics" will propose an approach to interpreting the Bible that links important Anabaptist concerns with recent developments in biblical interpretation, the philosophical hermeneutics of Hans-Georg Gadamer and the reading strategy of Latin American liberation theology. These three approaches share some key characteristics, most notably the belief that genuine understanding of the Bible requires commitment on the part of interpreters to live out what they learn from the Bible.

Chapter six, "The Core Message of the Bible: God's Healing Strategy," gives an overview of the main storyline of the Bible as read from an Anabaptist perspective. It proposes that the story the Bible tells may best be understood in terms of God calling into being a community of faith that is intended to know God's love and mercy, and to witness to that love and mercy to the whole world.

CHAPTER FIVE

Biblical Interpretation: Anabaptist Theology and Recent Hermeneutics[1]

HISTORIANS HAVE proposed that sixteenth-century Anabaptist theology and practice pioneered many changes now embraced by Christians throughout the world—believers baptism, separation of church and state, and conscientious objection to warfare among them. This pioneering dynamic may be seen with regard to biblical interpretation as well. The Anabaptist approach to the Bible has many affinities with recent developments.

In this chapter, I will use these convergences as a way of articulating an approach to biblical interpretation that builds on the insights of our sixteenth-century forebears and broadens them with help of philosophical hermeneutics and Latin American liberation theology.

Our age is not friendly to the authoritative use of writings from the past. We breathe the air of a skeptical, individualistic, and ahistorical worldview characterized by radical doubt regarding revelation, by suspicion of claims for loyalty and duty to people and communities outside our selves and maybe immediate family, and by a sense that only the present matters and that how we got to where we are today is irrelevant if not undiscoverable anyway.

Nevertheless, many believe that these issues, though daunting, are not insurmountable. In fact, their existence only underscores the need to construct and enact a biblical hermeneutics that makes available the immensely helpful resources of the biblical materials for Christian ethics.

One recently emergent tradition that has accepted this challenge and thereby made it much more real to the rest of the world has become known as "liberation theology." This movement's main center has been Latin America, but the label "liberation theology" has been used much more widely of groups such as blacks, feminists, Africans, etc. I will focus

---

[1] The first draft of this chapter was written in 1986 at the Graduate Theological Union, Berkeley, California.

57

on Latin American liberation theology from its "classical" period, the late 1960s through early 1980s.

I will explore the close affinity that liberation theology has in its attitude toward and use of the Bible with another recently emergent "school" of thought—"philosophical hermeneutics." In particular, I will consider the thought of German philosopher Hans-Georg Gadamer.

These two movements share significant common ground—and, I suggest, this common ground has close affinity with main characteristics of sixteenth-century Anabaptist biblical hermeneutics. Hence, both liberation theology and philosophical hermeneutics may help in the articulation of a present-day Anabaptist approach to the Bible.

Sixteenth-Century Anabaptism

The Anabaptists joined other Protestants in ascribing central authority to the Bible. However, the *way* they did that marks them off. For the Anabaptists, more than any other sixteenth-century group, their "focus on Jesus always took pre-eminence."[2]

Stuart Murray lists the following elements of the Anabaptists' distinctive central focus on Jesus:

> a focus on the person of Jesus; a willingness to start with Jesus and accept his deeds and words as normative on many more topics than the Reformers accepted; an extension of the principle of Christocentrism to embrace the whole of the New Testament; and an emphasis on the cruciality of a life-experience of the living Jesus as a prerequisite for all interpreters, a prerequisite that no amount of education could replace.[3]

Directly following from reading scripture with Jesus at the center, Anabaptists followed three principles that in many ways parallel what we see in recent liberation theology and, less directly, in philosophical hermeneutics.

(1) "Anabaptist hermeneutics is the hermeneutics of obedience."[4] That is, we read the Bible as people committed to *act* on what we learn. Following the demands God places on God's people provides our reason for reading the Bible—and only such a commitment enables us genuinely to hear the Bible's message.

---

[2] Murray, *Biblical*, 20–21.
[3] Murray, *Biblical*, 86.
[4] Ollenburger, "Hermeneutics," 59.

(2) Anabaptists affirmed "the hermeneutical privilege of the poor."[5] Many Anabaptists came from lower classes and understood God as having special concern for powerless and marginalized peoples. They believed that the message of scripture was clear, uncomplicated, accessible to socially powerless, uneducated people—and was a message of God's love and acceptance of such people.

(3) The congregation provides the most fundamental context for biblical interpretation.[6] The Bible yields meaning through the give and take of a community of interpreters, all sharing a common commitment to *acting* on the basis of what they learn from the Bible.

These three principles provide strong links between Anabaptist hermeneutics and the two schools of thought I will explore below.

The sixteenth-century Anabaptist principles have not necessarily been determinative for all contemporary Anabaptists. Norman Kraus helps us understand that many Anabaptists in the past century have had their approach to the biblical interpretation shaped more by fundamentalism than the Anabaptist tradition.[7] Philosophical hermeneutics and liberation theology may help us recover a more authentically Anabaptist approach.

In what follows, I will first examine the approach of philosophical hermeneutics, a more formal, theoretical perspective, then summarize the more engaged approach of liberation theology. After analyzing their similarities and differences, I will conclude by suggesting a few links with Anabaptist hermeneutics.

Philosophical Hermeneutics

A key issue with regard to the contemporary use of the Bible is the connection between what the Bible meant in its own time and what it mans today. Is there an unbridgeable gulf between then and now? No one would deny that there is distance—such as culture, language, geography, time, etc. Given this distance, can an ancient text speak to us, and if so, how?

I take it as an empirical fact that, indeed, the Bible does speak meaningfully to people today. Philosophical hermeneutics makes an important contribution in helping us understand *how* this happens. By "philosophical hermeneutics" I mean especially the work of German philosopher Hans-Georg Gadamer (most importantly in his book *Truth and Method*). I will

---

[5] Swartley, "Continuity," 327.

[6] Lind, "Reflections," 152.

[7] Kraus, "American."

summarize the perspective of philosophical hermeneutics in the following ten propositions.

1. Encountering the past is necessary for present-day understanding of reality. Our present-day viewpoint is always in formation, according to Gadamer. As we test our understandings we inevitably encounter the past and struggle with understanding the traditions from which we come. Hence, the "horizon" of the present, our understanding of present-day reality, cannot be formed without resources from the past.[8]

As "hermeneutical animals," we understand ourselves by interpreting a heritage and shared world bequeathed us from the past, a heritage constantly present and active in all our actions and decisions. Thus, we should not conceive of our understanding of reality simply as a product of our present self-awareness. Understanding requires placing ourselves within a process of tradition in which past *and* present are constantly fused.

Interacting with the past is possible. Certainly the historical "worlds" that succeed one another are different from each other and from the world of today. But they are all human worlds and thus open and available to each other.[9] Even when life changes dramatically, as in ages of revolution, far more of the old is preserved in the supposed transformation of everything than anyone realizes.[10] This continuity makes necessary, *and* possible, self-consciously encountering the past in formulating our present-day understanding of reality.

2. The interpreter must relate the text to the present in order to understand it. In Gadamer's words:

> In order to understand [what this text, this piece of tradition, says, what constitutes the meaning and importance of the text, the interpreter] must not try to disregard himself and his particular hermeneutical situation. He must relate the text to this situation if he wants to understand it at all.[11]

There must be a connection between the interpreter's world or horizon and that of the text for understanding to happen. If a text is to be understood, the interpreter must be able to relate one's own horizon to that of the text.

At the same time, the job of hermeneutics is not negating the distance between the text and the interpreter. Every encounter with tradition that takes place within history involves the experience of the tension between

---

[8] Gadamer, *Truth*, 306.
[9] Gadamer, *Truth*, 447.
[10] Gadamer, *Truth*, 281–82.
[11] Gadamer, *Truth*, 324.

the text and the present. The hermeneutical task consists in not covering up this tension but consciously bringing it out. The present and the past remain two distinct entities.

3. We especially gain a sense of identity through interacting with "classic" texts. For Gadamer, a "classic" text does not merely testify to something of the past but "says something to the present as if it were said specifically to it."[12] The reason for the classic's perennial quality is that it deals with matters of such human importance, and deals with them with such abundance of truth and beauty, that the classic remains vitally important for people of succeeding ages.

The classic is, in Gadamer's view, certainly "timeless," but this timelessness is a mode of being *in* history.[13] It is only as a historical entity that a classic text can speak to later historical situations. "Timeless" does not mean ahistorical; rather, it means that the text illumines truth within history time after time. It is "timelessly" valid, not just one time only.

The Bible, as a classic, suppresses the distance between its time and ours with its profound rootedness in our common humanity. The "authority" of the Bible is functional. It shows itself in *practice* to be a classic, profoundly illumining the human situation in ever-new ways.

4. The goal of interpretation is to understand the text for today more than focusing on its "original meaning." The fundamental issue is not what it meant *then*, but what it means *now*. The key issue is not what the author intended or what the text meant to its first audience or even what the text actually says, but what the text as it now stands means to the contemporary reader.

The text is not a depository of static meaning but a mediation of meaning. The reader's task is not finally simply to figure out what the author was trying to say but to understand what the text actually says (in the reader's present). Reconstructing the "original meaning" cannot be primary in interpretation of texts, because they all take on a life of their own when they become texts. Their meaning goes beyond that "original meaning" for that reason, so even if it could be recovered, it would not exhaust the present meaning of the text.

5. There is no pure "objectivity" in interpretation. Because, as interpreters, we are historical beings, we cannot remove ourselves from history and make a neutral, purely objective interpretation. Therefore, we cannot distinguish between "the meaning of a text" and the "meaning of a text as I understand it from my place history." Interpreters cannot simply step out

---

[12] Gadamer, *Truth,* 290.

[13] Gadamer, *Truth,* 290.

of their own horizons and look out at the text in way detached from their own context.

People unmodified by the custom of particular places have never existed, could not in the very nature of the case exist. To try to eliminate one's own biases in interpretation is impossible because to interpret means precisely to *use* one's own biases so that the meaning of the text can really be made to speak for us.[14]

Thus, there are no facts independent of our theories about them, and in consequence no one way of viewing, classifying, and explaining the world that all rational persons are obliged to accept. If there can be no presuppositionless interpretation, then the notion of one "right interpretation" as right in itself is a thoughtless ideal. There is no interpretation without relationship to the present, and this is never permanent and fixed.

However, that there is no pure "objectivity" does not mean that interpretation and understanding are impossible. As we seek to understand, we must not believe we may be preserved us from mixing in our own judgments and prejudices. Yet, at the same time, to acknowledge that one inevitably stands within a tradition does not limit the freedom of knowledge. Rather, this is what makes knowledge possible.[15]

The illusion of pure "objectivity" and denial of prejudice are themselves blind prejudices that distort interpretation and prevent understanding. People who imagine that they are free of prejudices, basing their knowledge on the objectivity of their procedures and denying that they are themselves influenced by historical circumstances, then are dominated by the power of prejudices that unconsciously dominate them.[16]

6. Language is finite. If all of life is historical rendering pure "objectivity" impossible, then it follows that human language cannot explain all of reality. Since interpretation and understanding involve intuition and the dynamic interplay of subjectivity and objectivity, they must be seen to be more than a matter of what can be explained by words.

Nevertheless, the limits of language do not imply that understanding is not possible. Understanding beyond language, in reality, *does* occur. Hence, understanding is not bound by language. Language is limited; it does not encompass all reality.

The goal of hermeneutics as understanding, therefore, goes beyond what can be expressed by words. Understanding is a dynamic, subjective, relational process stemming from the interpreter's commitments and social

---

[14] Gadamer, *Truth*, 397.

[15] Gadamer, *Truth*, 361.

[16] Gadamer, *Truth*, 360.

location. There is no exhaustive, absolute truth that only need by uncovered through the use of purely "objective," neutral tools.

7. A goal in interpretation is to separate one's valid biases from one's invalid biases. Our being anchored in specific human communities is a given for all of us. We must acknowledge our biases and seek to use them as helps and not hindrances in understanding. To deny them is to short-circuit one's potential before even getting started.

What distinguishes helpful biases from the countless unhelpful ones that it is the undeniable task of the critical reason to overcome?[17] The interpreter cannot separate in advance productive biases that make understanding possible from biases that lead to misunderstandings. This separation, rather, must take place in the process of interpretation itself.[18] We cannot first separate our biases, discard the invalid ones, and *then* begin the task of interpretation. We must begin the process of interpretation first. Through the *dialogical* encounter with tradition we discover which of our biases are blinding and which are enabling.

8. Understanding comes via dialogue with the text, not control over it. Understanding is not primarily a matter of trained, methodical, unprejudiced technique; understanding involves *engagement*. The keys to understanding are not manipulation and control, but participation and openness, not knowledge but experience, not methodology but dialectic.

Since understanding is a matter of dialogue with the text, Gadamer rejects the idea of "control" over the text via a strict interpretive *method*. Method implies control, that is, closed-mindedness regarding new awareness.

9. Questions, ours and *the text's, are central to interpretation.* Interpretation seeks to find the questions underlying the text. We cannot comprehend what texts are saying until we discover the questions to which they offer themselves as answers. Along with seeking the questions asked by the text, the interpreter also should seek the questions *not* asked. It is necessary to go behind the text to find what of relevance the text also did not say.

Besides seeking what questions do and do not underlie the text, we also need to be self-conscious regarding our own questions. Our understanding of a text is bound up with how we question it. There are true, legitimate questions for us to ask, according to Gadamer,[19] and there are also false questions. A true question is one capable of shaking the hold of our taken-for-granted opinions. It opens up a region of ignorance, of not

---

[17] Gadamer, *Truth*, 277.
[18] Gadamer, *Truth*, 295.
[19] Gadamer, *Truth*, 363–64.

knowing, without which genuine inquiry would not be possible. The question implies openness, but also self-awareness of limits.

Ultimately, for philosophical hermeneutics, the truthfulness of our questions has to do with our openness to reality. Are we asking the questions in order truly to gain understanding? Are we willing to change, to learn, to have our old ways of thinking and our old assumptions challenged. If so, we will be asking truthful questions and will have the possibility of understanding what we are interpreting. Our questions will be false to the extent that we are only seeking to buttress what we already know and thereby make *our* answers the text's answers.

10. The process of interpretation is interactive, circular—hence, the "hermeneutical circle." Gadamer thinks of understanding being achieved not so much through individual reflection, but through the placing of oneself within a dynamic process of tradition in which past and present are constantly interacting with one another.[20]

We understand something by comparing it to something we already know. What we understand forms itself into systematic unities, or circles made up of parts. The circle as a whole defines the individual part, and the parts together form a circle. We may call this process the "hermeneutical circle," referring to the interplay between the tradition and the interpreter. We have our perceptions and the tradition speaks to us from the outside. But as the interplay proceeds, we actually join the production of on-going tradition.[21]

Understanding happens with this continual interplay between present reality and tradition, not as two mutually exclusive entities but as inter-related parts of the whole. We are part of tradition ourselves and contribute to its growth. But it precedes us, and our understanding of it is necessary for us to understand our present and contribute to the formation of our future.

Common Ground: Liberation Theology and Philosophical Hermeneutics

Though formulated in quite different contexts, Latin American liberation theology shares striking similarities with philosophical hermeneutics.

1. They both assert the need to take the Bible seriously. Philosophical hermeneutics asserts that an encounter with the past, especially through

---

[20] Gadamer, *Truth*, 290.
[21] Gadamer, *Truth*, 293.

"classic" texts, is necessary for an understanding of the present. For theology, of course, *the* classic text is the Bible.

Latin American liberation theology, which emerged from changes in Roman Catholicism following Vatican II in the early 1960s, understands itself as biblically based. Juan-Luis Segundo, perhaps the most methodologically self-conscious of the liberation theologians, asserts that since Christianity is a biblical religion, Christian theology "must keep going back to its book and reinterpreting it." It "cannot swerve from its path in this respect."[22]

According to Gustavo Gutierrez, a commitment to the Bible goes hand-in-hand with a commitment to be devoted to service for justice in relation to oppression.

> Our purpose is . . . to let ourselves be judged by the word of the Lord, and to therein think through our faith, to strengthen our love, and to give a reason for our hope from within a commitment which seeks to become more radical, total, and efficacious.[23]

2. They both recognize our lack of "objectivity." Perhaps the clearest area of convergence between liberation theology and philosophical hermeneutics is in their common recognition that "neutrality" and total objectivity in interpretation are not possible and that it is precisely this lack of total objectivity that makes understanding possible.

We *all* have pre-understandings in the form of values, commitments, and concerns that are part of the very nature of being specific people living in a specific place in time as part of specific communities with specific traditions.[24] There can be no understanding apart from this non-neutral, non-absolutely objective specificity. Language itself reflects the values and beliefs of those who use it. Thus, our way of speaking, even our way of "seeing" is value-oriented. As Jon Sobrino sees it, understanding is never neutral either in practice or in intention, but it always has a practical and ethical character.[25]

When it poses as an "impartial" discipline, theology already is choosing for the status quo.[26] To assert that theology should choose for the poor and oppressed is not a new imposition of partisanship. It is rather simply posing an alternative partisanship to the one already chosen.

---

[22] Segundo, *Liberation*, 7.

[23] Gutierrez, *Theology*, ix.

[24] Gutierrez, *Theology*, 3.

[25] Sobrino, *True*, 9.

[26] Segundo, *Liberation*, 13.

3. Both accept the text's and our historicity. Gadamer asserts that there can be no real understanding of a text without the recognition that both we and the text are located in history. Thus, we do not read the text as if it is somehow above history. Nor do we assume that we can somehow find an objective spot "above" the text. We share this being-in-history with the text. This sharing is the basis for inter-communication between the text and us.

For liberation theologians, "entering into the historical particularity of our own situation"[27] means inserting ourselves *into* our historical situations as agents of liberation in the struggle for a more just society.[28] The Bible itself emerged from a particular historical situation of action for liberation. It is this common involvement in particular situations of oppression and injustice that forms a bridge between the biblical materials and the present.[29] Modern people not involved in action for liberation will find these biblical materials inaccessible.

To link our historical situation with the interpretation of the Bible, eschewing a universal, objective, neutral, ahistorical perspective for interpretation "above" the text is simply being honest. *Everyone* does this in actuality because such an ahistorical perspective does not and cannot exist. The true question is: *what* present-day historical reality does the interpreter's perspective reflect and how well does this correspond with that of the biblical writers?

4. Both assert the need to relate the text to the present. Philosophical hermeneutics views the Bible as a "classic" text that only lives in relation to the questions of the interpreters. It is not to be studied in a neutral fashion for its own sake. It speaks to those who ask of it, but only in relation to the interpreter's own horizon. Liberation theologians write of the need to interpret the Bible in light of their present social situation and the questions arising from that situation.

In focusing on one's present situation for the questions that make interpretation of the Bible and the doing of Christian theology possible, liberation theologians attempt to understand the Bible in the light of their contemporary situation. Miguez Bonino asserts that his theological method has to do with first developing questions "which arise out of the concrete historical praxis" and then looking "to the biblical and theological tradition."[30] These questions arise from the historical reality of oppression and injustice in Latin America.

---

[27] Assman, *Theology*, 105.
[28] Gutierrez, *Theology*, 262.
[29] Miguez Bonino, *Doing*, 102.
[30] Miguez Bonino, *Doing*, 165.

True understanding happens with an *ongoing* willingness to change one's interpretation of scripture in light of the continuing questions arising from analysis of the present. As Segundo writes: "If our interpretation of scripture does not change along with the problems, then the latter will go unsanswered; or worse, they will receive old, conservative, unserviceable answers."[31]

5. Both see knowledge as personal and practical. To liberationists, what we know is inextricably tied with what we do. Like Gadamer, they reject the idea of abstract, ahhistorical, objective, neutral "knowledge" existing apart from involvement in historical existence. In Gutierrez's terms, "history . . . can be known only by transforming it, and transforming oneself." To know the truth requires a commitment to modify reality according to that truth.[32] It is only by *practicing* what we know, only by living the truth, that we can truly gain knowledge.

Both recognize the need to encounter "classic" texts, especially the Bible, for help in understanding the present. Both see the impossibility of this encounter being unbiased, neutral, and totally objective, and both recognize that the interpreter *and* the text are historically specific. Both see the need to relate the texts to the present in order for them to "live."

Making the Hermeneutical Circle Specific

Liberation theology makes the hermeneutical circle quite specific and in the process articulates a "method" of interpretation. Philosophical hermeneutics focuses more on describing the context within which interpretations takes place than than on outlining how it should be done. Liberation theology is much more *directive* than philosophical hermeneutics.

1. Reality is experienced as oppressive. The theologian must recognize that most Latin Americans are poor and that their poverty is not simply a matter of bad luck or the "orders of creation," but rather the result of oppressive, even evil social structures.

According to Hugo Assmann:

> The starting-point of liberation theology is the present historical situation of domination and dependence in which the countries of the third world find themselves . . . . [We start here] because this is the situation of two-thirds of humanity and as such must impinge

---

[31] Segundo, *Liberation,* 9.
[32] Gutierrez, *Power,* 59.

on the historical consciousness of Christianity and pose radical questions about the nature of the church's mission.[33]

Starting from this experience leads to a more conflictual notion of reality and God's relation to that reality than customary in Christian theology. But this is the only way genuinely to "de-ideologize" the Christian message. Gutierrez writes, "theology seems to have avoided for a long time reflecting on the conflictual character of human history, the confrontations among people, social classes, and countries."[34] By doing so it has missed the central thrust of the Bible.

Truly to understand the Bible, the interpreter must share the biblical writers' awareness of the conflictual nature of reality exposed by the existence of oppression and poverty. The God of the Bible takes sides in these situations.

2. Our ideological superstucture is viewed with suspicion. An awareness of the unjust realities of their social situation leads liberation theologians to suspicion of the ideological superstructure of the social status quo. This suspicion is a fundamental component in the theological method of liberationists. As Segundo writes, "systematic suspicion would seem to be an integral part of the hermeneutical circle of any liberated and liberating theology."[35]

The phenomenon of *ideology* occurs when thinkers claim to be neutral. When we are unaware of how outside concerns shape our thinking, we are most vulnerable to oppression-justifying ideologies.[36] A truly liberative theology must start form the opposite assumption than that that sees the theologian as unaffected by surrounding society.[37] Liberation theologians recognize that theology is shaped by its social world and its institutions and worldview.

3. Traditional biblical interpretation is viewed with suspicion. Reflection upon human experience, especially the experience of the poor and oppressed, leads to a sense of suspicion, not only of one's social world but also of theology and the prevailing interpretation of the Bible.

Liberationists do not seek abstract, intellectual "understanding" of biblical texts, but question results of biblical scholarship that relegate the biblical message to "personal" or "spiritual" present-day relevance. Something is

---

[33] Assman, *Theology*, 53–54.
[34] Gutierrez, *Theology*, 35.
[35] Segundo, *Liberation*, 231.
[36] Segundo, *Historical*, 27.
[37] Segundo, *Liberation*, 56.

drastically wrong when Christians can study the Bible and come away with their involvement in an oppressive social order unchallenged.

The liberationist hermeneutical circle deconstructs traditional interpretations of Christianity and the Bible that buttress a socio-political reality in which the vast majority of Latin American people are "non-persons." Liberationists believe that a different interpretation of Christianity and the Bible is possible that demands commitment to liberating action.

4. Reinterpretation brings new insight. From this attitude of suspicion can flow new interpretations for these oppressive situations. A rejection of status quo interpretations frees one to see the full radicality of the biblical God. These conditions of sin and oppression may actually prove to be the context of an encounter with God.[38] As they facilitate rejecting traditional interpretations, they help foster a clearer vision of the biblical God as liberator of the oppressed.

As involvement in these conditions begins this new interpretative process, its fruit moves the interpreters to *change* these conditions, making clear that the Bible points toward liberation, justice, shalom, the poor, and love.[39] To be animated by these themes leads us to reject any acceptance of oppression and poverty as inevitable constituents of "the way things are."

The Central Point of Difference

In comparing liberationist and philosophical hermeneutics, we see many similarities. However, the two perspectives diverge regarding the "rights" of the text. A feminist theologian speaks more clearly to this point than the Latin Americans we have considered—but they likely would echo her comments.

> Feminist biblical hermeneutics stands in conflict with the dialogical-hermeneutical model developed by . . . Gadamer . . . because it cannot respect the "rights" of the androcentric *text* and seek for a "fusion" with the patriarchal-biblical horizon. Its goal is not "identification with" or "consent to" the androcentric text or process of biblical reception but faithful remembrance of and critical solidarity with women in biblical history.[40]

Commitment to present-day liberation requires that one be selective in reading the biblical materials. Some biblical passages are *accurately* read as buttressing the status quo. A hermeneutics of total openness to the bibli-

---

[38] Sobrino, *True,* 27.
[39] Miguez Bonino, *Doing,* 103–4.
[40] Schüssler Fiorenza, *Bread,* 140.

cal materials reflects an apolitical orientation; present-day commitments make it necessary to affirm some biblical teachings and to reject others.

On the other hand, the viewpoint of philosophical hermeneutics remains suspicious of any strict method—presumably even a liberationist one. Method, according to Gerald Bruns,

> is what we take recourse to when our learning fails us: it is an alternative to invention. Method tries to reduce rather than to amplify, for it wants always to determine what *cannot* be said in this or that case, and so by closure or the natural exclusiveness of its design it forbids all statements but those it can account for.[41]

So, these two perspectives diverge over the question of "method." The priority of the liberationists is on the use of the Bible as a means to the end of liberation. Because they believe the true message of the Bible supports liberation, they claim that their biblical study is seeking only to understand the Bible. But in practice it is clear that liberationist hermeneutics is a *method* for utilizing the Bible for the work of liberating the poor and the oppressed. Philosophical hermeneutics much more sees "understanding" the text and "understanding" our world as ends in themselves. A "method," which by definition exerts control over the text, hinders gaining understanding by asserting ahead of time what kinds of things the interpreter expects to find.

Conclusion: Implications for Anabaptists

Present-day Anabaptist biblical hermeneutics surely finds affinity with the common ground we see between philosophical hermeneutics and Latin American liberation theology. Sharing this common ground leads many Anabaptists to be suspicious of objectivist "scientific" approaches.

Anabaptists see the Bible as central to our faith and practice. We recognize that all people have interests, commitments, and biases that shape how they read the Bible. We affirm that only as we seek to *follow* Jesus will we be enabled truly to understand the Bible. Anabaptists also recognize that the Bible is a historical document and that we are, as well, ourselves historical creatures. Anabaptist theology cares much more for practical, concrete living than for ahistorical, abstract ideas. And the point of reading the Bible is to relate it to present-day life.

For Anabaptist theology, as for philosophical hermeneutics and liberation theology, knowledge is personal and practical. We know Jesus as we follow his way. Knowledge follows from commitment. Christian ethics

---

[41] Bruns, *Inventions*, 1.

have much more to do with face-to-face caring for actual human beings than with intellectualized, disembodied theories.

The *difference* between liberation theology and philosophical hermeneutics points to challenges for how Anabaptists read the Bible and challenges us to be self-conscious about our hermeneutics and to be careful about how we may uncritically echo the tendencies in mainstream Christianity that liberationists and philosophical hermeneutics challenge.

On the one hand, liberationists challenge a complacent biblicism that comfortably accepts the power and privilege accorded wealthy North Americans. Present-day Anabaptists may neglect the logic of their tradition and tend toward either a kind of individualistic reading strategy that focuses on personal piety or a scholarly, critical reading strategy that distances the interpreter from the text. Both strategies blunt the radical biblical call for transformative social engagement, a call echoed by the first Anabaptists.

On the other hand, philosophical hermeneutics challenge any comfortable melding of ideology with biblical interpretation—be it an ideology of social action or (much more likely in the U.S.) an ideology of Pax Americana. Present-day Anabaptists (like all other Christians) may minimize the core anti-idolatry message of the Bible that demythologizes *all* ideologies—again neglecting the anti-ideological logic of the first Anabaptists.

Resources from the Anabaptist heritage could foster a creative synthesis of liberation theology and philosophical hermeneutics. Most centrally, our peace tradition provides a basis for *non-coercive* engagement, transformative social involvement without coercive ideologies.

CHAPTER SIX

The Core Message of the Bible: God's Healing Strategy[1]

IN CONTINUITY with the Anabaptist tradition dating back to the sixteenth century, present-day Anabaptists understand their faith convictions as being rooted in the Bible. A major one of these convictions is the role of the community of faith in God's work of bringing healing to creation.

In this chapter, I present an Anabaptist reading of the Bible that sees its central message as the account of "God's healing strategy": God has called communities of God's people together to find healing themselves and to witness of this healing to the rest of the world.

The Need for Healing

Early on, the Bible tells us something has gone wrong. Loving relationships have been broken. Creation has been marred. Salvation is needed. However, God will not simply step in and by force, by coercion, make things right. God's healing strategy is much more subtle. *Love* shapes God's activity, patient, long lasting, persevering love.

The Genesis one creation story concludes, "everything . . . was very good." Then, Genesis three tells of a break in the relationship between human beings and God, the rise of "brokenness" among human beings. Genesis 4–11 tells more of brokenness: Cain's murder of Abel, Noah and the Flood, the Tower of Babel. At the end of Genesis eleven, we read of Sarah's barrenness.

Something new emerges with Genesis twelve. In the face of barrenness, God calls Abraham and Sarah to begin a community, to be the parents of a great people—and miraculously makes it possible by giving Sarah a child. Thus begins God's *strategy for healing* as summarized in the words in Genesis 12:3: "In you all the families of the earth shall be blessed."

---

[1] This chapter is a summary of the argument of Grimsrud, *God's Healing Strategy*. Used with permission of Cascadia Publishing House.

God establishes a community of people who will know God. Through people of faith living together, face to face, in *peaceable community life* God will make peace for all the families of the earth. This healing strategy proceeds through the Old Testament and the New, culminating in Revelation 21–22. A desire to be part of the on-going expression of God's faith community-centered healing strategy animates Anabaptist convictions, from the sixteenth century to the present.

In Genesis twelve, God *promises* Abraham and Sarah a future. And through that promise, God also promises all peoples a future. "In you, Abraham, all the families of the earth shall be blessed." God's healing strategy for the human race will be funneled through Abraham.

God's calling of a people included two elements. First, "I will bless you," God said, "so that [second] you will be a blessing." These remain the two elements of God's calling of people—"I will bless you . . . so that you may be a blessing." The Bible tells the winding story of the people of the promise. However, in the end, each piece points toward the continuance of this two-part strategy: "I will bless . . . so that you may be a blessing."

The last part of Genesis tells how Abraham's descendants went to Egypt. In time, they were enslaved. Exodus 2:23–5 tells of their plight. "The Israelites groaned under their slavery, and cried out. Out of the slavery their cry for help rose up to God. God heard their groaning, and God remembered God's covenant with Abraham." God remembered the promise to Abraham.

God's "remembering" (generally in the Bible, God "remembering" leads to saving acts) results in the call of Moses to lead the saving involvement of God with the people. Moses, Israel's great prophet-leader, challenges Pharaoh with the words of Yahweh, helps the Hebrew slaves coalesce as a coherent community, and leads the people in their escape from Egypt and slavery. The escape culminates with the miraculous flight through the parted Red Sea waters—that then crashed down on Pharaoh's pursuing armies.[2]

---

[2] For those who read the biblical story as culminating in God *healing* the nations, an incident such as the destruction of so many Egyptians raises numerous problems (as do, of course, many other examples of violence along the way). These problems are not easily dismissed, especially when we realize how often throughout history, stories of violence in the Old Testament have underwritten later human violence.

However, a couple of points are important to keep in mind. The first is the importance of our reading the parts of the story in light of the whole. Later elements of the story, especially the words of the Old Testament prophets, the message of Jesus, and the portrayal of the ultimate healing of the *nations* in Revelation 21–22, do point towards healing, meaning that the violence in these earlier stories is never an end in itself—and often, as in Exodus 1–15, the main violence comes from the oppressors as they hurtle themselves into situations

The God of the Exodus is *not* a God of people in power who lord it over others. This God, *unlike* other gods, does not merely reinforce the king's power. This God is a God of *slaves* who gives life to the life-less, hearing the cries of those being treated like non-persons.

God's will for salvation here is not expressed through human military action. God's human leader, Moses, is *not* a commander of weapons of war but a weapon*less* prophet whose authority is based solely on him speaking for God. The Israelites experience salvation by the direct involvement of God, not by having more powerful horses and chariots.

The Hebrews are called not simply to leave Egypt behind, but to *reject* Egypt's unjust ways. When God gives the Hebrews the Law following the exodus, much of the Law was explained in *opposition* to Egyptian cruelty. One of the harshest criticisms the prophets make of Israel later on is that Israel had become like Egypt—unjust, materialistic, oppressive.

The law comes *after* liberation—not as a means of earning salvation but as an additional work of God's grace, a resource for ordering peaceable living in the community of God's people. The intent, ultimately, is to lead to universal shalom, to bless all the families of the earth (God's healing strategy). Exodus 19:6 states: "The whole earth is mine. . . . You shall be for me a priestly kingdom." "Priestly" implies "mediator." Israel mediates God's presence to the "whole earth."

Kingship and the Need for Prophets

After the children of Israel were freed from Egypt, they wandered in the wilderness for forty years before settling in the land God provided for them. God's special calling for these people remained the same as it had been from the beginning when he called Abraham and Sarah: to be a *blessing* for all the families of the earth—by showing them a better way of living characterized by genuine justice. [3]

---

where those who kill by the sword end up with violent deaths themselves (a witness to the self-defeating nature of violence).

Second, the Exodus story explicitly makes the point that in this work of liberation God's people were not to use violence themselves. Moses' violence early on, when he murders an Egyptian, is condemned. This dynamic of the people of faith being required *not* to use violence is echoed, in the end, with Revelation's clear message that the followers of the Lamb must refuse the sword (Rev 13:10), even in the face of the Beast's oppression.

[3] Again, this is a complicated part of the story. The account of the Hebrews gaining the promise land famously includes extreme, God-ordained violence (see, for example, Josh 8:18–29). This part of the story needs to be taken seriously; it is indeed troubling—and not only for pacifists.

However, in terms of the argument of this chapter, the main point of the settling of the land

After Israel settled in the promise land, they lived as an association of tribes. When Israel needed them, "judges" would arise and unite the tribes for a while—Gideon and Deborah were two of the best. Gideon led Israel to victory. Then the people wanted to make him king. But he refused: "I will not rule over you, and my son will not rule over you; the Lord will rule over you" (Judges 8:23). *God* is the only king you need.

However, the system did not always work well. The book of Judges tells mostly of judges who were not that great. It concludes: "In those days there was no king in Israel; all the people did what was right in their own eyes" (21:25).

Then, under Samuel, a *good* judge, things get better—for a while. However, chaos returns: "When Samuel became old, he made his sons judges over Israel. . . . His sons did not follow in his ways, but turned aside after gain; they took bribes and perverted justice" (1 Sam 8:1–3).

Israel's elders ask for a warrior-king in the face of a threat from their enemies. "Appoint for us a king to govern us, like the *other nations*" (1 Sam 8:5). Samuel insists that Israel's elders will regret their choice:

> These will be the ways of the king who will reign over you: he will *take* your sons and appoint them to his chariots and to be his horsemen, and to run before his chariots. . . . He will *take* your daughters to be perfumers and cooks and bakers. He will *take* the best of your fields and vineyards and olive orchards and give them to *his* courtiers. He will *take* one-tenth of your grain and of your vineyards and give it to his officers and courtiers. He will *take* . . . the best of your cattle and donkeys, and put them to his work. You shall be his *slaves*. In that day you will cry out because of your king, whom you have chosen for yourselves; but *the Lord will not answer you* in that day (1 Sam 8:11–8, emphases added).]

Samuel finds it shocking that the elders don't realize what they would be getting into. He tells the elders that, under their king, they will return to "Egypt." "You shall be his slaves." Having a king will result in a radical change in Israel's society: (1) the concentration of wealth in only a few hands with poverty for the many as a result (in contrast to the ideal of *each* family having its own land); (2) the establishment of a permanent standing army and a warrior class (in contrast to a society which trusted in God for its security); and (3) general conformity with the social patterns of the sur-

---

is the call for the Hebrews to live *justly* (implicitly, in contrast to the injustices of the nations they displaced as well, of course, of Egypt) for the sake of their calling to bless all the families of the earth. The spread of *injustice* within Israel leads to prophetic condemnation and, ultimately, the portrayal of the experiment of channeling God's healing strategy through a nation-state as a *failure*.

rounding nations (instead of being the alternative society God had created from the freed slaves to be a light to the nations). Samuel's voice, though, is not the only one in Israel. God grudgingly gives Israel a king.

As it turns out, even the Hebrews' greatest king, David, tends too strongly toward the ways of Pharaoh, as seen in his infamous action with Bathsheba. David becomes infatuated with the beautiful woman, takes her, and has her husband killed. The prophet Nathan does confront David, and the king repents. However, great damage had been done. The community of faith moves much further from its call to be a blessing.

David's style of kingship carried over to his son Solomon, the next king of Israel. If we look at the story from the perspective of the Bible's message of God's healing strategy (and from the portrait of valid kingship in Deut 17:14–7), we see Solomon as a power-seeking, merciless leader, who moved ancient Israel toward its tragic ending. Solomon ruthlessly eliminated his opponents, built a standing army, began forced labor, gathered wealth for himself, and entered alliances with other nations and worshiped their Gods.

God warns Solomon in 1 Kings 9:6–8:

> If you turn aside from following me . . . and do not keep my commandments . . . , but go and serve other gods and worship them, then I will cut Israel off from the land . . . ; and the [Temple] I will cast out of my sight. . . . This [Temple] will become a heap of ruins.

This is indeed what happens. Solomon did turn aside from following God. "His wives turned away his heart after other gods; and his heart was not true to the Lord his God" (1 Kings 11:4). In time Israel is cut off from the land and the Temple becomes a heap of ruins.

Prophetic Critique of Communal Injustice

The kings after Solomon tended even more towards injustice. The story in 1 Kings 21 shows typical problems. King Ahab has an Israelite, Naboth, killed so he may take possession of his vineyard. However, Ahab meets the prophet Elijah when he gets to the vineyard. "Have you found me, O my enemy, you troubler of Israel?" Indeed, says Elijah. The Lord has told me the injustice you have done. *You* are the troubler of Israel and will suffer the consequences.

The society had changed tremendously from the views of Moses, Joshua, and Samuel of God's will that the society would be most healthy when *all* the people prospered. Only an Israel that embodied health across the society would fulfill its vocation. In time, though, some became quite rich, and many others were very poor. The prophet Amos speaks God's words of indictment for a society that had become *unhealthy*:

> They sell the righteous for silver, and the needy for a pair of sandals—they who trample the head of the poor into the dust of the earth, and push the afflicted out of the way; father and son go in to the same girl, so that my holy name is profaned (Amos 2:6–7).

Amos calls for justice, challenging an unjust society to turn back to God as their only hope of finding life. "Let justice roll down like waters, and righteousness like an ever-flowing stream" (Amos 5:24). Justice has to do with water, with life. To do justice is to support life.

The prophets' also teach, as seen in Hosea eleven, that no matter what, God continues to love God's people and desire their healing. At the beginning of that chapter, Hosea draws on Israel's memory. "When Israel was a child, I loved him, and out of Egypt I called my child" (Hos 11:1). The exodus revealed Israel's identity and Israel's understanding of God. God freed the poor enslaved Hebrews from Egypt.

God did *not* demand that the children of Israel earn his love. However, God *did* ask that they live with the care and respect God had shown them, thus living in relationship with God. Israel was not able to remain committed to God's ways. "The more I called them, the more they went from me; they kept sacrificing to the Baals, and offering incense to idols" (Hos 11:2).

God, though, speaks of more than judgment following disobedience. "How can I give you up, Ephraim? How can I hand you over, O Israel?" God asks this question of the people: Can I simply let you go, my child, after all that I have done for you? Can I simply write you off? "My heart recoils within me; my *compassion* grows warm and tender. I will *not* execute my fierce anger; I will not again destroy Ephraim; for I am God and no mortal, the Holy One in your midst, and I will not come in wrath" (Hos 11:8–9). This God acts with mercy and compassion because it is part of God's very *nature* to do so.

God Remains Committed to Healing

The Hebrews did not heed the message of the prophets. The kings did not turn from injustice toward justice. The prophesied consequences came to pass. With the book of Jeremiah, we read that the center of their religious life, the Temple, was destroyed as was the center of their political life, the king's palace. Many were killed and others shipped away to Babylon in exile.

Jeremiah especially linked Israel's conformity with the injustices and idolatries of the nations with the end of their nation state. His own life symbolizes Israel's fate when he travels to Egypt, symbolizing the return to the pre-exodus dynamics of their society.

However, even with his dark words and profound grief, Jeremiah also provides words pointing forward, words that indicate that God's healing strategy is not ended. Jeremiah's words may have served to help the Israelites survive as a people. He encouraged them to seek the wellbeing of whatever society they were part of (Jer 29:7) while at the same time maintaining their distinct identity as people of Torah—remembering God's blessing in order to be a blessing.

In light of Jeremiah's witness, the entire Old Testament may be read as a cautionary tale. Nation-state-centered, sword-oriented politics failed to be a viable vehicle for sustaining the people of God's calling to bless all the families of the earth.

The vocation to spread peace will be fulfilled not through the violence of the standard nation-state, but through the peaceable witness of counter-cultures scattered throughout the world in *various* nation-states—counter-cultures that center their lives on the consistent embodiment of the command to respond to God's creative love with creative love of their own.

The survival of the people did not require the assumed pillars of identity—the king's palace and the temple. These pillars lay in ruins. But the peoplehood, the call to be a blessing to all the families of the earth, *remained*, even after their nation-state bit the dust.

Through this failure, the true nature of God's promise became more clear to prophets such as Jeremiah, with his exhortation to the people of the promise to seek the peace of the city wherever they were living (29:7). This was actually a call for the people to embrace their existence in Diaspora—an existence that did indeed continue for generation upon generation *separate* from any kind of Israelite nation-state.

Jesus and the Liberating Kingdom of God

When Jesus enters the scene, Israel is again dominated by a large empire. In Jeremiah's time it was Babylon, the followed by Persia, then Greece. About one hundred years before Jesus began his public ministry, the Roman Empire took over control of Palestine.

Economic injustice remained widespread. So, too, did poverty and a large disinherited peasant class. The inheritance regulations that Elijah had defended in the time of King Ahab were long gone. Religion generally supported this unjust status quo, as it had in the time of Solomon and in the generations following.

Jesus' message echoed many prophetic themes. God gives life as a gift *and* expects that those who know God's mercy share it with others. Jesus critiqued power politics, trusting in weapons of war, and people seeking wealth and worldly success above all else. Jesus proclaimed God's healing strategy through the calling of a people who would know God and who would share that knowledge with others—blessing all the families of the earth.

Jesus' time of ministry begins John the Baptist's baptism. As he came out of baptismal waters, "he saw the Spirit descending like a dove on him. And a voice came from heaven, 'You are my Son, the Beloved; with you I am well pleased.'" What follows is a time of discernment; what kind of "Son" (a royal title) will Jesus be?

Jesus first moves deeper into the wilderness. After forty days of fasting, Satan tempts him, a foretaste of his struggle for the rest of his life. How will you respond to brokenness most effectively and do the most good? How will you function as God's Son? Satan offered Jesus several options for kingly power. Jesus says no to each. He will trust in God's ways.

In Mark, Jesus starts with a simple proclamation. "The time is fulfilled, and the kingdom of God is at hand; repent and believe in the good news" (1:15). These words summarize Jesus' mission. God's plan in calling Abraham and Sarah and in liberating the children of Israel from slavery in Egypt remains in effect. God calls for a people to live with God as their only king, and by doing so to bless all the families of the earth. Jesus calls upon his listeners to repent of misplaced priorities and to believe the good news of God's mercy and love.

After proclaiming the good news, Jesus then showed that that was indeed true; he healed diseases, cast out demons, forgave sins, welcomed people seen to be unclean by the religious authorities. He founded a community of followers to provide the needed critical mass to live free from the domination systems of his day—both Empire and institutional religion.

Jesus *combined* his teaching with his healing activity. Jesus conveyed God's abundant compassion. Jesus taught that, and he *showed* that. Jesus says "kingdom of God" and people think great, new, political revolution, big transformations. However, Jesus' images challenge their expectations. Do not expect the kingdom of God to be something all-powerful. The kingdom is at-hand already. We see it in the mustard bush. A healthy mustard bush serves just fine as a nesting home for the birds. God's rule does not have to appear in the grandiose; a mustard seed growing into a mustard bush will do just as well. You can live the way of the kingdom right now, in *this* life.

The Cost of Faithfulness to God

Still, Jesus' healing acts will not simply bring about heaven on earth. "Many believed in Jesus' name because they saw the signs that [Jesus] was doing. But Jesus on his part would not entrust himself to them, because he knew all people" (John 2:23–4). Are the people following Jesus only as one who does wonders? Do they genuinely want to know God?

Jesus realized that living out his message includes suffering. This becomes clear in the passage that is at the center of Mark, 8:27–38. Jesus has just cured a blind man, and he and the disciples are on the road. Jesus asks the disciples, "Who do the people say that I am?" And they answered him, "John the Baptist; and others, Elijah; and still others, one of the prophets." He asked them, "But who do you say that I am?" Peter answered, "You are the Messiah (King)."

Jesus accepts Peter's answer, but he then goes on to teach them that the Son of Man must undergo great suffering, be rejected by the elders, the chief priests, and the scribes, and be killed. Peter took him aside and began to rebuke him. But Jesus responded to Peter, "Get behind me, Satan! For you are setting your mind not on divine things but on human things." Jesus rebukes Peter because Peter fails to understand the type of Messiah Jesus is. Jesus is not the kind of almighty king who would never face suffering. Jesus will be a king whose saving faithfulness leads to his death. Peter cannot understand that, at least not yet.

Jesus links his suffering with the suffering his followers will face. "If any want to become my followers, let them deny themselves and take up their cross and follow me. For those who want to save their life will lose it, and those who lose their life for my sake, and for the sake of the gospel, will save it" (Mk 8:34–5).

Jesus realizes that through his willingness to suffer and die, God's salvation will be made known. Jesus will not fight back, relying on God to vindicate him. Jesus taught his followers that they too must be willing to take up their crosses. He challenged them to remain committed to love and mercy even when it is rejected, even when such a commitment leads to suffering.

Jesus' ministry reaches its climax in Jerusalem, triggered by his symbolic act of cleansing the temple that shows his disdain for the corrupt religious institutions. In response, the religious leaders began to look "for a way to *kill* Jesus" (Mk 11:18). And, in a few days, in cooperation with the Roman political leaders, they succeed. The religious leaders could not accept Jesus' critique of their corruption.

The Roman governor, Pontius Pilate, oversaw Jesus' death by crucifixion. From Pilate's perspective, Jesus was merely a pawn, an insignificant irritant. Pilate *used* the religious leaders' hostility toward Jesus as a means to humiliate those leaders. Pilate manipulated the leaders into proclaiming, "We have no king but Caesar!" (Jn 19:13). Pilate, interrogating Jesus, asked a rhetorical question, "What is truth?" But he is not actually interested in the answer. Jesus replies, "Everyone who belongs to the truth listens to my voice." Pilate does not listen. He simply walks away. Pilate has not interest in Jesus' truth. He orders Jesus killed.

Some of the people who loved Jesus the most, his mother and a couple of other women, watched him die. Two days later, they go to his tomb to anoint his body, a Jewish custom. When they get there, Jesus is *gone*. In time, he appears in his resurrected body to his followers, and reinvigorates their community.

With Jesus' resurrection, God vindicates Jesus' life as truth and shows that God's love is stronger than death. Jesus lives on and promises that those who trust in him will also live on and need not fear death. Jesus' resurrection keeps God's healing strategy going. It brings new hope, the possibility of life even in the face of death and despair.

The community of disciples was in complete disarray after Jesus' arrest. Peter, in terror denied he ever knew Jesus. Then, Jesus' post-resurrection appearances brought the community back together. And the blessing they received, that Jesus lives on and that his way is God's way, became their message. This blessing they shared with others.

The Church Expands

The Book of the Acts of the Apostles begins with Jesus' farewell statement to his followers. Just before he ascends to heaven, Jesus tells them: "You will receive power when the Holy Spirit has come upon you; and you will be my witnesses in Jerusalem, in all Judea and Samaria, and to the ends of the earth" (Acts 1:8).

Acts then tells of the carrying out of Jesus' words. The Holy Spirit, a few days after Jesus' ascension, visited the followers of Jesus in a powerful way. They then began to spread the word of God's salvation offered through Jesus far and wide.

The first seven chapters of Acts tell of Peter's preaching in Jerusalem, the witness of many other Christians—and scores of people in Jerusalem trusting in Jesus. The also met with opposition. One of their leaders, Stephen, is put to death by stoning. Like with Jesus, these Christians had conflicts with the religious leaders who saw the Christians as rejecting standard religious procedures and threatening the status quo and with the political leaders who saw them threatening the social order. Christians were violently driven out of Jerusalem, and thus began to preach the gospel in the surrounding areas—in Judea and Samaria.

The rest of Acts tells of the ever wider area reached by the gospel, concluding when, after many tribulations, the Apostle Paul reaches the city of Rome, the heart of the Empire—witnessing to the ends of the earth.

The Book of Acts tells of the carrying out of the promise to Abraham, that Abraham's descendants would bless all the families of the earth. Peter gave one of his sermons in an area near the Jerusalem Temple. As he often did, he stressed the belief that Jesus fulfilled the Old Testament. "The God of Abraham, the God of Isaac, the God of Jacob, the God of our ancestors has glorified his servant Jesus" (Acts 3:13).

He called upon his Jewish listeners to accept Jesus as their savior. "All the prophets from Samuel and those after him also predicted these days. You are the descendants of the prophets and of the covenant that God gave to your ancestors, saying to Abraham, 'And in your descendants all the families of the earth shall be blessed'" (Acts 3:24–5).

Paul, the Missionary

Paul, the most important writer in the history of Christianity, summarizes his vocation in Romans 1:5. He exhorts his readers to "the obedience of faith." The obedience God wants has to do with two things—first, *trust* in God's mercy, *accept* Jesus Christ as our savior from the power of sin. Second, *respond* to God's love for us by actively loving others.

Paul learned about God's mercy through desperately needing it himself. Paul was a Jew by birth, named "Saul." By the time he was a young adult he established himself as a leader. He joined the Pharisees, was well educated and strongly committed to a quite strict understanding of religious faith. Like other Pharisees, Paul found himself in conflict with Jesus and his followers.

After Jesus' death, conflict between the Christians and the Pharisees reached its height when Stephen was stoned to death. When "they dragged [Stephen] out of the city and began to stone him, the witnesses laid their coats at the feet of a young man named Saul" (Acts 7:58) who obviously supported the crowd's action.

This Saul soon became a leader among the Pharisees, specializing in persecuting Christians. He regularly breathed "threats and murder against the disciples of the Lord" (Acts 9:1). Saul sought to follow the ways of God. His hostility toward the Christians was *because* of his commitment to protecting God's honor. Later, he wrote this about himself: "You have heard, no doubt, of my earlier life in Judaism. I was violently persecuting the church of God and was trying to destroy it. I advanced in Judaism beyond many among my people of the same age, for I was far more zealous for the traditions of my ancestors" (Gal 1:13–4).

Then, something amazing happened.

> Now as [Saul] was going along and approaching Damascus, suddenly a light from heaven flashed around him. He fell to the ground and heard a voice saying to him, "Saul, Saul, why do you persecute me?" He asked, "Who are you, Lord?" The reply came. "I am Jesus, whom you are persecuting. But get up and enter the city, and you will be told what you are to do." The men who were traveling with him stood speechless because they heard the voice but saw no one. Saul got up from the ground, and though his eyes were open, he could see nothing; so they led him by the hand and brought him into Damascus. For three days he was without sight, and neither ate nor drank (Acts 9:3–9).

Saul had his life turned completely around. He, in time, took on a new name—*Paul*. Paul, the Apostle. His old world came apart. Then he started to put the pieces together. Because Paul did sincerely want to do God's will, he was able to receive God's direct revelation to him. This Jesus who you hate in fact truly reveals your God.

One of the questions Paul surely struggled with is this—how could I have been so *violent* in the name of God? How can I now understand God and God's will in a way that will overcome such sacred violence? Paul speaks out of his own experience when he writes Romans. As an alternative to doing violence in the name of obedience to God, he writes of obedience that comes from faith. The obedience that comes from faith is what the "gospel of God" produces.

The "gospel of God" is the good news that more than anything else, God loves us and wants us to be whole. In *response* to God's love, we are challenged ourselves to love. This is the most important law or commandment. Paul makes this clear later in Romans. "The one who loves another has fulfilled the law" (Rom 13:8).

Paul argues in Romans 1–3 that all people are sinful—blatant sinners *and* morally upright sinners. All need God's mercy. The final part of Paul's argument is that God's mercy *is* available, to everyone, without distinction. To God we are all loved people who can, and must, accept God's mercy *and* who can, and must, share this mercy with others.

Paul finishes with this: "But now, apart from the law, the righteousness [or justice] of God has been disclosed [in order to justify,] by God's grace as a gift, [all who trust in that grace, which God has made known through Jesus]" (3:21). The answer to sin is trusting in God's *mercy*.

The *justice* of God is not primarily expressed by works of the law—strict boundary lines between us and them *showing* (through circumcision, kosher, Sabbath) that *we* are righteous. It is expressed by *trusting* in God's mercy shown through Jesus Christ. Justice has to do with healing. This point takes on much more weight when we think of Paul's own story—moving from *violence* toward *shalom* as a result of meeting Jesus.

These who genuinely know God's justice will form communities of healing that overcome alienating distinctions that heretofore have separated Jews and Gentiles, male and female, slave and free. And they will witness to this healing, as Paul did, to the ends of the earth.

Christian Faith Under Fire

The early Christians continued to face persecution. As time went on, this came mostly from the Roman Empire. The problem with the Rome was *religious*. Who would the people worship—the God of Jesus Christ or the emperor-as-god? A common religion of emperor worship helped unify the various peoples of the empire. Faithful Christians could not worship the emperor, for them, an act of blatant idolatry. By refusing such worship, they threatened the social unity based on common religious practices. The Christians paid a price for this refusal. The stress of living in this context of constant danger challenged the faith of many Christians.

The book of Revelation sought to encourage Christians in the face of these dangers. In its visions, Revelation challenges the hearts of its readers. Follow the way of Jesus. Find your strength in communities of the Lamb, not communities of the Beast (Empire). Turn from the allurements of Roman civilization because it is based not on trust in God but on trust in the powers of evil (symbolized by characters such as the Beast, the Dragon, and the Great Whore).

One of the common motifs in Revelation is that of conquering. In face of the seemingly all-conquering power of the Roman Empire to deal out death, Christians are told of another type of conquering. Conquer not by killing others, but rather by remaining faithful to Jesus even to the point of profound suffering. How is this "conquering"? It can be seen as conquering *only* if one believes this is precisely how Jesus won his victory—remaining faithful, not resorting to violence, facing death itself—and being vindicated by God.

Revelation five presents the most crucial image of the book. The chapter envisions a scroll that has some large meaning. At first we are told that no one can be found to open the scroll. The writer weeps. But then—"Do not weep, one has been found." Who has the kind of power needed to open the great scroll? The Lion of the Tribe of Judah (an image of a military conqueror). Here is the crucial moment. The conqueror is . . . "a Lamb standing as if it had been slain" (Rev 5:6). Jesus Christ, slain but now risen from the dead. The "king" is a lamb!

The power that truly matters is not the power to kill others (Rome's kind of power), but the power to trust in God, facing death faithfully, trusting in God's vindication. This trust is worth giving because the Lamb that was slain now stands.

In chapter thirteen, we are introduced to the terrible Beast whose power is that of government with its "crowns" and "throne". His authority is worldwide. This symbolizes the spiritual power of the Roman Empire. Rome's demand that people worship the emperor was blasphemy for Christians. Revelation 13:4 tells of this: "The whole earth . . . worshiped the dragon [meaning Satan], for he had given his authority to the Beast [meaning the Empire], and they worshiped the Beast, saying 'Who is like the Beast, and who can fight against it?'"

John says do not go along with this worship—and expect to pay a cost for your refusal. Do not fight back with violence (Rev 13:10). Follow Jesus and stick to the path of non-retaliation even in the face of violence. Refusing violent resistance to the conquering attack of the Beast shows the only way the spiral of violence might be broken.

The first few verses in chapter fourteen show, in contrast to the Beast's power, the deeper reality that the Lamb is victorious and that those who follow him are also victorious. The Beast's conquering was only temporary. The faithful followers' final fate will be to sing with the community of the faithful on Mt. Zion.

These visions of the Beast and of the faithful ones singing praise to God reveal the reality of Revelation's readers. The persecuting Roman Empire is aligned with Satan and must not be worshiped. As Jesus' followers faithfully follow the Lamb, they will be present with God.

The concluding vision in Revelation 21–22, the New Jerusalem, reveals God's completed healing strategy. This enlivening hope helps Christians remain strong and faithful.

The New Jerusalem is cleansed of the forces of evil. It is creation as it was intended to be. Healing completed. It is made up of *people*. "On the gates are inscribed the names of the twelve tribes of Israel" (Rev 21:12), and "on the foundations are inscribed the twelve names of the twelve apostles of the Lamb" (Rev 21:14); the entire people of God.

Along with the end of evil and the direct presence of God, the vision promises the *healing* of the nations. The human enemies of God's people are not, in the final event, to be destroyed. They, too, find life when the dragon's spell is broken. Part of the reason Jesus' followers do not fight back and join the spiral of violence is this hope that even the nations might find healing. Persevering love is the method—not brute force.

The New Jerusalem (Rev 22:1–2) contains a river with the water of life. On each side of the river is the tree of life. "The leaves of this tree are for the healing of the nations."

Most of Revelation portrays the spiritual forces of evil, symbolized by the dragon and his cohorts, as powerful and greatly influencing life on earth. They are behind the persecutions, injustice, and sufferings that plague people of faith. The conclusion, though, in chapters 21–22, is that this evil will not last forever. God is not powerless to stop it. The power of everlasting love will win out. God's healing strategy will *conclude* with its mission accomplished.

God's Healing Strategy Today

Reading the Bible as the story of "God's healing strategy" may buttress Anabaptist convictions in several ways. These are some key points that emerge for Anabaptist convictions from the Bible:

(1) The world is all too often characterized by brokenness and alienation. This alienation corrupts, even communities of people of faith who worship the God of the Bible. However, God's intention is not to establish these communities as a remnant that remains comfortably detached amidst the brokenness, nor, even less, simply to escape this "vale of tears." Rather, God has established communities of faith so that people who know God's

healing love might *enter* the brokenness of the world, being agents for healing wherever healing is needed.

(2) The community witnesses to a message of peace and healing, not of condemnation and fear. God, in intervening in the world most profoundly through the witness of people shaped by God's mercy, offers the world a carrot more than a stick. Thus, God calls the community to manifest authentic peace in its common life and to speak of this peace to the wider world, rather than to speak of "justifiable violence" and religiously underwritten conflict and judgmentalism.

(3) The faith community holds a double-sided perspective concerning the wider world. The empires are to be seen as God's *rivals* for people's loyalties. The empires are to be viewed with great suspicion. Yet, at the same time, the Bible promises *healing* to the nations. The critique of power politics, the formation of counter-cultural faith communities, and the clear awareness of the contrast between Torah and gospel versus the ideologies of empire, should, *for the sake* of the nations, foster their genuine healing.

The prophets, like Jesus, modeled this double-sided perspective (as did many sixteenth-century Anabaptists). They preached God's justice, formed and cultivated the life of communities *countering* Empire, engaged the nations to the point even of suffering martyrdom—and trusted in God's vindication, a vindication that culminates not in human beings being punished but in human beings, even the kings of the earth (Rev 21–22), being transformed and healed.

So, we see a close connection between the core values of the biblical story and those of the sixteenth-century Anabaptist story. This correlation remains extraordinarily instructive for those who seek today to live as part of these same stories.

PART THREE: Tradition

THE INTERPLAY of biblical interpretation with the heritage of the Christian tradition in general, and more specifically the Anabaptist tradition since its beginnings in the sixteenth century, engenders much that is distinctive about Anabaptist convictions today.

Chapter seven, "From Sixteenth-Century Anabaptists to Mennonite Church U.S.A.," traces the trajectory beginning during the Reformation and culminating in the formation of the largest North American Mennonite denomination with the merger of the Mennonite Church and the General Conference Mennonite Church.

Chapter eight, "Practice-Centered Convictions: Some Central Themes" offers a descriptive account of what Mennonites tend to see as distinctive about historical Anabaptist convictions in relation to the broader Christian tradition—an emphasis on practice over theoretical reflection.

CHAPTER SEVEN

From Sixteenth-Century Anabaptism to Mennonite Church U.S.A.[1]

THE ANABAPTIST movement included diverse expressions in its first decades. However, by the end of the sixteenth century the movement had settled into small communities scattered across Europe, most numerous in Holland, parts of Germany, Moravia, and Switzerland. Except for the Hutterites, who maintained a distinct identity from the 1530s to the present, just about all the Anabaptist groups in Europe in 1600 were (or eventually became) known as Mennonites. The other modern group that directly traces it lineage to the sixteenth century, the Amish, split off from Mennonites in Switzerland in the late 1600s.

Other groups have arisen that have been deeply influenced by the Anabaptist tradition but never affiliated with Mennonites, most notably the movement that became known as the Church of the Brethren. In recent years, numerous theologians and church members from a variety of traditions identify themselves as, in some sense, being Anabaptist (or at least express strong affinities with Anabaptism).[2] So, "Anabaptist" is a broader category than "Mennonite."

Mennonites, though, do understand themselves as direct spiritual descendants of sixteenth-century Anabaptists and generally affirm "Anabaptist" as a rubric that characterizes their values and aspirations. For all present-day Anabaptists, considering the history of Mennonites is instructive; here we have the thickest real-life embodiment of Anabaptist ideals and convictions.

In this chapter, I will trace the story from sixteenth-century Anabaptists to the largest contemporary North American body, Mennonite

---

[1] This chapter is based on lectures presented at Salem Mennonite Church, Freeman, SD, in 1995.

[2] Roth, ed., *Engaging*, collects essays from various theologians discussing their attraction to the Anabaptist tradition.

Church U.S.A. (which shares a history and retains a formal connection with Mennonite Church Canada).

I will consider the Anabaptist/Mennonite story in four parts. First, I will look at the origins of the Anabaptists of the sixteenth century. Second, I will consider the first couple of hundred years in Europe and the evolution from being the core of the Radical Reformation to being the "Quiet in the Land." Third, I will focus on the time of Mennonite migrations—to North America, and to Russia, then again to North America—down through World War II. Fourth, I will focus on the recent past, the present, and the future.

Origins of Anabaptist Convictions (1525–1555)

The Anabaptist movement emerged in the 1520s as a part of the Protestant Reformation, especially in Switzerland, Germany, and Holland. The first Anabaptists were several young men who were supporters of Ulrich Zwingli, a church leader in Zurich, Switzerland, who in 1522 led the church at Zurich to separate from the Catholic Church.[3]

These young supporters challenged Zwingli to make his reforms more radical, urging him to baptize only *adult* believers and to separate the church from the dominance of the Zurich city council. Zwingli said no, and the young "radicals" broke with him. In 1525, they instituted the practice of believers baptism, separating themselves from Zwingli's church. They thus began what turned out to be the Reformation's first free church (i.e., church free from state control).

These "radicals" early on, called "Anabaptists" for re-baptizers, preferred to call each other "Brethren." They did not believe they were re-baptizers, since they did not recognize the validity of infant baptism. This movement, in several discrete expressions, early on spread rapidly across Western Europe.

Anabaptist theology emerged out of a great deal of ferment during these eventful years of the 1520s and 1530s. I will mention three distinct movements that all contributed to the formation of key Anabaptist values.

(1) *The Protestant Reformation*—In 1517, Martin Luther, a German Catholic priest of the Augustinian order and a popular theology professor, posted his Ninety-five Theses in Wittenberg door, leading to his break with Catholicism. Luther's movement gained allies among many of the local po-

---

[3] Basic treatments of early Anabaptist movement include: Dyck, *Introduction*; Williams, *Radical*; Weaver, *Becoming*; and Snyder, *Anabaptist*.

litical leaders. The Magisterial Reformation (so called because of alliances with their nation's government leaders, the magistrates) grew quickly, fueled in large part by strong disillusionment with the Catholic Church.

A few years after Luther's movement emerged, a Catholic priest in Zurich, Switzerland, Ulrich Zwingli, also broke with Catholicism and established, with the city's political leadership, another Protestant Church. Though influenced by Luther, Zwingli never became a Lutheran. His significant theological differences with Luther kept them apart. So, Zwingli founded the Swiss Reformed Church, independent both from Catholicism and Lutheranism.

Typically at that time, few church members could read; even fewer could read Latin, the language in which the Bible was available. To counter this problem, Luther translated the Bible into popular German. Luther's translation spread widely in all German-speaking areas. Now the Bible could be read in the language of the people. Zwingli shared Luther's commitment to giving all Christians direct access to the Bible. In fact, Zwingli accused Luther of not following the Bible closely enough.

The Anabaptists who broke with Zwingli shared his biblicism (basing belief and practice directly on the Bible). They strove to get the Bible into the hands of common church-goers. The early Anabaptists emphasized literacy more than most other Protestants. Christians need to read the Bible and apply its teaching to all of life for themselves. The Protestant Reformation contributed especially to Anabaptist biblicism. Out of this biblicism came the Anabaptist focus on the life and teaching of Jesus, especially the Sermon on the Mount. A key dynamic of church life for the Anabaptists was the exercise of communal discernment in studying the Bible.

(2) *Peasants Revolt*—In the 1520s, general unrest among the poor peasants of Western Europe erupted in violence, the "Peasants War."[4] This conflict emerged out of horrendous living and working conditions for the masses of Western Europe. Resentment over these conditions led to hostility toward church and political leaders who enforced and benefited from the exploitative conditions. The leaders smashed this revolt, with much bloodshed. In one major "battle," approximately six thousand peasants lost their lives—compared to six of the government soldiers.[5]

These events shaped Anabaptists' tendency to reject control by hierarchies, their recognition of the futility of revolutionary violence to correct injustice, and their concern for the lives of common people. The Anabaptist

---

[4] See especially Stayer, *German*.

[5] Williams, *Radical*, 24.

movement, in general, emerged as a grassroots movement that appealed to many disillusioned Peasant Revolt supporters. This contributed to an attitude of suspicion toward the powers-that-be and openness to new expressions of faith.

(3) *Monasticism*—An influential early Anabaptist leader, Michael Sattler, drafted the Schleitheim Confession of 1527 that cemented pacifism and discipleship as core Anabaptist beliefs. Sattler had been a monk in the Benedictine order before becoming an Anabaptist. This background significantly shaped his theology, and through him the theology of Anabaptism.[6]

Monasticism began when a few devout Christians separated themselves from the wider culture, moving into small, isolated monasteries. One of the early monastic leaders, Benedict of Nursia (480–543), formed an order in 529 that eventually took his name, the Benedictines. In 1209, Francis of Assisi (1182–1226) founded the Franciscans. Benedict and Francis shared similar values (simplicity, peaceableness), values the monasteries kept alive.

In 1525, Michael Sattler left the Benedictines because he did not want to be so separate from the world. He found kindred spirits among the Anabaptists, and contributed to the movement strong values about community, service, and the love ethic.

These various currents came together to produce the Anabaptist movement. The movement, chaotic and decentralized, tended to attract at least a few people prone toward over-enthusiasm. It also, from the beginning in Zurich, met with extraordinarily harsh persecution from the powers-that-be. Many Anabaptists met with martyrs' deaths.

Nonetheless, the movement spread rapidly. It *never* had complete unity, suffering from the very start from internal conflicts and splits. We can't look back to a "Golden Age" when all Mennonites or Anabaptists were unified under one roof. Our present-day diversity is not new.

The extreme persecution surely contributed the most to the fragmentation of the Anabaptist movement. The Anabaptists found precious little breathing space. A tragic number of early leaders faced imprisonment, exile, and death. This extreme persecution left an indelible stamp on movement, especially in the withdrawal attitude that we will look at in the next section.

Even given the diversity that characterized the movement from the beginning, despite the persecution that decimated the ranks and kept the survivors constantly on the move, the Anabaptist movement by the 1550s

---

[6] See Snyder, *Life*.

did have common features. Six key values may be mentioned as broadly characteristic of all the Anabaptist groups.[7]

(1) *All who believe in Christ are priests.* All Christians have direct and equal access to the Bible and to God. This includes a much lower view of the priesthood and sacraments than the Catholic Church of the sixteenth century.

(2) *Discipleship is central to faith.* Faith without works is dead. The only way to know Christ is by following him in life.

(3) *Bible is supreme authority.* The teachings of the Bible, especially the words and deeds of Jesus, are the basic material for understanding Christian theology and ethics. The Bible carries a much higher authority than church tradition.

(4) *Only believers are to be baptized.* Baptism is for Christians who themselves have made a conscious decision to follow Christ. To be baptized, a person must be able to understand what the Christian life is about and to be willing to participate in the life of the church, giving and receiving counsel with fellow church members.

(5) *Violence is rejected.* Christians are expected to follow Jesus' way of peace, refusing to fight in wars. The church is free of state control, offenders within the church receive church discipline and not the state's sword, and God is seen to transcend national boundaries.

(6) *Christians are not to conform to the wider world.* Separate from the ways of the world, such as materialism, frivolity, seeking power and prestige, competition, coercive way of relating. Such separation leads to living simply.

The Quiet in the Land (1555–1700)

For the development of the Anabaptist tradition, the significance of the persecution that the first generation faced cannot be overstated. From very early on, the expression of those values met with harsh resistance. That resistance determined the direction this radical movement would go for generations afterwards, down to the present.

The state and state churches persecuted the Anabaptists as a threat to very fabric of western European society. The Anabaptists denied the ages-long assumption that church and state must be tied inextricably together. In a day when European civilization lived in terror of invasions from the

---

[7] My summary here is my own synthesis, influenced by, among other writings, Yoder, "Summary;" Weaver, *Becoming,* 113–41; and Snyder, *Anabaptist,* 379–96.

Turks, the Anabaptists rejected any responsibility to join in military resistance. The Anabaptists also rejected hierarchical structures in church and society.

In response to the persecution, Anabaptists sought to remain faithful to their central values. Often they faced two choices—repudiate their faith (which doubtlessly many did) or flee to new locations.

The Anabaptist movement evolved after the first generation into a migrating people, seeking tolerance and the possibility of practicing their faith with a minimum of resistance from the outside. By the mid-sixteenth century, when many of the Brethren came to be called Mennonites (after an important and relatively long-lived Dutch Anabaptist leader named Menno Simons), they had given up the confrontive, evangelistic style of the early Anabaptists, evolving toward becoming the "Quiet in the Land."

This era of harsh persecution and the resultant evolution of the group into a migrating people, primarily seeking tolerance and security, served as a crucial defining time. Out of the experience of persecution came dynamics that reshaped the Anabaptist movement and determined how the original creative values would be expressed.

What are some changes wrought by this era of persecution on the Anabaptist movement?

(1) A change from voluntary membership to membership by birth. Theologically, one of the largest innovations for the Anabaptist movement was the rejection of infant baptism for believers baptism. They believed that membership in the church is not for everyone in the society, but only for genuine Christians who *voluntarily* join the church.

However, in practice, their focus on voluntary membership did not last long. The effect of living as a migrating people, separate from the wider culture, meant that they became somewhat self-contained societies. In general, all in these mini-societies became church members, being born into it. Few people from outside these mini-societies joined their churches. In numerous situations, governments gave Anabaptists tolerance with the understanding that they would not try to convert outsiders.

(2) From urban to rural. The first Anabaptists often lived in cities. Before long, though, the focus turned to the countryside, as the more likely environment conducive to tolerance. Before long, Anabaptists' skill as farmers and their willingness to cultivate unsettled countryside became their main attraction to potentially tolerant princes.

(3) From adult baptism to baptizing children of the church. The practice of baptizing adults who made a clear and conscious choice to move from the world of darkness to the world of light changed after the first

generation. This change came in conjunction with the rapid evolution of the Anabaptist movement toward self-contained, ghetto-like communities. After the first generation, the practice of baptism centered much more on the integration of children of the church into the adults' church. Baptism become more of an initiation rite set at a somewhat arbitrary age to mark the full membership of children whose faith generally evolved gradually.

(4) From evangelism to seeking toleration. The first Anabaptists zealous evangelized outsiders with the claims of Christ. In face of extraordinarily hostile reactions from their societies' powers-that-be, the later Anabaptists soon became much more concerned with finding tolerant locales quietly to practice their faith within their isolated communities. Often, part of the agreements they made with estate owners included the promise *not* to evangelize.

(5) From open membership to ethnicity. The first Anabaptists came from the wider society in which the movement arose. They shared their neighbors' language and cultural practices. However, in time the Anabaptist religious community and the Anabaptist cultural community (which were basically identical) became distinct from the surrounding culture. This led to the emergence of Anabapt ethnicism.

An ethnic enclave is a group of people distinct from surrounding groups not only in terms of theology but also distinct in terms of various other characteristics, most notably language, but also dietary practices, dress, and other folkways.

Anabaptists became an ethnic enclave largely as a response to the intense persecution they faced. This persecution caused them to turn inward, to band together in migrations where they took along their native language and folkways to a new environment. Their different language and folkways marked them off as different from the surrounding culture. Over several generations, these differences became ingrained and they evolved into a distinct *ethnic* group.

(6) From a more personal orientation to a more communal orientation. The first Anabaptists, though certainly community-oriented, generally had a strong sense of individuality that allowed them to differentiate themselves from their wider culture and consciously choose to join a different church. Over time though, this individuality became increasingly diminished as children were socialized to identify first of all with their separated, self-contained community.

(7) The emergence of the powerful dynamic of Gelassenheit. The word *Gelassenheit* refers to a spiritual attitude of yieldedness, submission, humility, openness to martyrdom. The value placed on this attitude increased

significantly over time in the Anabaptist communities in response to persecution and marginalization. Anabaptists had little external power and hence the ideal of transforming the wider world diminished. The focus of their faithfulness became more oriented around something they could do—live submissively and with their wills yielded to God's will, even when that meant suffering and martyrdom. The Hutterites used the notion of *Gelassenheit* in a very concrete way—the ideal of community of goods.

These developments shaped the history of Anabaptists down to the present, especially those who continued to face persecution and the need to maintain a separated identity.

Holland provided an exception. After the last Dutch martyrdom in 1574, Anabaptists increasingly found toleration in Dutch society. The high tolerance led Dutch Anabaptists to increased acculturation that in some ways modified many of the dynamics that marked Anabaptism's evolution. Unlike the Anabaptist populations elsewhere in Western Europe, Anabaptists in Holland in the seventeenth century and later rarely migrated. They lost membership not through people leaving with the hope of finding increased tolerance elsewhere so much as through the processes of assimilation, inter-marriage, secularism, and joining other churches.

Thinking in terms of Anabaptist groups that eventually ended up in North America, the changes from sixteenth-century Anabaptism significantly effected their expression of the key Anabaptist values noted above.

(1) Priesthood of believers—The sense of community strengthened with the increased sense of separation from the wider culture. Also, though, the communities tended toward stronger internal leadership, and many conflicts resulted. The Anabaptist movement as a whole remained decentralized, with no unified leadership that encompassed all groups.

(2) Discipleship—The focus of energy turned away from transforming the world. The focus turned inward toward seeking for community purity and a personal sense of submission to God and the community. Instead of evangelism, the focus became more works of service, especially mutual aid (i.e., service of others inside the community).

(3) Bible-centered—The Bible remained central, but the focus became more one of repeating first generation interpretations and insights into biblical teaching than of continuing to seek new applications of biblical teaching to new settings.

(4) Believers baptism—The survival of the church came to depend on retaining children of the church instead of gaining new converts. Hence, baptism served more as an initiation rite for bringing in children of the church into the community than as a sign of conversion.

(5) *Rejection of violence*—The commitment to pacifism became perhaps Anabaptism's most distinctive characteristic, accompanied by solidifying a two-kingdom orientation holding that governmental activities are not appropriate for Anabaptists. They assumed a clear distinction between church and world, and their responsibilities lay exclusively in the former.

(6) *Non-conformity*—The sense of separation from the wider world was strengthened (in part due to the development of Anabaptist ethnicism). Anabaptists grew in self-consciousness as people who did not conform to the wider world. Along with non-conformity, the strengthening of community-consciousness led to a decrease in the *internal* non-conformity that was allowed. Anabaptists were becoming more different from the outside world but more like each other.

The Migrations (1683–1945)

The first known Anabaptists to move to North America came from Holland and from all appearances crossed the ocean in search of economic opportunity more than religious toleration. Scattered references may be found to Anabaptist settlers, the first being in 1644 in the Dutch settlements in New York. Dutch Mennonites established the first permanent congregation of Anabaptists in North America in the Germantown area near Philadelphia in 1683.

The first larger influx of Anabaptists migrating to North America came in the first half of the eighteenth century. They mostly originated in Switzerland and South Germany, and migrated to escape the persecution they still faced in Europe. Dutch Anabaptists assisted their brethren on the way, but few desired to leave Holland at that time.

These migrating Swiss at first settled in Pennsylvania, finding welcome from the Quakers who promised them religious freedom and respect for their pacifist practices. Between 1700 and 1756, approximately four thousand Swiss and South German Mennonites came to the United States, until immigration was halted during the French and Indian War.[8] After 1815 and the conclusion of the Napoleonic wars, another influx of immigrants came to North America. Approximately three thousand Swiss and South German Anabaptists immigrated. Many of these also settled in Pennsylvania, but some moved further west to Ohio, Indiana, and Illinois, and north to Ontario.

---

[8] See MacMaster, *Land*.

For generations these Anabaptists lived an isolated existence in the United States, maintaining many of the ethnic practices of their European forebears, including the use of the German language (or "Pennsylvania Dutch"). This isolation lasted throughout the nineteenth century and beyond in some communities, though gradually they did become more acculturated—a process that has greatly accelerated in the twentieth century.

The various wars of the US, especially the Revolutionary War and the Civil War tested Anabaptist pacifism, though in many ways Anabaptist convictions were strengthened.[9]

In the late 1800s, many Anabaptists began a process of assimilating with the broader American culture that has continued to gain momentum down to the present-day. Probably the main factor contributing to this process has been the religious toleration they have found in the United States and Canada. North American toleration contrasts with the harsh persecution Anabaptists earlier faced in Western Europe.

The first steps in this acculturation process began when many Anabaptist congregations adopted church practices used by more mainstream churches such as revival meetings, foreign missions, beginning of Sunday school programs, and the publication of religious literature.

A more recent influx of Anabaptist to North America came from Russia. In the years of strong persecution before Holland granted toleration to Anabaptists (ca. 1580), many Dutch Anabaptists migrated to the Danzig area on the Baltic Sea. Though they originally spoke Dutch, over the years they spent in the Danzig area they began speaking the local German dialect known as Low German. Low German became the language for their descendants.

The Low Germans found a measure of tolerance in the Danzig area in the late sixteenth and seventeenth centuries. Anabaptists from throughout Europe continued settling there through much of the eighteenth century. In 1772 sovereignty over this area was transferred from Poland to Prussia and the toleration lessened. The new overseers exerted pressure on the Anabaptists to participate in the military and placed increasing restrictions on their land ownership. As military demands increased and the Anabaptist population also increased, the difficulty in maintaining a viable way of life and holding to their convictions as the same time increased significantly.

These dynamics led many to consider another migration. Beginning in 1762, Catherine II of Russia had invited Germans and other western Europeans to move to Russia and occupy land vacated by Turks in south-

---

[9] See Brock, *Pacifism*; MacMaster, et al, *Conscience*; MacMaster, *Land*; Schlabach, *Peace*; and Horst, *Mennonites*.

ern Russia.[10] In the 1780s, Danzig-area Anabaptists showed interest in Catherine's offer. They had farming skills to offer Russia. Russia offered them assurances of autonomy, freedom of religion, and no military involvement. Besides their farming success, all the government asked of the Anabaptists was that they not recruit local Orthodox Christians.

The Mennonites established two main colonies in Russia, first Chortitza followed by Molotschna. These colonies thrived throughout the nineteenth century, growing increasingly prosperous until the transformation of Russian society that came with World War I, the Russian Revolution, and the establishment of Stalinism.

Along with the growth and prosperity of the two main colonies in Russia came some tensions. Over time, the colonies grew more and more stratified between wealthy landowners and landless laborers who struggled to make a living. Also, the Russian government began to pressure the colonies in the second half of the nineteenth century to integrate more with the Russian society, especially by participating in the military and integrating with the Russian educational system (including the use of the Russian language). Throughout Anabaptist history, language has been a central factor in the maintenance of a distinct identity in relation to the wider culture. These Mennonites resisted these pressures, but they caused significant stress within the colonies.

A third tension stemmed from controversy within the churches following the emergence of a reform movement that eventually separated to form the Mennonite Brethren church.

The pressures from the Russian government on Mennonites to assimilate more with the wider culture echoed similar earlier pressures from the Prussian government, the main factor in migration to Russia. So, many began to consider the migration option once more, understanding the issue as a choice between staying in Russia and facing the trials of increasing governmental pressure to accommodate or facing the trials of uprooting and seeking new life in a foreign land.

In response to these threats of Mennonites to leave, the Russian government relented somewhat and lessened their pressures. They established the world's first thoroughgoing alternative service program that allowed Mennonites to stay out of the military. They also allowed the Mennonite schools to continue to teach German and Anabaptist religion.

These changes were not enough for many. About one-third of the Russian Mennonites (ca. eighteen thousand) migrated to North America,

---

[10] For Mennonites in Russia, see J. Friesen, ed., *Mennonites*; Urry, *None*; and J. Toews, *Czars*.

settling mostly in the Midwest, from Manitoba in the north down to Oklahoma in the south, with the largest settlements established in Kansas.[11]

As it turned out, neither the Mennonites who stayed in Russia nor the Mennonites who migrated to North America sustained the Russian Mennonite way of life for long. Those who stayed faced incredible trauma with World War I, the Russian Revolution, and the establishment of Stalinism. By the end of the 1930s, the Mennonite churches in Russia had pretty much ceased to exist as openly-meeting congregations, thousands of Mennonites had lost their lives, hundreds more had been exiled to Siberia, and the Soviet government forbade those who remained to practice their faith. Recent research indicates that even in face of such violence, the Anabaptist faith did survive in Russia—but at great cost and in great secrecy.[12] A group of about twenty thousand Russian Mennonites did migrate, mostly to Canada, in the 1920s.

The Mennonites who migrated to North America did prosper. They accommodated rapidly to the wider culture, largely due to the religious toleration that they found. In some ways, their experience in North America paralleled the experience of Anabaptists in Holland after they gained toleration—the loss of much that was distinctive about the Anabaptist faith tradition.[13]

These series of migrations shaped the expression of key Anabaptist convictions. Up until the twentieth century, the migrations solidified Anabaptist ethnicity. As Anabaptist groups migrated to new areas, they tended to take their language (e.g., Pennsylvania Dutch and Low German) and folkways with them, remaining distinct from their new surroundings, often for generations.

Did this ethnically based separation from the world reflect the same concerns as the sixteenth-century Anabaptists commitment to non-conformity? Certainly separation from the outside world was much easier when the outside world was so clearly different in various ways (most obviously language) from the church-community.

The migrants often selected themselves by the strength of their convictions. This dynamic surely had the effect of helping those convictions to remain viable. The people who stayed behind tended to be the people more comfortable with their environment and more open to accommodation with the wider culture.

---

[11] Schlabach, 231–94.

[12] Sawatsky, "Historical."

[13] See Juhnke, *Vision,* and P. Toews, *Mennonites.*

An example of this can be seen with regard to the commitment to pacifism. Mennonites who remained in Holland, Switzerland, Prussia, and Germany had mostly given up on pacifism by the nineteenth century. The pacifist ideal in Europe essentially remained limited to the Russian Mennonites—descendants of those who had left Prussia in large part in order to maintain their freedom from military involvement. Quite likely, the migration of one-third of the Russian Mennonites in the 1870s repeated this process. Those who left probably felt more commitment to the peace position than did those who stayed.

The migrations stimulated much mutual aid among Anabaptists—including Anabaptists of different nationalities. Dutch Mennonites provided significant assistance to the Swiss and South Germans who migrated to North America. In the 1870s, North Americans helped Russians in their move to North America. The prime twentieth-century case of Anabaptist mutual aid was the establishment of the Mennonite Central Committee (MCC) in the 1920s. MCC offered life-saving assistance to Russian Mennonites facing starvation in the aftermath of the Russian Civil War. As it turned out, MCC also was the channel for invaluable assistance for the twenty thousand Russian Mennonites who migrated to North America during this time.

The Twentieth-Century and Beyond

In the 1870s, Anabaptists in North America began to open up to the wider culture through the influence of revival meetings, missions, Sunday Schools, and the publication of religious literature. Around this same time, about eighteen thousand Russian Mennonites moved to North America and found the most hospitable environment their people had ever known.

The two World Wars brought out some tensions between Anabaptists and surrounding culture. However, the dynamics changed a great deal between the two wars. Anabaptists experienced World War I as a much more difficult and alienating experience. By the time of World War II several factors reduced the tensions.

North American society was not nearly as militant in its pro-war fervor. Anti-German sentiment had fueled resentment toward German-speaking Anabaptists during World War I (many not realizing that many German-speaking Anabaptists were *hundreds* of years removed from residence in Germany). By the time of World War II, many fewer Anabaptists spoke German as their first language. Also, peace church leadership saw World War II on the horizon and did a great deal of effective work with the US government to establish more acceptable provisions for conscientious objectors. As result, a generally mutually acceptable program (Civilian Public Service) was set up.[14]

Consequently, even the evolution of Anabaptist relations with military actions in North America shows that basically Anabaptists have found a safe haven in the North American cultural melting pot. Anabaptists have settled in and found a home here over the past one hundred thirty years, more than any other situation they have faced (except for Mennonites in Holland).

Anabaptists have become increasingly acculturated in North America, most clearly seen in the adoption of the language of the surrounding culture. After speaking their various forms of German for hundreds of years in several different locations, North American Anabaptists have now become mainly English speaking (with the exception of churches established among recent immigrants). This removal of the language barrier has opened Anabaptists to outside influences, both from secular society and other Christian traditions, more than any other development.

Another indication of acculturation has been Anabaptist commitment to higher education, both in terms of the establishment of Anabaptist colleges and seminaries and in Anabaptists' widespread attendance at non-Anabaptist colleges, universities, and graduate schools.

Somewhat connected with the commitment to higher education, Anabaptists have increasingly chosen to enter the professional (e.g., medicine, law, education) and business worlds, leaving the farms behind. This has led to a reversal of the sixteenth-century ruralization of Anabaptist culture. Anabaptists are becoming increasingly urbanized. One important effect of this movement to the city has been the growing scarcity of distinct Anabaptist communities. Without the distinct language and distinct communities, Anabaptist ethnicity is dying out.

Another factor leading to acculturation and loss of ethnicity has been increased inter-marriage between Anabaptists and non-Anabaptists. While often these marriages result in the Anabaptist spouse leaving the home church, such marriages also contribute to an increase of non-ethnic Anabaptists joining Anabaptist churches. As well, greater acculturation also has resulted in greater visibility of Anabaptists in American culture, leading to many non-ethnic Anabaptists joining Anabaptist churches by choice.

The process begun in the late nineteenth century of borrowing religious techniques such as revival meetings, Sunday school, and publications from non-Anabaptists has continued apace. Along with the increased

---

[14] See chapter nine below.

stability and security Anabaptists have found in North America has come increased prosperity. Anabaptists have generally joined with their North American neighbors in accumulating possessions.

Another indication of the accommodation of Anabaptists can be seen in their response to World War II. Even with the generally attractive provisions for COs and strong support from church leadership for conscientious objection, approximately fifty per cent of American Mennonite young men who were drafted during the War joined the military. This certainly served to reflect the loyalty that Anabaptists had come to feel for their adopted nation.

The Anabaptist group I am focusing on, the Mennonite Church USA has evolved into a full-fledged denomination, also reflecting cultural accommodation.

Among the Anabaptists who came to North America in the eighteenth and early nineteenth century and formed the Mennonite Church, another sign has been the loss of distinctive dress. Until well into the twentieth century, these Mennonites adhered to the practice of "plain dress," characterized, in part, by head coverings for the women and plain coats for the men. Starting in the 1950s and accelerating in the 1960s and 1970s, fewer and fewer Mennonites have been dressing plain.

A final example of Anabaptist acculturation is the increase of Anabaptist participation in politics. For years many Anabaptists did not vote, nor try to influence policy makers or run for office. Again, this was more true for the earlier immigrants. However, this withdrawal stance has been fading away. Mennonite Central Committee has an office in Washington, DC, and Anabaptists are much more likely than before to vote, to write letters, even to run for office.

How has this acculturation of affected key Anabaptist convictions?

Anabaptists remain committed to the Bible; however, their interpretations are shaped much more by outside influences. These influences include TV and radio ministries and non-Anabaptist Bible colleges on the one hand, and universities and critical Bible scholarship on the other hand. These influences have fostered a growing gap between the views of Anabaptist professors and their students on the one hand, and the "people in the pews" on other hand.

With the loss of ethnicity, the sense of community has become more voluntary. The priesthood of believers more than ever relies on choice, and as a result is much more fragile, especially in areas with little social pressure to be involved in church.

The practice of believers baptism has evolved. Many Anabaptists accept membership transfers from churches that baptize infants without rebaptism. The age for baptizing children of the church has tended to get younger. In some cases, under the influence of evangelical churches, congregations have connected baptism to conversion more closely. All of these tendencies have contributed to baptism being separated more from mutual accountability within the church and from the call to discipleship.

The peace tradition has evolved in several ways. Possibly as a result of the wider cross-fertilization with other Christian traditions, Anabaptists less strictly adhere to the peace position. It is hard to gauge commitment to pacifism as long as it is mostly an abstract belief in the absence of a military draft. Certainly Anabaptist churches still teach and profess pacifism. The outside world more highly respects Anabaptist pacifism. Probably the clearest development has been the increase in Anabaptist nonviolent political activism. This style of involvement has not been widespread, but it has gotten wide exposure and reflects a sense of responsibility for the affairs of the wider world that was not characteristic on earlier generations of Anabaptists.[15]

As would be expected, the ideal of non-conformity has been less central the more Anabaptists have assimilated with North American culture.

In light of this general acculturation, what might the future hold for the Anabaptist faith?

It seems clear that the Anabaptist church will increasingly become multi-cultural. The significance of stable, generations-long, rural Anabaptist communities will continue to shrink in the midst of increasingly mobile North American culture. As a result, the perpetuation of the key Anabaptist ideals will no longer depend on a sustained, concrete "community of memory."

Certainly these values have always been evolving and being shaped by historical events. This process will surely only accelerate as Anabaptist communities become more and more changeable, fluid, and oriented around centers other than ethnicity. Due to the influence of the media and the education of Anabaptists in non-Anabaptist colleges and graduate schools, the influence of non-Anabaptist theological orientations will continue to grow. This factor also will serve to make the adherence to traditional Anabaptist ideals more tenuous.

---

[15] Driedger and Kraybill, *Mennonite,* and Sampson and Lederach, eds., *From,* especially Kathleen Kern, "From Haiti to Hebron with a Brief Stop in Washington, DC: The Christian Peacemaker Teams Experiment," 183–200.

From Sixteenth-Century Anabaptism to Mennonite Church U.S.A.

At the same time, these ideals continue to be widely held in Anabaptist churches and are gaining increasing respect outside of Anabaptist circles. The ideals will not die, just as they have not died since the time of Jesus. The big question facing Anabaptist churches is not whether we can keep these values alive—God will see to that. The big question is whether we will continue to be used by God as a carrier of these values.

CHAPTER EIGHT

Practice-Centered Convictions: Some Central Themes[1]

AFTER TRACING the historical evolution of the Anabaptist movement in chapter seven, here I will focus on describing some of the central convictions that have characterized this tradition.

Throughout this book I use the term "Anabaptist" both in relation to the sixteenth-century Radical Reformation movement and in relation to on-going ideals rooted in that movement. I use "Mennonite" generally to refer to one specific expression of the Anabaptist tradition—though by far the largest. I do not see these two terms as being in tension.

Of all Christian traditions, Anabaptism recognizes that traditions require embodiment. I focus on the Mennonite expression of Anabaptism partly because that is my own context, partly because it is the largest, and partly simply to provide a sense of how Anabaptism "meets the actual world."

Mennonite theology, as expressed in the mainstream of Mennonite Church USA, generally agrees with other Protestant traditions (e.g., Baptists, Methodists, Lutherans, Presbyterians). And yet, in important ways, Mennonite beliefs stand as a *distinctive* approach within the broader Protestant world. In a phrase, this distinctiveness may be characterized in this way: Mennonite beliefs are *practice-centered*. Mennonites, as a rule, do not focus on abstract theological ideas but more on day-to-day life. Mennonites hold *together* belief and actions.

In what follows in this chapter, I will present what I understand to be, as a rule, consensus Mennonite beliefs. These are basic beliefs reflected in Mennonite confessions and other official statements, articulated by theologians affiliated with Mennonite institutions, and expressed in Mennonite

---

[1] This chapter originated as Sunday School classes led at various times for Eugene (Oregon) Mennonite Church, Trinity Mennonite Church (Phoenix, Arizona), and Salem Mennonite Church (Freeman, South Dakota).

pulpits. I offer this chapter as a *descriptive* portrayal of Mennonite convictions.

Mennonite Beliefs in Harmony with the Protestant Mainstream

At the joint assembly of the General Conference Mennonite Church and the Mennonite Church in Wichita, Kansas, summer 1995, the two denominations prepared for their eventual merger into Mennonite Church USA by approving a confession of faith, entitled *Confession of Faith in a Mennonite Perspective (CofF)*. The *CofF* writers noted that Mennonites have typically placed *less* emphasis on creeds and official confessions than many other Protestant traditions.

Two key early Anabaptist/Mennonite confessions—Schleitheim, Switzerland (1528) and Dordtrecht, Holland (1632)—have been influential, but they were not intended as comprehensive. Both served as attempts to unify Mennonites, asserting "this is what we agree on." The General Conference Mennonite Church in North America *never* had an official confession until 1995. The Mennonite Church adopted an official confession in 1962, but it was not used widely.[2]

The *CofF* shows how theologically similar Mennonites are to other Protestants. The *CofF*'s twenty-four articles are divided into three sets of eight. The first eight focus on basic general theological affirmations—God, Jesus Christ, Holy Spirit, Scripture, et al. The second eight focus on beliefs concerning the church, and the final eight focus on discipleship and ethics.

The distinctiveness of Mennonite beliefs becomes more clear in the second and third groups of articles. The first eight articles could be affirmed by most other Protestants.

The *CofF*'s summary begins as follows:

> We believe in God, Creator and Sustainer of the universe, who in love and holiness has called forth a people of faith, who has spoken to us in Jesus Christ, the Word of God become flesh, in whom Scripture has its center, the one crucified, resurrected, and exalted for our sake, our Savior from the dominion of sin and evil, our peace and our reconciliation, our Lord and the head of the church,

---

[2] For a brief history of the role of Confessions in Mennonite churches see Loewen, *One*, 21–60. See also Finger, "Confessions," and Koop, *Anabaptist-Mennonite*.

through whom God sends the Holy Spirit, the source of our life and the guarantee of our redemption.³

The *CofF* uses the language of traditional Christian orthodoxy: "We believe this only true and triune God has created all things visible and invisible" (Article one). "We believe in Jesus Christ, the Word of God incarnate" (Article two). "Because of sin, all have fallen short of the Creator's intent, marred the image of God in which we were created, disrupted the order in the world around us, and limited our love for others" (Article six). "We believe that, through the life, death, and resurrection of Jesus Christ, whose faithfulness put into effect the new covenant, God offers salvation from sin and a new way of life to all people" (Article seven).

The *CofF* articulates beliefs in a way that Christians from most denominations would affirm, presenting Mennonite faith as firmly in the mainstream of Protestant Christianity. At the same time, as we will see in what follows, we may also accurately refer to a *distinctively* Mennonite approach to Christian convictions. From their sixteenth-century beginnings—and down to the present—Anabaptists have operated both within the general parameters of Protestant theology and on their own as a distinct expression of *practice-centered* beliefs.

Scripture

Mennonites have always closely tied their theology with the teaching of the Bible.

Mennonites have traditionally been "biblicists," using scripture as the basis for all of their doctrines and practices. In defending their distinctive positions on pacifism and baptism, they cite Bible passages as their basis. Mennonites have denied that human reason, secular science, or common sense carry the same weight as the Bible in determining Christian beliefs. They have also refused to give church tradition equal weight as the Bible in guiding Christians.

The studying of scripture by *all* church members has been given high priority. Mennonites expect each person, in the context of the church community, to be able to gain from such study the knowledge necessary to know how she or he should walk as Christ's follower.

This biblicism has also resulted in some problems. Although ostensibly freed from church hierarchies and calcified traditions to appropriate biblical teachings directly, Mennonites have developed their own hierarchies and traditions. Parts of the Bible that support the desired position

---

³ *Confession*, 101.

have often been emphasized, while other biblical viewpoints have been ignored. Beginning in the late nineteenth century, many Mennonites were attracted to the biblicism of North American fundamentalism in ways that have fostered many conflicts over the years.[4]

Though biblicists, Mennonites do not read the Bible as a "flat book," weighting all parts equally. They take Jesus as the center. The Old Testament has secondary authority when it contradicts what Jesus said and did. Only that in the Old Testament that is consistent with Jesus remains authoritative. This view reflects not so much a negative attitude toward the Old Testament as a positive attitude toward Jesus as the fullest and clearest revelation of God.

Mennonites have traditionally started with the Sermon on the Mount and gone on from there in interpreting the rest of the Bible. This approach may lead them to value the Old Testament less than they should.[5] However, it has also protected them from the pitfalls many Christians have fallen into of using Old Testament morality (for example, in the area of the use of violence and warfare) to justify not obeying Jesus' moral teaching.

Along with seeing Jesus as central, Mennonites have placed a high premium on the role of God's Spirit in understanding the Bible. The written scripture (the "outer word") *must* be supplemented and activated by the Spirit in the believer's life (the "inner word"). But both remain essential. The "inner word" illumines the "outer word;" it is not a different word.

The "inner word" is necessary for a person genuinely to meet God in the Bible. Without the Holy Spirit in a person's life, the Bible is only an interesting book of stories.

The early Anabaptists struggled over this issue, because some believed that the gift of the Holy Spirit freed them from the Bible altogether. Most, however, while recognizing that the Spirit gives some people special visions, remained firmly committed to letting the Bible always be the judge of the validity of the vision.

In light of seeing Jesus as central, Mennonites say the purpose of the biblical teaching is not primarily to satisfy people's intellects but to instruct people on how to live. Mennonites have not traditionally devoted energy to abstract theologizing. To some degree, they have manifested a regrettable anti-intellectualism. However, their antipathy toward abstractions has followed mostly from placing the priority on trying to understand how the Bible speaks to day-to-day life.

---

[4] Kniss, *Disquiet* and Schlabach, *Gospel*.

[5] See the critique by Mennonite Old Testament scholar, Waldemar Janzen, "Canonical."

For Mennonites, the Bible's home has been in the fellowship of believers who *together* discern the Bible's message. People *produced* the Bible in community (including letters to churches, materials written for public worship, stories of the community of faith, and teachings to the community), people in community are best situated to understand the Bible.

It is inadequate simply to read the Bible as an individual or simply to study the Bible as a scholar. The meaning of the Bible among Mennonites comes most clearly to the congregation as the people together seek God's word for them, with an open dependence upon the Holy Spirit and a clear willingness to obey the word of God that comes to them.

The point considered by many to be the most crucial in the Mennonite approach to the Bible is that genuinely to understand the Bible, one must be reading it with the intent of *living* a faithful life. When people read the Bible with this intent, they will be open to obeying the truths they encounter there. One finds understanding only when one willingly obeys what is revealed.

Jesus directs us on the path that we should follow. Mennonites assume the *clarity* of Jesus' teaching. People's *unwillingness* to obey, not the obtuseness of the message, most hinders understanding. Mennonites have also said that if people harden their hearts long enough against Jesus' teaching, that teaching will no longer be clear to them and it will become foolishness.

Jesus Christ

Early Anabaptists confessed Jesus Christ as the center of their faith. We cannot truly know Christ unless we follow him in life. We cannot follow him unless we first have known him. Mennonites have firmly believed that faithful living serves as a requirement for Christians formulating an adequate theology.

The first Anabaptists generally focused more on biblical categories than traditional creedal formulations. They emphasized Jesus as the *model* for believers. They affirmed his deity *and* his humanity, teaching and actions. They taught his atoning work on the cross, but they also emphasized Jesus' way of the cross as the model for Christian discipleship.

Since the sixteenth century, Mennonites have continued to consider practical life as central to theology. The basic Mennonite belief about Jesus is that in him, we see God. In Jesus' birth, we see God entering the world on behalf of hurting humanity. In Jesus' life, we see God's chosen one revealing human life as it is meant to be lived. In Jesus' death, we see Jesus' faithfulness standing the ultimate test, the "rulers of this age" crucifying him (1 Cor 2:8). And in Jesus' resurrection, we see God's vindication of Jesus' life, and we learn just how faithful God is to his promise of life everlasting for those who trust in his mercy.

Discipleship

Mennonite convictions begin with this basic question: "what does it mean to follow Jesus?" Mennonites seek to walk the way Jesus walked. The key words for them have not been "faith" or "grace" or "incarnation" so much as "following" or "discipleship."

For Mennonites, Jesus has been seen to be quite clear about what he wanted from his followers—turn the other cheek, share with those in need, love your enemies, and so on. The reason few human beings obey these commands is not because the commands are not clear;we do not follow because most of us think it is too hard to follow them.

From their beginnings, Mennonites have had confidence that it is indeed possible to be obedient to Christ. His teachings are not simply ideals that we seek for but have no chance ever to come close actually to practicing. Rather, it *is* possible to be a disciple. A person of faith may, to a large extent, experience deliverance from sin and evil in this life.

Mennonites have certainly believed in the sinfulness of human beings, but they have not seen that as an unconquerable barrier. Even as sinners, people still have the ability to respond to Jesus, be transformed by his grace, and obediently to follow his commands. They have believed that if God commands something, then it must be possible for the person of faith to obey.

The path to discipleship begins with a faith commitment to Jesus Christ. The believer makes this commitment concrete and public through the act of baptism. Baptism inaugurates the believer into the way of discipleship. The baptized person publicly commits to the way of Jesus, making a solemn vow to seek to "go and sin no more."

The voluntary baptism of believers emphasizes that discipleship is a *choice* that a person must make. Mennonites do not expect discipleship of the unbaptized or those baptized as infants without choice and who have never consciously made the choice to follow the way of Jesus. A person cannot choose to follow Jesus before one is capable of counting the cost.

Baptism

At the time of the beginning of the Anabaptist movement in Europe (1525), the state church baptized infants for two main reasons. First, the church taught that a person needed to be baptized to gain salvation. Baptism provided a means of countering the infant's inborn (or "original") sin. People were condemned without baptism.

Second, baptism provided the means of incorporating the person into the general Christian society. The church baptized the entire population in order to maintain social unity. Baptism served, in effect, as one of the central ways in which society was kept "Christian." For the society to be Christian everyone in the society must be baptized.

The first Anabaptists saw both ideas as problematic. They believed that children are *innocent* until the "age of accountability" and thus are not condemned if not baptized. People would be condemned only when they chose to turn from God. So they rejected the idea of an inborn sinful nature that understood everyone as born condemned and needing to be baptized in order to avoid that condemnation.

Likewise, an *external* act such as baptism could not provide the means of salvation. Salvation was gained through a faith-commitment to Christ. Baptism only had meaning when it came due to this faith-commitment. Baptism should result from people's choice to follow Christ and not be something done to people before they had faith and chose to be baptized.

The Anabaptists also rejected the idea of a state-controlled church, especially when the membership of the church included everyone in the state regardless of their present faith-commitment. When people without faith make up much if not most of the membership of the church, the ideal of discipleship becomes quite unrealistic.

The very first Anabaptists hoped to reform the entire church along these lines—so that membership to all churches would include only adult believers. Their efforts were rebuffed, so they broke with the state church. Baptism, as an obvious, external act, was recognized as a central distinctive of these new "radicals," becoming the basis for intense persecution. If the state knew people to have been rebaptized or to have refused to have their babies baptized, it marked those people for persecution.

The Anabaptists actually spoke of three baptisms. They spoke first of the baptism of the Spirit. What followed in a believer's life required this initial baptism. When a person makes a freely chosen faith commitment to trust in Christ and to follow him, that person receives the gift of the Holy Spirit. This gift empowers the Christian to see the truth and to live according to it, and facilitates fellowship and the mutual up building of people in the church.

They spoke of a second baptism, the baptism with water. After a person trusts in Christ, one undergoes water baptism as a sign of Spirit baptism and as an initiation into the fellowship of believers. This fellowship becomes the earthly "home" for the new believer and provides the context of support and encouragement necessary for lives of discipleship. Water baptism publicly affirms the willingness of the new believer to walk the path of discipleship.

They then spoke of a third baptism that results from discipleship. Early Anabaptists called this the baptism of blood or fire. The early Anabaptists literally experienced baptisms of blood. Many lost their lives for their beliefs. Being faithful to the commitment made with water baptism led to inevitable suffering at the hands of a hostile state and state church. The baptism of the Spirit and water baptism as entrée to the community of faith both provided resources for remaining strong in the midst of suffering.

Mennonites have sought to maintain this vision of the meaning of baptism, continuing to see baptism as following repentance and confession of faith in Christ. Baptism initiates the believer into membership in the congregation; a baptized person will be encouraged and admonished and called forth to contribute to the work of the church. Baptism makes a public statement of one's willingness to follow Christ in discipleship, even to suffer for his sake.

However, in the years since the first Anabaptist baptisms, much has changed. Like with the early church, the first Anabaptist churches were made up of "first-generation" believers self-aware of their conversion experiences and of making a clear break with former beliefs and ways of life. Early Anabaptists did not say much about the issue of what to do with children of the church, those born into the faith.

In later generations, many children of the church do not have a clear sense of turning from a life of sin to a life of faith, since they have grown up in the faith. They may not have a moment of conversion. The question of when these people should be baptized is vexing.

The severing of the church from state control and the resultant ending of the practice of baptizing all infants in a given country has removed a major issue of contention and a main justification for infant baptism. Some churches emphasize infant baptism less and place more emphasis on nurture for baptized children. The practice of infant baptism and adolescent catechism closely resembles Mennonites' practice of baby dedication and adolescent baptism. Those who practice each kind of baptism tolerate the other's views more. Many on both sides know that faithful Christians practice either.

However, recognizing the importance of ecumenical respect, Mennonites still make the case for believers baptism. In Paul's imagery in Romans 6:1–4, baptism identifies the believer with Christ's death so that we, like Christ, may be raised to newness of life. In the Mennonite view, baptism expresses that God's grace has been made known to us and enables us to die to our seeking to control others and our acquiescence to the powers of violence. In baptism, we affirm that we want to throw in our lot with other people who also know this grace and death to sin, so that *together* we may know, as well, something of resurrection in our lives right now.

Church members benefit from having grace concretized. We benefit from having some tangible expression of what is by its nature an essentially heart-oriented, somewhat mysterious and dynamic reality—the experience of the grace of God. We also benefit from going through an initiation that allows us publicly to identify with others who have shared an experience of God's grace and who promise to help us along the way. Baptism helps to make concrete this powerful yet mysterious experience of grace. And baptism helps to reflect the reality that others share in this experience and that we all are promising to walk together in the life of faith.

The Community of Faith

For Mennonites, God's message comes to the congregation in many ways, including through the teaching and discernment of recognized leaders. God's message also comes through mutual discussion and exhortation among all members. Every individual in the church may and should add to the discernment process.

Mennonites believe that the Old Testament priesthood, where only the set-apart priest could approach God in the Temple and everyone was separated from God, has ended. Every person of faith could now directly approach God. God regards no one more highly than others.

Each may approach God through faith in Christ directly with no need for human mediation. The individual does this in the context of the community of faith. We are not isolated priests; we are a nation of priests. If we are each a priest, that also means that all areas of our lives are sacred. Whatever we do matters to God and is related to our worship of God.

The implications of these convictions for Mennonites have shaped many practices over the years. If *all* of our activity matters to God, we should work hard and seek to, say, be the best farmers possible. We also should question the government's right to ask us to do things that we believe are contrary to worshiping God in life such as fighting in wars.

Mennonites have formally recognized leaders in the church, but they have attempted to emphasize qualities such as humility, simplicity of life, and a servant's heart in choosing leaders. They believe that the officers in the church are not a different class of person, are not mediators between people and God, and are not called to a higher righteousness than anyone else in the church. This is not to say that pastors are *not* called to a high level of discipleship. It is to say the opposite; *everyone* in the church is called to an equally high level of discipleship.

The Mennonite understanding of the community of faith places a premium on mutual accountability. Mennonites require a high level of commitment and discipleship from everyone in the church. Since everyone, supposedly, joins the church by one's free choice, the church expects each one to have counted the cost and to be willing to live a disciplined, faithful life.

Early Anabaptists accused state churches of laxity with regard to the moral lives of their members. They said that the state churches, made up of everyone in the country, practiced a lowest common denominator style of church life. The expectations for the lives of church members were no stricter than standards attainable by anyone regardless of faith commitment.

On the other hand, the state church would kick "heretics" out of the city, imprison them, even kill them, utilizing the state's sword. The Anabaptists would disfellowship wayward brothers and sisters, holding open the invitation to return following repentance.

The challenge of maintaining meaningful practices of mutual accountability has been a large one. The Anabaptists had conflicts with each other over the proper styles of discipline. Anabaptists in Holland experienced a major split near the end of Menno Simons' life over church discipline. The Amish began in the seventeenth century largely due to a belief that the existing Mennonite churches in Switzerland were too lax in their use of church discipline.

Many older Mennonites today have "horror stories" about various uses and misuses of church discipline. In reaction against those perceived misuses, present-day Mennonites have often found it difficult to articulate a positive, creative vision of practical mutual accountability.

Some people still make the case that Christians have a definite need for mutual accountability in all churches at all times. I will summarize the perspective of Marlin Jeschke in his book, *Discipling the Brother*. Where churches in the past have gone wrong with regard to mutual accountability is when they have had the wrong motives and goals. All too often, motivations have had to do with pride and fear of change, fear of innovation, fear of individuality. The churches' sense of holiness and faithfulness have at times reflected a narrow and legalistic adherence to rigid rules more than creativity, honesty, and growth.

More appropriately, according to Jeschke, the church, in its treatment of troubled members, should be motivated by the need to express God's grace and forgiveness. It is not loving to people who are running from God's mercy to let those people continue on destructive paths. It is more loving sensitively to confront such people, to invite them back and to let them become aware of the consequences of their actions.

Jeschke argues for a priority on people over "institutions" or "doctrines." God's justice is relational, with the goal being to set right what has been broken, to restore relationships where there has been alienation. As church discipline reflects God's justice, its goals will not be on extracting an eye for an eye nor on maintaining "purity" by making sure to kick out unsavory members. Its goals will be restoring broken relationships.

Finally, Jeschke points out that Matthew eighteen has traditionally been used by Mennonites to guide the practice of church discipline. Jesus concludes his instructions with the statement that if a person does not repent, he or she should be treated as a "pagan or tax collector." Jesus treated pagans and tax collectors with love them invited them to become part of his people (Matthew himself was apparently a tax collector). So, when there is a breaking of fellowship due to a church member deciding not to share in the common life of the congregation, the result should be renewed efforts to love that person and inviting him or her to return.

The church best sees accountability as being part of a community where people have the freedom *voluntarily* to be honest about their beliefs, their doubts, their hopes, their hurts in a context of others also being honest. Accountability has to do with being lovingly encouraged to discover and cultivate one's best self, more by seeing others do this than by having people overtly demand this. That is, accountability has to do with working with others to grow and mature as human beings living before God.

Nonconformity

Early Anabaptists understood the call to nonconformity to be the Bible's direct command expressed most succinctly in Romans 12:1–2:

> I appeal to you brethren, by the mercies of God, to present your bodies as a living sacrifice, holy and acceptable to God, which is your spiritual worship. *Do not be conformed to this world* but be transformed by the renewal of your mind, that you way prove what is the will of God, what is good and acceptable and perfect.

Nonconformity in this general sense seems to be a direct consequence of the Anabaptist understanding of the Christian faith. However, the positive thrust to understandings of nonconformity has not always dominated Mennonite consciousness. Though Mennonites have valued nonconformity to the wider culture, they have often been resistant to nonconformity within their own communities.[6] Independence of thought and action, unprecedented expressions of creativity, new theological and other intellectual expressions have often met with great resistance in Mennonite communities amidst strong pressure toward internal *conformity*.

Also nonconformity with the outside world has often been expressed as hostility toward the outside world. Mennonites at times have struggled with being able to appreciate the positive things in the outside world. And even when they have accepted some of these things, at times people have done so with a bad conscience—feeling defensive or trying to hide.

The issue of nonconformity may be connected with the need of communities to have "boundary markers" to help sustain their sense of identity. If we dress distinctively, if we speak a different language, it is easier to have a distinct sense of identity. Such boundary markers are inevitable and certainly have a legitimate role in facilitating a sense of internal cohesion, self-identity, connectedness with a particular tradition, and a coherent value structure. However, boundary markers easily become problematic when they become too rigid, when they are used to facilitate a sense of the superiority of "insiders," and when they are (implicitly, at least) associated with "direct revelation from God" for all times and places.

Present day Mennonite identity appears to be in a state of flux, in part due to a shaking of boundary markers. Some Mennonites hold on to the old boundary markers in a legalistic way. Others, hastily escaping "oppressive" traditional nonconformity, pretty much blend in with the surrounding culture. The challenge remains to find ways to positively express Christian faith, sustaining creativity and innovation, while also benefiting from the strengths of one's tradition.

The early Anabaptist notion of nonconformity served a *transforming* (not withdrawing) agenda. Present-day Mennonite non-conformity should seek to echo that emphasis. Consider Paul's words in Romans 12, where he

---

[6] See C. Redekop, "Power."

writes *do not* be conformed to the world and *do* have your mind renewed. Paul's words demand a holding together of two elements—a nonconformity with this world and a renewal of the mind. Paul's is not a call for closed-mindedness, for anti-intellectualism, for utter rejection of everything the world has to offer, including the life of the mind. Nor is it a call for uncritical acceptance of thought forms from the wider world.

Part of the problem with many expressions of non-conformity arises when we do not remember how Paul couples not being conformed with this world with having one's mind *renewed*. In many cases in Mennonite communities, people's minds have not been renewed but instead stifled, repressed, forced to fit into a certain ideological mode allowing little room for creativity and openness to new ideas and new perspectives on old problems.

Nonconformity without mind renewal expresses itself primarily as rejectionism, defensiveness, fearfulness, intellectual narrowness, and—perhaps most ironic of all—as fostering strong pressure for total conformity within the group. Pressures both to be clearly different from the outside world and to be very much like others inside the community tend to stifle intellectual creativity and the renewing of the mind.

As in the time of the first Anabaptists and in Mennonite history, the call to transformative nonconformity remains. When the wider world's values include glorifying violence and acquisitiveness and self-protectiveness, creative nonconformity becomes crucial for followers of Jesus. This kind of nonconformity goes hand in hand with the renewal of our minds.

Growing in freedom from bondage to fearfulness, selfishness, and lust for power, leads one to grow in freedom genuinely to think clearly. As people of faith grow in this freedom even while remaining part of a broken world, they also grow in their ability to respond to that brokenness in new ways.[7]

Mennonites' most profound expressions of nonconformity are shaped by a positive vision of what they are living for much more than being dominated by what they reject. We live for relationships of love and respect. We live for intellectual and spiritual growth, never ending as long as we live. We are tempted by many things that block us from such growth. We need to say no to those—but only as a means of clearing the way for our yes for life.

---

[7] See below, chapter nine, for an account of one instance of a creative response in a time of fearfulness, violence, and brokenness.

Outreach: Evangelism and Service

In the history of Christian evangelism, the Anabaptist movement did not directly change the way the majority of Christians did things, but they represented the future. In the sixteenth century, evangelism was a minor part of the life of the mainstream church. There was no need to evangelize your neighbor when that neighbor was a baptized member of the state church.

The Anabaptist practice of believers baptism and voluntary church membership meant that the future survival of the church depended upon evangelism. Each new generation represents a need for mission since in their view no person could be a Christian except by personal faith commitment to Jesus. From the start, the Anabaptists were active in their outreach. That was why they early on experienced such rapid growth.

For the Anabaptists, all of Europe was a mission field. Even children of church members needed to make their own choice to be baptized and follow Christ. The Anabaptists, though, definitely did not limit themselves to children of the church. They were the first people for centuries in Europe to assume that people in Europe were not necessarily genuinely Christians in spite of formally belonging to the church.

So, the Anabaptists were to some degree pioneers in the area of missions and evangelism. However, their strong evangelistic push did not last long. They soon became much less evangelistic, largely due to the violent resistance they met at the hands of the political and religious leaders of Europe. They were, perhaps we could say, simply beaten into submission with regard to their outreach. Quite often they received tolerance and freedom to live and work in certain areas of Europe only on the condition that they not try to convert any of the non-Mennonite people in the area into which they moved.

The loss of the outreach drive went hand-in-hand with the growth of a sense of being a separated community, essentially self-contained and different from the world around them. This continued with the Mennonites who settled in North America. They held on to their German language and their various cultural practices and resisted acculturation with the surrounding American society. They succeeded at this for at least two centuries up to the end of the 1800s, thereby maintaining a sense of community and a strong adherence to practices such as mutual aid and non-resistance. However, such inwardness limited their reaching out with the message of the gospel to the world around them.

The past one hundred twenty five years have seen tremendous changes in Mennonite churches. As Mennonites have been more open to influence from other Christians, they have adopted new practices such as Sunday Schools, church periodicals, church colleges, and foreign missionaries.

At the same time, Mennonites have apparently done something a little different than other groups in their mission work. One indication of this is the close relationships they have established with a number of African churches that have arisen seemingly spontaneously in recent years independent of any missionary activity. Perhaps a little more than most North American missionaries, Mennonites have not been closely identified with the United States government. Perhaps Mennonites have typically worked a little harder at understanding the native environment of places into which they have gone.

Mennonite priorities on discipleship have shaped how they do evangelism. If you do not separate discipleship from belief, you tend to avoid quick, emotional, and likely fleeting conversions of belief only and try to include an awareness of the costs of discipleship in one's evangelistic message.

While Mennonite churches in recent years have had a number of well-known evangelists, they also have tried to emphasize the belief that *each* Christian is a missionary. The missionary is someone who is ready for whatever sacrifice is involved in carrying the gospel in the most faithful way. And, according to Anabaptist thought, this should be *all* Christians.

From their sixteenth-century beginnings, Mennonites generally understood outreach to include acts of caring and help toward all people in need. That is, service and evangelism have gone hand-in-hand. Hans Leopold, a Swiss Brethren martyr of 1528, said of his brethren: "If they know of anyone who is in need, whether or not he is a member of their church, they believe it their duty, out of love to God, to render help and aid." Menno Simons, in an enumeration of qualities of the saints, says: "They show mercy and love. . . . They entertain those in distress. They take the stranger into their houses. They comfort the afflicted; clothe the naked; feed the hungry." Two Mennonite confessions of faith, Dordrecht (1632) and Ris (1766), in their statements on nonresistance emphasize the duty of Christians to feed, clothe, and help the needy.

Anabaptist-Mennonite history is filled with illustrations of this brotherhood and "Good Samaritan" faith in action. In 1553, the followers of Menno Simons at Wismar in North Germany gave asylum to a group of English Calvinist refugees who had been driven from home by the Catholic queen and then were refused admission to Denmark by its Lutheran king. The Hutterite chronicles of the seventeenth century record the presence in these Anabaptist communities of numerous strangers receiving aid during a time of famine.

Mennonites in North America continued the tradition of helping the needy. As early as 1756 Mennonites in Pennsylvania organized a relief program to help Moravian communities who had suffered loss in conflicts. During the Revolutionary War, Mennonites set up a hospital to help war victims. During the Civil War, many Mennonites also performed hospital service. The Mennonite Relief Commission for War Sufferers, organized in 1917, was the official agency through which the Mennonite Church supported Quaker reconstruction work in France and other European Relief projects as well as the Near East relief following World War I.

In June 1920, a group of four Mennonite delegates from Russia came to North America to solicit help for their people who were suffering from famine, many of whom desired to emigrate. In response to this need and appeal the Mennonite Central Committee (MCC) was organized. The various relief committees of numerous Mennonite groups now joined forces.

With the coming of World War II, the Mennonite relief ministry was expanded beyond anything that had been conceived in World War I. MCC developed into an agency coordinating the relief work of Mennonites everywhere. By 2003, MCC had a budget of $61.6 million and had over one thousand two hundred people working in fifty-seven countries.

For Mennonites, service often has been identified with the will of God for God's people. In service men and women have confirmed God's abiding principle of life and also pointed others to God, the source of life. Service has been a way of saying that the gospel is indeed good news, it is a message of life.

Conclusion

Mennonite convictions characteristically take a practical thrust. The Mennonite vision of Christian faith has at its center *faithful living*.

As the *CofF* makes clear, on central doctrinal issues, Mennonites share many commonalities with other Protestants, and, for that matter, with Catholics and Orthodox as well. However, in holding to this strong practical thrust Mennonites have, at least implicitly, articulated a distinctive approach to basic Christian beliefs.

PART FOUR: Experience

Along with the Bible and tradition, experience is the third key element in the constructing of Anabaptist theology. "Experience" can have several senses. The three chapters in this section each reflect on experience in different ways.

Chapter nine, "The Significance of Civilian Public Service for Anabaptist Pacifism," tells the story of the experience of Anabaptists in the United States during World War II. Thousands of young men served as conscientious objectors during the war, an experience that illumines a great deal about the outworking of the peace traditions of these Christians.

Chapter ten, "Anabaptist Faith and American Democracy," reflects on the relevance for social ethics of the experience of seeking to hold together the Anabaptist tradition and its suspicion of national politics with the realities of citizenship in one of the world's pioneering democracies—that also happens to be the world's current reigning great empire.

Chapter eleven, "Who is Part of the Conversation? 'Neo-Mennonites' and Anabaptist Theology," deals with experience in a different sense, looking at a segment of Anabaptist faith communities in North American (the "neo-Mennonites") that in some sense privileges present experience as the core source for Anabaptist theology.

CHAPTER NINE

The Significance of Civilian Public Service for Understanding Anabaptist Pacifism[1]

ONE OF the most distinctive convictions that has been central for most Anabaptists since the movement's sixteenth-century beginnings has been pacifism, following Jesus' message of love even for enemies, refusing in principle to participate in warfare. Understanding principled opposition to warfare requires understanding *ideas*—theology, philosophy, principles, beliefs. However, it also requires looking at what happens in actual *life*, in human *experience*.

The experience of American conscientious objectors to World War II serves as a particularly helpful test case for understanding Anabaptist pacifism. This was a test for pacifist principles that affected the entire American Anabaptist community. Here we see what pacifism meant in *practice* for Anabaptists. The need to respond to America's call to arms touched everyone's *actual* life. Pacifism at that time had to do not only with the theories of theologians and pastors and denominational leaders or only to do with the practices of a few activists or those who found themselves caught in the crossfire of a local conflict. It had to do with *everyone*.

I will focus on what happened during World War II, the Anabaptist experience in alternative service. I also want to raise questions of how that experience might sharpen our reflections on the meaning of pacifism for us today.

The First World War had tested American pacifists. Peace church people did not realize until too late that the government would induct conscientious objectors (COs) into the military. Only then would people be allowed to take a CO stand. By taking that stand *within* the military, COs faced hostility, harassment, and worse. In the most extreme case, two young Hutterite men lost their lives due to the treatment they received

---

[1] This essay is drawn from my Ph.D. dissertation, "Saying No to the 'Good' War."

from the U.S. military. Horrified peace church leaders worked hard during the 1920s and 1930s to prepare their young people for war's return.[2]

In the late 1930s, as war grew imminent, peace church leaders lobbied Congress for liberal CO provisions. Legislation in 1940 allowed for Civilian Public Service camps (CPS) as an alternative to military service. This saved pacifists from having to join the military. However, instead of a *civilian* governmental agency (such as the Interior Department) providing oversight for CPS, Congress put Selective Service in charge. Hence, CPS stood in ambiguous territory, operated by an agency whose first priority was procuring soldiers for the military.

Selective Service placed COs in remote camps doing forest and agricultural conservation. Near the end of the War, some gained permission to work in mental hospitals, public health, and a few other forms of "detached service." The director of Selective Service, General Lewis Hershey, stated that he wanted to keep the COs out of the public eye. He would not allow them to do work that would appear too attractive. If alternative service became too well known or too appealing, more people might opt for alternative service instead of the military.[3]

The draft began in early 1941, almost a year before the December 7 Japanese attack on Pearl Harbor and the formal beginning of American involvement in the War. From the beginning, peace church people faced surprises. On the one hand, many fewer men from their churches than expected chose CPS. Only about 50% of the drafted and inducted men from the various Mennonite groups performed alternative service. The other 50% joined the military as combatants and non-combatants. Fewer than 10% of Quaker and Brethren draftees joined CPS.

On the other hand, draftees from a large diversity of other church groups chose to perform alternative service. This number included men from mainline groups such as Methodists, Catholics, and Episcopalians. However, it also included men from dozens of obscure groups such as Black Muslims, Christadelphians, Russian Molokans, and various Pentecostal groups. As well, several hundred Jehovah's Witnesses joined CPS.

Nearly twelve thousand men took part in CPS. About forty percent were Mennonites. Brethren, Quakers, and Methodists each made up about ten percent. Six thousand COs went to prison, either because their draft boards did not recognize their CO claims or they chose not to cooperate with the draft in any way. Jehovah's Witnesses made up about seventy-five percent of the number of COs in prison.

[2] See Juhnke, *Vision*, 208–42; Bush, 26–55; and Homan, *American*.
[3] Wherry, *Conscientious*, 1–2.

Now, let's look more closely at Mennonites in CPS. I will consider three main themes: their attitude toward the state, their major sources of influence, and the most distinctive fruits of their experience. As I go along, I will make a few comparisons with COs from other traditions. I am speaking of "typical Mennonites;" certainly not all Mennonites fit with my description.

Attitude toward the State, Social Change, and CPS

Mennonites rejected direct involvement in the state's military activities. Yet, they did not oppose the government's right to institute conscription, even in peacetime. Mennonites believed that they could give their testimony of love even within the framework of conscription. They voiced a philosophy of responding to governmental authority by "going the second mile."

A Mennonite CPS leader described this philosophy.

> In place of gaining its point by law . . . [our pacifism] operates on the level of love which restores the broken fellowship. It does not insist on personal rights, but rather gives thought to the obligations and duties that one has when under the Spirit and direction of Christ. When compelled to go one mile, the non-resistant Christian does not resist the compulsion, but rather stands prepared to volunteer the services of the second mile.[4]

Mennonites respected state authority. They readily cooperated with Selective Service in CPS. Mennonite Central Committee (MCC) served as the Mennonite agency for administering work camps. Mennonites willingly accepted the government's terms. MCC did reserve the "right of conscience to reject forms of service which contribute to war or coercion in any form or to any other social evil." However, it did not feel a "nonresistant church" could appropriately make further demands of Selective Service or actively oppose it.[5]

Mennonites generally supported alternative civilian service in place of military service. Most officially preferred, on the one hand, to reject noncombatant military service (such as being medics) as being too militaristic. On the other hand, they also rejected resistance to alternative service itself as being too rebellious. Some non-Mennonite COs felt the government

---

[4] Quoted in Sibley and Jacob, *Conscription*, 310. This book remains the authoritative history of conscientious objection to World War II. More recent and quite helpful studies of CPS include Robinson, "Civilian," and Keim, *CPS*.

[5] Quoted in Sibley and Jacob, *Conscription*, 313.

had no right to conscript people at all. Most Mennonites, though, objected to war, not to conscription *per se*.[6]

Mennonites posed no threat to the alternative service system. One of the MCC camp newspapers contained an editorial declaring: "CPS is a privilege! . . . We intend to serve our country to the best of our ability. And we intend to do that without the unjustified grumbling and complaining that has been evidenced among some COs."[7]

Some Mennonites even expressed gratitude to the government for its tolerance. Some Mennonite bishops wrote as follows to General Hershey at the close of the War.

> We must thank God that we live in a nation whose Constitution grants us the precious privilege of religious freedom. We appreciate the work that your department has done in setting up the Public Service camps. We are happy that amicable relations existed between our unit and the Government so that defenseless Christians had no need of violating their consciences and could do something that was of National importance.[8]

Mennonites commitment to non-involvement in warfare took priority over social change. They strongly emphasized performance of deeds of service to people in need and to the land. They did not directly connect this concern for service with notions of social change.

This contrasted with the attitudes of many non-Mennonite COs. For these, conscientious objection was part of a broader agenda of transforming the world. These COs hoped that CPS would prove to be a means of significant political activism.

CPSer Walter Forster, a Methodist, expressed these sentiments:

> We must indelibly impress upon our minds the fact that we are only a few thousand in number who must convert millions to our way of thinking. . . . We must change the hearts and minds of [people] all over the world so that they will believe this also. It is up to us in CPS to germinate the seeds for such a dynamic aggressive peace movement on an international scale so that in the not too distant future the militarists, rather than the pacifist, will be the minority.[9]

---

[6] Keim and Stoltzfus, *Politics*, 121.
[7] Quoted in Wittner, *Rebels*, 82–83.
[8] Cited in Hunsberger, *Franconia*, 137.
[9] Forster, "Place," 7.

Mennonites did not typically think in such global terms. They viewed war and conscription as part of the basic pattern of society as it actually existed. They focused on doing works of service within the framework of such a society more than dramatically changing that society. Mennonites generally had little concern with applying their pacifism to affairs of state. Vocational and relief training blossomed, but not attempts to raise political concerns.

Many Mennonites worked on educational programs in CPS. Mennonites focused on Bible study and church history, particularly the history of their tradition. One Mennonite CPSer referred to his CPS experience being "as educational as going to college."[10] However, the education he referred to did not include political action.

An incident that illustrates Mennonites' approach to a major social problem (i.e., racism) occurred in 1944. MCC agreed to set up and administer a new public health unit in Mississippi limited to white assignees. It argued that an interracial camp would be impossible in that situation. MCC argued for carrying on a program that served both white and black families, and quietly demonstrating a belief in human solidarity. In this way, they could accomplish more toward solving the race problem in the South than by having no project at all. Mennonite assignees appear to have supported this stand. The unit had full staffing and continued after the War was over as a volunteer service of MCC.

Dallas Voran, the educational director of a Mennonite CPS camp, explained the rationale for MCC's attitude about the unit in Mississippi.

> We do not agree that if we cannot have an ideal arrangement—in this case racial equality—at the outset, we should stay out. We do not agree that more good can be done by refusing to go into such a situation than by going in and trying to improve conditions by working on the local scene. Just as men in CPS must believe that by being in CPS they are doing the most possible under existing conditions to live their convictions about war, so we believe that by going into Mississippi rather than staying out, we can live our ideals on race most effectively under existing conditions.[11]

Mennonites did not deny the existence of injustices in the CPS system, but they still felt it was the best of *possible* choices. They hoped through the work projects to contribute materially to the conservation of both the human and the natural resources of the world.

CPSer Dwight V. Yoder issued a representative endorsement.

---

[10] Interview with Ralph Kauffman, Phoenix, Arizona, December, 1986.

[11] Voran, "CPS," 2, 4.

> There is a positive side to CPS. To us, it is an expression of our willingness to serve our country so long as the service does not contradict Jesus' teaching. It gives us an opportunity to show that living our convictions is more important than where, or under what circumstances we are permitted to live them, and that following in Jesus' steps is more important than gratification and fulfillment of selfish desire. To the world it is proof of the strength of our faith while we stand the test of the pressure of war and public ridicule. For the church it gives opportunity to rethink in practical ways our principles of peace as based on the word, and preserves for the church of the future a principle that has been a major factor in its origin, growth, and witness. To men in CPS it gives opportunity to apply the principles of peace and nonresistance in their close association with others of various beliefs and practices who have been thrown together because of this strong common interest.[12]

Elmer Ediger's statement characterizes Mennonites' acceptance of the CPS system.

> I am convinced that I can and should accept CPS under wartime or peacetime conscription. Even if I were fully convinced that conscription in itself would inevitably lead to great evils, I would still accept CPS. The basic Christian principles that helped me most: (1) As a Christian I can obey and comply with unchristian methods used on me, even though it would be a sin for me to use those methods on others. (2) The "second mile" and "good for evil" principles teach me as a Christian to accept compulsory service and then seek to reconstruct this compulsion into a voluntary service of good will. (3) I believe government (not anarchy) is desired by God to make for orderly group living, and therefore I obey government except when I am asked to sin.[13]

So, Mennonite pacifism during World War II focused not so much on political activism as on finding ways to do peaceable service in a warring society. Mennonites were respectful toward the state so long as they were not asked to fight in the War.

Sources of Central Influence

Mennonites emphasized the New Testament, especially the teaching of Jesus, as their most important influence. Nevertheless, for most of them this reading occurred through the eyes of their church tradition. Their ex-

---

[12] D. Yoder, "CPS," 3.
[13] Ediger, "Is," 2.

perience of growing up in pacifist communities and retaining the strong support of those communities influenced them decisively. These influences shaped both how they read the Bible and how they put that reading into practice.

Most Mennonite COs were conditioned from an early age to make the CO commitment. When asked later why they chose to be COs, many spoke of expectations of their churches and families.[14] Still, often Mennonite COs had brothers who went into the military. This step usually came *after* a decision not to join the church. Hence, a Mennonite did not automatically become a CO. However, once he joined the church, he most likely would refuse to join the military.

Wilbur Miller represents many Mennonites' experience. He had a conversion experience at age 18, just before facing the draft. This experience emboldened him to take a CO stand.[15] Mennonites usually assumed, based on church teaching, that God's will required them to be nonresistant. A personal conversion experience would move a person toward that stance. The Mennonite not taking that stance likely did not claim a close spiritual relationship with God. Spirituality served as the crucial locus of a commitment to nonresistance—much more than formal theology, ethical principles, or political convictions.

Mennonites had a practical spirituality, stemming from teaching and example seen beginning in early childhood. Mennonite CPSer J. Mark Martin recognized this reality:

> Why am I a conscientious objector? First, I was taught to live peaceably with all men from childhood. Certainly, I am grateful for the fact of having Christian parents who instilled in me the principles of a nonresistance stance. Second, I have witnessed the practice of the nonresistant life as exemplified in the lives of others. Third, I have found the principle of nonresistance to be practical in my own life. Truly the practice of nonresistance is essential to a happy Christian life.[16]

Of the factors that contributed to maintenance of Mennonites' positive attitude toward CPS, the support of their home communities had enormous importance. Knowing the support of family, friends, and fellow church members significantly affected morale. This contrasted with many non-Mennonite COs. For them, the decision to become a CO was usually

---

[14] E.g., interviews with Paul Davidhizer, Vincent Krabill, Eugene Hershberger, and Ralph Kauffman, Phoenix, Arizona, December, 1986.

[15] Interview with Wilbur Miller, Phoenix, Arizona, April 1987.

[16] Martin, "That's," 5.

a *lonely* decision, often made in *opposition* to the wishes of family, friends, and fellow church members.[17]

Mennonite CPSers received many tangible expressions of support from their home communities. For example, they often received food from home communities. A CPSer might open his lunch out on project and see on the label of some canned fruit the name of someone he knew, perhaps even his mother. This proved to the young man that he did not carry his conviction alone. It showed to him that the church, the folks at home, and he were all in a cooperative way practicing their pacifist faith.[18]

Mennonite communities and their CPS camps both worked at maintaining a sense of connectedness. They did this by publishing and distributing camp newspapers. They also see it by sending campers to churches to speak. This is one typical report:

> Furlough time was used to good advantage by campers who appeared on the conference programs at Tabor College and Hesston College during the past week. The annual Tabor Bible Conference featured a session devoted to the discussion of CPS. Campers from Denison, IA, gave a picture of their camp in the Saturday session. Sunday afternoon men from both camps joined in a forum discussion about the camps. On Monday afternoon the men from this camp appeared on the program. Jesse Harder discussed the peace testimony and the CO position. Ray Schlichting reviewed CPS history and discussed the community relationships of the camp. Robert Kreider spoke on the values of camp life. The annual Christian life conference at Hesston provided an opportunity for Ernest Kauffman, Glen Greaser, and Orie Gingerich to participate in discussions of CPS. The young people's group voted to include in its budget $125 for the support of CPS camps. The conclusion of the campers who had these experiences was that the home communities are eager to know more about the challenges and the possibilities of CPS.[19]

Roman Catholic sociologist Gordon Zahn, himself a World War II CO, confirms this communal support. He surveyed the responses draftees made on the forms Selective Service required them to fill out to substantiate their CO claims. Mennonites' replies to questions asking COs to substantiate their claims show a distinct contrast to those given by the Friends. Instead of being intellectualized arguments for a personal stand against war,

---

[17] See Gara and Gara, eds., *Few*.
[18] Hunsberger, *Franconia*, 102, 104.
[19] "Campers," 1.

the Mennonite statements are brief and direct. They are often limited to scriptural quotations citing chapter and verse, giving the impression of being "form answers" prepared in advance and made available for draftees.

Many draftees stated that they received help from their pastors or other official advisors provided by the church. This trend may account for the close similarity of expression among the different Mennonites. These men likely received strong encouragement and support in their stand against the war. Hence, they could confidently turn to members of their religious community for direct aid in the preparation of these crucial documents.[20]

Many Mennonite COs surveyed after the War said the church had not provided adequate peace education. In Zahn's view, this reflects how these respondents had internalized their peace traditions.[21] They did not fully recognize the education they had received.

A personal account that highlights the communal nature of Mennonite CPSers comes from Richard C. Hunter. He was a CPSer from a Methodist background who found himself in a Mennonite CPS camp early in the War.

> I began to recognize that [CPS] Camp #5 [in Colorado Springs] was not just a camp for a collection of unrelated COs operated by MCC, but that it was a Mennonite community, within which non-Mennonites were permitted to reside. I began to see that "Mennonite" was not just a name of a church denomination. It was a church-centered culture which commanded far greater loyalty and allegiance among its constituents than I had ever experienced as a member of the Methodist Church. I could tell the difference between Kansas, Oklahoma, and Nebraska Mennonites. However, there were some well-defined and encompassing boundaries which brought together those who were on the inside and established for me my place on the outside.[22]

Hunter questioned the reality of true personal commitment to pacifism among the bulk of the Mennonite campers at first. This was due in large part to their apparent lack of individual focus and expressiveness.

> I was developing a great deal of respect for the leadership of the church as I had an opportunity to observe it in people like Albert Gaeddert, our first camp director and fellow campers such as Robert Kreider, Ray Schlichting, and Elmer Ediger. However, I had questions about whether the rank and file among the campers who

---

[20] G. Zahn, "Descriptive," 117–18.
[21] G. Zahn, "Descriptive," 285.
[22] Richard C. Hunter, "From," 296.

had grown up in a tightly controlled culture were objectors on the basis of their own conscience or of the community from which they came. Pacifism was not actively discussed as it might have been in a college dorm. It was difficult to comprehend the depth of a conviction that was never verbalized. I tended to question the personal commitment of people who seemed to be able to go on day after day patiently putting up with the discomforts of camp and the disruption of their lives. It was then a revelation when one day, an Amish crew leader out in the field on an assignment, proceeded without any discussion to load his crew into the trucks at midday and bring them back to camp when he and others realized that they were involved in the initial stages of preparing for what later became Ft. Carson. There was not a lot of talk and debate, nor was the action dramatized for public consumption. When conviction called for action, it was taken quietly and effectively.[23]

A later CPS assignment helped Hunter to see in a deeper way the value of the communal orientation of Mennonite CPS.

[After Colorado Springs,] for a year I served in the Methodist-operated unit in Asheville, NC, as a ward attendant. Working conditions were reasonably good. Living conditions were certainly better than barracks. The members of the unit and the hospital staff were congenial and intellectually stimulating. However, it was a situation in which I was neither an insider nor an outsider, for there was no group standard or expectation. I was one of several individuals, each having his own personal convictions. It was a group lacking in the strength and character of an organized culture. Consequently, when, after ten months in Asheville, I received an inquiry from MCC about my possible interest in a position in the Marlboro, NJ, State Hospital, I accepted without hesitation [in order] to return again to the happy role of "outsider" in a Mennonite unit.[24]

Mennonite COs would usually cite the New Testament as their central influence. However, what most distinguished Mennonites from other COs was the strong *community* support they had for their pacifism. The practical and emotional support they received was central to their expression of pacifism.[25]

---

[23] Hunter, "From," 297.

[24] Hunter, "From," 297–98.

[25] Bush, *Two*, 102.

Distinctive Fruits

For Mennonite COs, we can see two types of distinctive fruit that came out of their experience. The amount of work done at the base camps is one fruit. Mennonites committed themselves to the work more than many other CPSers. A second fruit emerged from their work in mental hospitals. This was the establishment of *alternative* mental health institutions, in contrast to other COs' efforts to transform the existing mental health system.

The conditions they found in mental hospitals appalled the COs who worked in them. Many came to the conclusion that changes were necessary. Some founded the Mental Hygiene Program of CPS to focus on seeking changes in the existing system. This Program evolved into the National Mental Health Foundation. The Foundation continued after the War ended as a tool for reforming the U.S. mental health system. This became the life work of several COs.

MCC supported this program and provided four staff people for the program from MCC-administered camps. However, only one of those staff people was a Mennonite, and that person did not continue in that position after the War ended. The other three staff people came from other traditions. Mennonites themselves took a different approach. They developed parallel institutions, a different kind of response to social problems.[26]

This approach reflects Mennonites' tendency not to make attempts to *force* institutions to change. Rather, Mennonites would simply focus on creating alternative institutions. They have seen this approach to provide a better context for doing works of service.

Mennonites saw an opportunity in the mental health area to do something constructive. About 1,500 Mennonite men and many of these men's spouses had served in mental health institutions by 1946. Many emerged from this experience convinced that they must, as Christians, do something for those unfortunate people in the hospitals. By 1947, MCC started Mennonite Mental Health Services (MMHS). MMHS began work to open three mental hospitals, one in the East, one in the Midwest, and the other on the West Coast. This happened in 1954—and several more have opened since.[27]

So, out of this encounter with an area of human need, we see two responses. A reformist response, focused on changing existing institutions. A second, that Mennonites took, focused on creating *alternative* institutions. In general, reformists tended to see pacifism as a tactic for social change.

---

[26] Keeney, "Experiences," 15.

[27] Pannabecker, *Open*, 250–51. See also Neufeld, ed., *If*.

Mennonites focused on positive service possibilities more than directly changing the social system. Faithfulness to their tradition took priority over political effectiveness.

Conclusions and Implications

In looking at the experience of Mennonites with CPS, we may note several strengths in the pacifist tradition of this group.

(1) Strong community roots. Mennonite churches formed communities that together, in some sense, stood against the state. Mennonite COs gained power from the sense that they did not stand alone. They shared their commitment with many other COs and had the backing of family, friends, and church communities. This support system might have meant Mennonites need not have as much personal strength to maintain their commitment as did other, more isolated COs. However, the support system also meant that many *more* Mennonites were able to withstand the pressures that pushed other COs to give up their commitment.

For Mennonites, being a CO during World War II usually meant being in harmony with the values of their church. Hence, they were able to gain full emotional and material support from that community. Virtually everyone in most Mennonite churches actively supported CPS. Church members gave millions of dollars and uncounted pounds of food and clothing. They also gave strong emotional support via letters, visits, pastoral support, and aid for families of COs. This reality supports the thesis that pacifism needs a communal context to flourish during adversity and across generations. Pacifism requires more than simply an individual choice.

(2) Realism about the state and social change. Many non-Mennonite COs bumped up against an intransigent state during the war and suffered as a result. They saw their stance as a means to construct a new social order. The Selective Service, on the other hand, saw alternative service as at most a way to have work done that might not be done otherwise. Mostly, Selective Service wanted ways to remove dissidents from the public eye. In this conflict between idealism and reality, the idealists usually found themselves frustrated by Selective Service intransigence.

Mennonites certainly did not accept that it was legitimate for them to be out of sight and out of mind during wartime. Nonetheless, they did not expect the government to embrace their values either. Consequently, they spent less time bumping against Selective Service, focusing more on the work they *were* able to get done.[28] They had a productive experience

---

[28] P. Toews, *Mennonites*, 140–41.

in CPS and, in time, did contribute to social change, both by creating alternative mental health facilities and by their long-range contribution to liberalizing the conscription practices of the US government.

(3) Mennonite peace theology. The point here is not that Mennonite theologians had developed a sophisticated rationale for pacifism, because essentially they had not.[29] However, Mennonite COs exhibited an impressive unanimity of theological rationale for their pacifism, impressive considering the diversity among the various Mennonite groups.

We might criticize their lack of theological sophistication. However, we should look at their theology in the context of the communal strength of the Mennonite tradition and its realism about the world Mennonites lived in. Mennonites understood God to be revealed in Jesus and as best understood in pacifist terms. This theological affirmation helped to buttress and sustain Mennonite pacifism in the face of great pressure to give it up.

Along with these strengths, however, I need to identify some questions.

Mennonites worked creatively within government restrictions because they never really expected much more. However, Mennonites may also have been naïve about the state. They realistically doubted that COs could use CPS as a direct tool for social change in effecting a "pacifist revolution." However, in naïvely assuming that the government did them a favor in allowing alternative service due to a tolerant respect for religious liberty, they failed to see the anti-democratic character of a government at war. This warring government used Mennonites themselves actually to support some of those anti-democratic tendencies through CPS.

Certainly Mennonites' strong communal sense strengthened their pacifism. However, we may wonder about the role of shame and external expectations in enforcing pacifism. How many COs took that stand simply out of fear of their church community condemning them if they did otherwise? How much *personal* ownership did Mennonite COs have?

Such personal ownership often emerged over time. Many Mennonite families sent one or more sons to the military as well as to CPS, indicating CPS was a *choice*. Many COs evolved in their views during their alternative service, taking a CO stand due to external expectations but developing more and more personal ownership as time went on. Many CPSers years later spoke of sustaining of a strong, and clearly deeply personal, pacifist commitment over the decades following the War, often expressed in various service activities.

---

[29] The first comprehensive theological rationale for the Mennonite peace position was only published near the end of World War II: Hershberger, *War*.

Related to the strength concerning Mennonites' simple but effective peace theology, we wonder about the intellectual basis for their pacifism. Mennonites had little to say that would be persuasive to outsiders. We might wonder if their influence might have been broader. Had they had more intellectual content to go with their impressive peaceable way of life and service involvement they might have more of an impact. They certainly had an unprecedented audience.

CHAPTER TEN

Anabaptist Faith and American Democracy[1]

ANABAPTISTS LIVING in America[2] are challenged by questions of citizenship in complex ways. We find ourselves in the land of freedom. The first Anabaptist generations faced severe persecutions and desperately sought safety; migrating widely in this quest. Beginning in the late seventeenth century many came to America. We may look back with gratitude for our forebears' opportunity to find a safe home here.

We have a great deal to be grateful for in terms of religious toleration. We also, not coincidentally, have opportunities, unimaginable for the sixteenth-century Anabaptists, to participate in the political life of one of the world's pioneering democracies. Not only are Anabaptists tolerated, we may vote, run for office, speak out, serve on school boards and in other ways be fully participating members in American democratic processes.

At the same time, American Anabaptists are also tax-paying citizens in a great empire, if we define "empire" in terms of a country's exercise of domination over many other parts of the world. America is now the world's one great superpower, spreading military bases spread far and wide,[3] spending more on our military than nearly all of the world's countries combined.

From its beginnings the Anabaptist tradition expressed a strong suspicion of empires. Present-day Anabaptists surely are being faithful to that tradition when we refuse to participate in, or even support, the wars of America.

However, what about the "good America"—the America of religious freedom and participatory democracy? Is the traditional Anabaptist "two-

---

[1] This chapter originally appeared in *Mennonite Quarterly Review* (July 2004). Used with permission.

[2] I use "America" (reluctantly) in this essay to refer to the United States of America. I recognize that the U.S.A. is not the only country in "America." Perhaps the ambivalence we may feel about using "America" as a synonym with the U.S.A. is appropriate for an essay that attempts to address the ambivalence some Anabaptist citizens of the U.S.A. currently feel about that citizenship.

[3] See Johnson, *Sorrows*.

kingdom" stance in which Christian convictions are understood primarily to be directly relevant for the faith community's inner existence and not the broader society's existence adequate for determining our understanding of citizenship today? In our time, people throughout the world plead for participants in American civil society to seek to influence American foreign policy to be more peaceable. Do American Anabaptists have responsibility aggressively to seek to take their pacifist convictions into the public square in a way that might influence the shape of American democracy?

We have three distinct stories to take into account as we reflect on these questions. The first I call the "Anabaptist Story." The second story talks of America welcoming migrating Anabaptists and serving as a beacon of hope for self-determination and freedom for people around the world. We may call this the "Democracy Story." The third, the story of the "other America," is a story of conquest, domination and widespread violence—the "Empire Story."

As pacifist followers of Jesus, those adhering to the Anabaptist Story appropriately seek to distance themselves from the Empire Story. Does such distancing also require of present-day Anabaptists a deep suspicion of the Democracy Story?

Anabaptist Faith

Recent writing on sixteenth-century Anabaptism highlights extreme diversity in the first fifty years of the Anabaptist movement. Such writing helpfully corrects simplistic generalizations about Anabaptist uniformity. However, it provides little clarity for those who would find it useful to draw upon the radicality of that movement for help in negotiating our current citizenship challenges.

If we want to go beyond the portrayals that focus on Anabaptist diversity, how might we draw upon the Anabaptist legacy to help discern how to respond to the citizenship issues I raise in this essay? Let me suggest a parallel. Scholars of the "historical Jesus" point out that the one incontrovertible "fact" about Jesus that is not dependent upon the biases of reports from his followers is that the Roman state executed Jesus as a political criminal.[4] Whatever else we might want to ascertain about Jesus' life and teaching, it needs to be understood in light of that one fact. So, they assert, we must ask what in Jesus' life and teaching led to his execution.

We may follow a similar path in seeking to understand the Anabaptists— as a means of better appropriating their legacy today. Amidst their diversity,

---

[4] See, e.g., Wright, *Jesus*, 106–9.

perhaps we may identify one commonality. Could we say that nearly every movement and leader was looked upon with suspicion, and usually hostility, by the state governments and state churches of Western Europe?

If so, then maybe the diversities among the Anabaptists pale when compared to this profound common ground. What about these movements and personalities led many of them to become enemies of the state? The answer to this question may provide us with a core of convictions to be carried on and applied to various times and places.

The four points summarized here should be seen as elements of such a core. Although not every point is equally true for each Anabaptist group or leader, they do apply widely enough to be seen as characteristic of the movement as a whole. The Anabaptists understood themselves as committed, above all else, to following Jesus' way in all areas of life. As they confessed him as Lord, they sought to follow him. As a consequence of that central commitment, they found themselves in conflict with the states and state churches of Western Europe.[5]

(1) By establishing themselves as a free church the Anabaptists asserted an unprecedented (and unacceptable) level of independence from the state and challenged the top-down social uniformity that political and religious leaders understood to be foundational for social order. The Anabaptists refused to accept the prince as ultimate authority. They gave their ultimate loyalty to God's call for how to live, not that of the government.

(2) By asserting that it is never God's will for Christians to fight, Anabaptists challenged governmental appeals to God as the basis for war. Such governmental appeals play a crucial role garnering citizens' support for warfare. Because of their rejection of participation in warfare, many Anabaptists also tended to reject participation in government altogether, insofar as they accepted the common assumption that human government without violence was inconceivable.[6]

---

[5] Present-day Anabaptists should also recognize that other sixteenth-century Christians often saw the Anabaptists as direct threats to the preservation of their societies in the face of chaos and anarchy, and that these perceptions were not always evidence of bad faith. The sixteenth-century was no less ambiguous in its political dynamics than the twenty-first.

[6] The later emergence of the Democracy Story, especially with pacifist Quakers playing a significant role, raised the possibility that violence and human government need not be inextricably linked. Certainly, actual democratic societies have remained dependent upon violence for their "defense" (and the Quaker leadership of the Pennsylvania colony ended after a few generations). However, the *idea* that political decisions might be based on consent and not coercion, even that forms of national defense that rely on nonviolent resistance might be possible, does enter the realm of imagination with modern democracy and makes it thinkable that a pacifist could participate in human government and remain pacifist.

(3) By rejecting the domination of political and religious hierarchies, Anabaptists pointed toward an upside-down notion of power. In their view, the gathered community of believers provided the best context for hearing Jesus. So, genuine power does not flow from the top of the social pyramid down, nor does it flow through the use of the sword. Discernment of God's will for human beings is not filtered through establishment mediators such as a prince or bishop. Rather, it comes directly to the community that then determines its own approach to faithfulness.

(4) By insisting on an alternative approach to economics, separating themselves from worldly materialism by advocating simplicity, economic sharing, mutual aid and, in a few famous cases, common ownership of all property, the Anabaptists challenged the emerging economic basis for the Empire Story. Probably the central driving point behind the nascent Spanish conquest in the Americas, which began at the same time as the Reformation, launching the great European empires, was the quest for gold and other sources of material wealth.

These core Anabaptist convictions—the church as free from state control, the refusal to fight in wars, the affirmation of upside-down social power and the commitment to an alternative economics—provide a basis for seeing Anabaptist faith in clear tension with the Empire Story. The opposition to warfare and exploitative economics clearly apply today. So do upside-down social power and the commitment to forming a counter-culture that would remain clearly committed to an identity as followers of Jesus, even though such commitment might be costly.

What, though, about the relationship of Anabaptist convictions to the Democracy Story? Do we gain direction from these core convictions that would also support deep suspicion toward active participation in the public conversation that makes up American democracy? Are the Anabaptist Story and the Democracy Story by necessity separate, even incompatible, stories?

The first Anabaptist generations, while certainly suspicious of the state and willing to separate themselves from activities, such as bearing the sword, that they saw contradicting the way of Jesus, seem nonetheless to have operated with assumptions that they could speak directly to prince, bishop and all others in their society. They believed they spoke a common language with others; hence, they could proclaim their religiously based convictions without apology—and they expected their interlocutors to be able to understand their proclamations.

A question we cannot answer is how sixteenth-century Anabaptists would respond to today's American democratic society. They may have shrunk from involvement, believing their commitment to Jesus precluded taking active roles in a society resting on the power of the sword. Just as plausible, though, would be to imagine at least some grasping the opportunity to proclaim their core convictions as widely as possible and to practice their vision for a society following Jesus as far as they would be allowed to—the limits to their proclamation not coming because of Anabaptists' self-imposed restrictions but because the society at some point stopped them.

John Howard Yoder hinted at this latter possibility when he wrote that the main difference between the more widely active Quakers and the more withdrawn Anabaptists lay not so much in different core convictions as in different sets of opportunities. Quakers had more freedom to express and implement their convictions in their social context than Anabaptists did.[7]

In America, Anabaptists found a place of toleration after generations of persecution in Europe. They became a part of the religious mosaic here. From its beginning, the U.S. had no established state church and made allowance for conscientious objection during times of war. Anabaptists have experienced (and have even helped to foster[8]) the American ideals of tolerance, freedom of religion, economic opportunity, protection of rights, free speech—the stuff of the Democracy Story. For this we must be grateful. Do we Anabaptists, in turn, have the responsibility to speak out openly and assertively in contributing to democracy by playing a role in the public conversation by which our society arrives at governmental policies?

---

[7] Yoder, *Christian*, 232–33.

[8] For example, in their steadfast quest for legal recognition for conscientious objection, Mennonites have made a significant contribution to the practice of democracy in the United States. Conscientious objection has not been so much a gift from a respectful government as a demand stemming from implacable convictions that meant that Mennonite pacifists would suffer a great deal rather than take up arms. Mennonites' perseverance in their peace convictions, even at the cost of great hardship (including, in a few cases, death), in time played a major role in widening the compass of legal recognition for conscientious objectors.

This widening in turn, during the Vietnam War era, led to an extraordinarily large number of claims for CO status (reportedly as many as fifty percent of draftees by 1973). It would not seem to be a stretch to argue that the popularity of the CO option played a major role in the decision by the U.S. government to end the draft and ultimately withdraw from Vietnam. Perhaps we could also say that this "threat" of widespread claims for CO status has played a large role in preventing the reinstatement of the draft and, in turn, has had a restraining impact on U.S. military activities.

The Two Americas: The Democracy Story and the Empire Story

The distinction between the Democracy Story and the Empire Story might be helpful in clarifying the question of our responsibilities in public policy conversations in that it helps us think about participating in democracy as an issue separate from our potential complicity in militaristic state violence. The Democracy Story/Empire Story distinction reflects the thought of many observers of American society and is reflected in a common refrain heard by Americans traveling abroad: "We love the American people and the ideals you stand for, but we do not like your government's foreign policy."

Historian Walter Karp, in his essay "The Two Americas,"[9] drew the distinction between "the American republic" (that has sought to embody the ideals of, for example, the Declaration of Independence and the Bill of Rights) and "the American nation" (that has sought dominance, wealth and power). Karp believed that these two are "deadly rivals for the love and loyalty of the American people."[10] He characterized the "nation" as a "poor dim thing, assembled as a corporate entity, sustained by an artificial patriotism, and given the semblance of meaning only when puffed up with the parade music of a foreign war."[11]

Noam Chomsky, critic of Empire, while condemning that story with great analytical prowess, also affirms that the United States is the freest society in the world.[12] Chomsky's main hope, in the face of the destructive power of the Empire, lies in the expansion of the Democracy Story. He cites solidarity movements in America that opposed U.S. Central American wars in the mid-1980s, the unprecedented worldwide demonstrations opposing the U.S. war on Iraq, and global justice movements that gather annually at the World Social Forum as elements of this needed expansion. Chomsky asserts, "The planet's 'second superpower,' which could no longer be ignored in early 2003, has deep roots in these developments, and considerable promise."[13]

Jonathan Schell, a journalist whose classic book *The Fate of the Earth* inspired the Nuclear Freeze Movement in the early 1980s, in his more recent book, *The Unconquerable World,* also draws the contrast between the

---

[9] Karp, *Buried*, 13–26.
[10] Karp, *Buried*, 14.
[11] Karp, *Politics*, ix.
[12] Chomsky, *Understanding*, 268–69.
[13] Chomsky, *Hegemony*, 235–36.

Empire Story and the Democracy Story. "For Americans, the choice is at once between two Americas," he observes, an "imperial America" and a "republican America."[14]

Schell shares Chomsky's use of the image of the world's "second superpower." Schell links these two "superpowers" with two kinds of power, drawing on Gandhi's distinction. "'One is obtained by the fear of punishment,' [Gandhi] said, 'and the other by acts of love.'" Schell calls these "cooperative power" and "coercive power."[15] His book demonstrates the viability of this second kind of power and presents the case for harnessing cooperative power for the sake of overcoming the destructiveness of coercive power.

Environmental writer Richard Nelson recounts his own evolution in a way that further highlights the distinction between the Democracy Story and the Empire Story. During the 1960s, Nelson found himself quite uncomfortable with the idea of patriotism and he joined movements opposing the Vietnam War, the denial of civil rights, and the power of corporations.[16]

More recently, though, Nelson has come to understand that the conservation work in the United States that he is involved with requires engagement with and affirmation of the process of democracy. As he sees positive results from citizen engagement in democratic movements to protect the environment, he has grown in his gratitude for the U.S. political system. That is, he has felt "a growing sense of patriotism."[17] He explains:

> By this I do not mean zealous loyalty toward a flag, veneration for a governmental system, or blind faith in "my country right or wrong." I am simply acknowledging the blessed good fortune to live in a democracy, a place where citizens can substantively influence decisions about society and land. And I am expressing my growing sense of allegiance to this living nation.[18]

Writers loyal to the Democracy Story insist on making the *distinction* between their loyalty to America as a democracy and to America as an empire. The first loyalty provides the basis for denying the second loyalty.

Certainly most of these thinkers have not been full-blown pacifists. However, their vision of democracy understands imperialistic violence to

---

[14] Schell, *Unconquerable*, 346–47.
[15] Schell, *Unconquerable*, 226.
[16] Nelson, *Patriotism*, 10.
[17] Nelson, *Patriotism*, 10–11.
[18] Nelson, *Patriotism*, 11.

be antithetical to genuine democracy. And, as a rule, they would affirm that pacifists within a genuine democracy have the right, even the responsibility, to seek to influence society to move in more pacifist directions. Again, the role of Quakers in American history testifies to this openness.

The current American Empire impacts the entire world; hence, the "death struggle" between our Empire Story and our Democracy Story has tremendous significance far beyond our country's borders.

Novelist and social critic Arundati Roy, from India, speaks for many around the world who seek to resist the destructive impact of U.S. imperialism. She argues that the people with the most potential to effectively challenge this imperialism are the citizens of the Empire itself:

> The only institution more powerful than the US government is American civil society. The rest of us are subjects of slave nations. We are by no means powerless, but you [Americans] have the power of proximity. You have access to the Imperial Palace and the emperor's chambers. Empire's conquests are being carried out in your name, and you have the right to refuse. You could refuse to fight. Refuse to move those missiles from the warehouse to the dock. Refuse to wave that flag. Refuse the victory parade.[19]

To the extent that Roy's perceptions are accurate, Anabaptist Americans are faced with a direct challenge. As members of our "powerful" civil society and as pacifists with theological convictions and a long history that point toward a rejection of the Empire Story, do we have a special responsibility to become politically active as an expression of our Anabaptist faith?

Faith and Citizenship in a Democracy

Let us grant Roy's assumption that American people have an indispensable role to play in fostering world peace through the mechanisms of our democratic system. How does this call toward active participation in public affairs fit (or not fit) with our Anabaptist convictions that we must not compromise in our commitment to follow the way of Jesus? May we do both—participate in American public affairs *and* remain consistent in our adherence to Jesus' way?

A recent discussion between two religious ethicists helps illumine our present context for reflecting on these questions. Jeffrey Stout, in his book *Democracy and Tradition*, offers a challenge to Anabaptists to seek to find a way to participate in American democracy even while maintaining our abhorrence of war and Empire. He does this by overtly engaging the thought

---

[19] Roy, "Seize," 17.

of Stanley Hauerwas. Hauerwas affirms Mennonite John Howard Yoder as having a profound influence on his social ethics and has categorized himself as a "high church Mennonite."[20] So, Stout's challenge to Hauerwas may be seen as a challenge to American Anabaptists.

Stout also makes a clear distinction between the two Americas:

> We tend to confuse the civic nation—the people—with the nation-state. In this book, I have been encouraging identification with the civic nation, with the community of reason-givers constituted by the democratic practice of holding one another responsible. This implies no affection for the massive institutional configuration of the nation-state, of which we should always remain suspicious. The American nation-state has proven itself especially worthy of suspicion in recent decades.[21]

Stout uses the term "democracy" for the "civic nation" of the United States that he passionately seeks to help thrive. Central to this democracy for Stout lies the practice of public conversation, wherein citizens take an active role in reasoning together to shape their society.[22] "Citizens" are characterized as those who accept some measure of responsibility for the condition of society[23]—and in a genuine democracy, this possibility is available to all, regardless of wealth, ethnicity, gender and class.

Stout seeks to make the case that the authentic democratic conversation *welcomes* all conversing citizens openly to express whatever premises ground their claims.[24] That is, for example, Christians should not bracket their faith-based convictions insofar as these convictions lead to certain social perspectives. Democracy seeks to bring as many groups as possible into the conversation, to encourage each group to be honest and straightforward in making their case for their particular perspective, to make sure to allow voice to each perspective and then to seek to arrive at the best possible public policies.[25]

This conversation is difficult, even under the best of circumstances, because the participants do not share a common agreement on how the

---

[20] See Hauerwas, "Confessions."

[21] Stout, *Democracy*, 297. Unfortunately, this clear statement of such a crucial distinction comes near the end of Stout's book. If he had placed it earlier, his argument would have been made even more clearly.

[22] Stout, *Democracy*, 6.

[23] Stout, *Democracy*, 5.

[24] Stout, *Democracy*, 10.

[25] Stout, *Democracy*, 226.

most important values should be ranked.[26] However, Stout believes that in practice this has never been an insurmountable problem in the United States. Analogously to how informal groups of athletes play sandlot baseball or street soccer without umpires or referees, our democratic society, without a monolithic authority recognized by all, still makes sense of commitment, and adjudicates right and wrong.[27]

Stout's passion for defending democracy stems in large part from his sense that U.S. democratic practices are presently at risk. The impact of the growth of the power of corporations and the national security state has directly challenged the sustainability of hard-earned democratic traditions in the U.S. Stout believes that all people of good will must join together in efforts to protect and reinvigorate these democratic traditions.

Hence, what he perceives to be antipathy toward the practices of democracy on the part of influential thinkers such as Stanley Hauerwas troubles him. Stout believes that Hauerwas's critique of "liberalism" often translates into hostility toward the civic nation and, hence, toward conversational democratic practices.[28] As represented by Stout, Hauerwas sees liberalism as a "secularist ideology" that discriminates against religion, forcing Christians to enter into public discourse only if they leave their Christian convictions behind. Hence, Stout thinks that Hauerwas seems to see "freedom and the democratic struggle for justice as 'bad ideas' for the church."[29] This antipathy of Hauerwas's, then, pushes Christians who identify most centrally with their faith community away from engagement with participatory democracy in the broader society—at precisely the moment when such engagement has become particularly important, in our age of anti-democratic responses to "terrorism" and corporate domination of civic life.

As read by Stout, Hauerwas, in emphasizing the difference between Christians and non-Christians, tends to foster suspicion toward those outside of the church.[30] In seeing his particular religious tradition as seeking to be a community of virtue over against the sinfulness of the world, Hauerwas undercuts Christian identification with the Democracy Story.[31]

---

[26] Stout, *Democracy*, 201.

[27] Stout, *Democracy*, 271–72.

[28] Stout, *Democracy*, 118.

[29] Stout, *Democracy*, 76. Stout cites the title of Hauerwas's book, *After Christendom? How the Church is to Behave If Freedom, Justice, and a Christian Nation Are Bad Ideas*.

[30] Stout, *Democracy*, 146.

[31] Stout, *Democracy*, 84.

Hauerwas's approach, claims Stout, leads to a lessening of concern about justice in the broader culture.

Stout recognizes that Hauerwas tends toward provocative rhetoric that does not always reflect the nuances of his actual arguments. While the subtitle of Hauerwas's book *After Christendom?* asserts that justice may be a "bad idea," in the book itself Hauerwas's argument more subtly focuses its critique on a narrow, Enlightenment-shaped notion of justice abstracted from faith convictions.[32] However, Stout sees the rhetoric itself as providing comfort to those in the churches who are relieved to hear a message that they are to be concerned only with the church's internal life and not with the risky task of seeking justice in the wider world.[33]

In Hauerwas's response to Stout, he actually affirms much of Stout's argument, taking issue primarily with Stout's account of the influence of moral philosopher Alasdair MacIntyre on Hauerwas's critique of liberal democracy—a point not central to our concerns here.[34] Hauerwas affirms the value of Christians being involved in what Stout calls the "civic nation." "I see nothing that prohibits Christians from using anything they find helpful—such as the kind of democratic conversation Stout desires—to engage in the work of living in a more peaceable and just society."[35] He further agrees with Stout's distinction between the "civic nation" and the nation-state "that we both believe is anything but 'democratic,'"[36] and cites his own involvement in the public debate prior to the 2003 U.S. war on Iraq as evidence that his approach is certainly not "withdrawal" from the democratic conversation.[37]

However, Hauerwas disagrees with Stout's assertion that by focusing on the internal life of the church, he refuses to care adequately for the wider world. Drawing on Yoder's insistence that the church best contributes to American political life by being "itself," Hauerwas calls on the church to do this by making sure to hear the voice of the "weakest member" and

---

[32] Hauerwas, *After*, 58.

[33] Stout, *Democracy*, 158.

[34] Hauerwas, *Performing*, 215–42. I will focus only on this one essay. I recognize that Hauerwas has written extensively on these themes elsewhere. I am not trying to examine Hauerwas's thought as a whole but simply highlight his particular conversation with Stout's book.

[35] Hauerwas, *Performing*, 237.

[36] Hauerwas, *Performing*, 238.

[37] Hauerwas, *Performing*, 239.

by engaging in "democratic conversation" because of its commitment to nonviolence.[38]

At the same time Hauerwas also rejects a view of the church that would imply that its concern with its internal life is an end in itself. "The call for the church to be the church is meant as a reminder that the church is in the world to serve the world." He denies believing that "the boundary between the church and world is impermeable."[39]

So, Hauerwas seems to be more or less agreeing with Stout's call for Christians to take their convictions into the public square—as Christians. Both reject the idea commonly attributed to liberal theorists such as John Rawls that Christians and other religious people should leave their faith convictions behind when they join the democratic conversation.

Hauerwas, however, remains more concerned than Stout about Christians joining this conversation wholeheartedly and still remaining truly Christian in their ways of thinking. He implies that at some point in the public conversation Christians are likely to reach the end of their ability to remain intelligible about their convictions to those who do not share their bases for those convictions. At that point, Christians will be tempted to leave out those bases—and then lose the distinctive content of their convictions.

Hauerwas quotes one of his earlier writings to make this point:

> Big words like "peace" and "justice," slogans the church adopts under the presumption that even if people do not know what "Jesus Christ is Lord" means, they will know what peace and justice mean, are words awaiting content. The church really does not know what these words mean apart from the life and death of Jesus of Nazareth. It is Jesus' story that gives content to our faith, and teaches us to be suspicious of any political slogan that does not need God to make itself intelligible.[40]

This is not the occasion to delve further into Hauerwas's thought. My concern is to note Stout's critique of Hauerwas's reluctance to affirm Christian participation in public discussion with the enthusiastic commitment to the Democracy Story that Stout would wish for.

Hauerwas acknowledges disagreement with Stout about the appropriate level of commitment to the Democracy Story even while agreeing with much of Stout's concern for the need to work for peace and justice in the

---

[38] Hauerwas, *Performing*, 227, 229.

[39] Hauerwas, *Performing*, 231.

[40] Hauerwas, *Performing*, 229, quoting Hauerwas and Willimon, *Resident*, 38.

world. But he sees more tension than Stout between peacemaking efforts focused on the faithful church and peacemaking efforts through an intentional, overt participation in public affairs. Stout asserts that Christians may do the latter without seriously compromising the former; Hauerwas is not so sure.

Two Distinct Languages?

Since my concern is primarily with Anabaptist understandings of citizenship, I turn to an Anabaptist writer who addresses these issues. While not directly mentioning Hauerwas, Ted Koontz, Associated Mennonite Biblical Seminary peace studies professor, echoes Hauerwas's concern with Christians proceeding too far into public policy discussions in his essay, "Thinking Theologically About War Against Iraq."

While supporting Anabaptists who publicly opposed the U.S war on Iraq "largely in terms of pragmatic or secular considerations" (such as just war, national self-interest, and general humanitarian concerns),[41] Koontz argues for the importance of Christian pacifists thinking and speaking in explicitly Christian terms. He distinguishes between the "first language" of pacifist Christians (the language of faith, most centrally based on our convictions about God and Jesus Christ) and our "second language" (the language of pragmatic considerations), and gives four reasons why using the "first language" is so important.

First, because "Christians should always reject all wars" even when there are not strong "second language" reasons for doing so, we may at times have to rely on our "first language" reasons as the only reasons for remaining committed to pacifism. Second, if we spend too much time speaking and thinking in our "second language," we may actually lose our "first language." Third, we do best to speak from our strength; few Christian pacifists are experts in the "second language." "We likely will make more of an impact speaking our first language than speaking 'their' language with a foreign accent." Fourth, our allies who speak our "second language" as their "first language" have more expertise to speak against war on pragmatic grounds.[42]

Certainly, Koontz's distinction between "first" and "second" languages helps us be clear about our convictions and articulate in how we communicate them. However, this distinction is ultimately not very coherent.

---

[41] Koontz, "Thinking," 93.
[42] Koontz, "Thinking," 95–96.

Koontz states, the "first language" includes "all those who name themselves Christian."[43] But, then, when he fleshes out Christian doctrinal convictions, he sounds specifically Anabaptist. For example, he writes, "our calling is to offer this message of salvation to all, particularly those who resist or reject that offer. This winsome offer is incompatible with killing them."[44] Yet, clearly the vast majority of Christians have *not* understood their soteriology to forbid their use of deadly force. This "first language" Koontz articulates seems to be only the "first language" of *pacifist* Christians. Thus, although Koontz claims all Christians speak the same "first language" because they all share a common confession concerning Jesus Christ, when he articulates his Christology, it is strongly pacifist in a way that most Christians would *not* agree with.

From another angle, Koontz implies that public policy actors are not Christians (since they cannot understand our "first language"), ignoring the fact that the vast majority of U.S. presidents and legislators continue to be professing Christians. At least two of the main advocates for Empire, Woodrow Wilson and George W. Bush, have especially professed overtly Christian commitments.

A more coherent "two language" motif would distinguish between the language of Empire and the language of Democracy or the language of Pacifism and the language of Justifiable War. If we do so, though, we will have Christians on both sides of the distinction.

With the assertion that "often our 'first language' of Christian theology will be unintelligible or unacceptable to our neighbors and our policy-makers,"[45] Koontz implies that it simply cannot be understood by people who are not Christians. However, if Christians do indeed have a problem with their convictions being understood, perhaps it is due to the fact that many Christians wrap their so-called "first language" of Christian faith in unintelligible jargon. The jargon creates an artificial divide not related to the intelligibility of our convictions so much as our own inability to speak clearly and concretely about them.

The model of Jesus, who presented his core theology in concrete, accessible language, provides us with a different kind of challenge. Christian pacifists need not construct a "first language"/"second language" distinction that may inhibit our engagement in the much-needed conversation in our broader culture concerning war and peace. Rather, we should learn better how to speak of our faith convictions in the same kind of concrete,

---

[43] Koontz, "Thinking," 96.
[44] Koontz, "Thinking," 99.
[45] Koontz, "Thinking," 94.

accessible way that Jesus did—to anyone who will listen in any available context.

Koontz worries that if we do not make a careful distinction between our "first language" and our "second language," and focus our energies on the former, we run the risk of losing our "first language." Let us grant his premise that Christian pacifists do commonly lose their "first language," and, as he implies, their pacifism with it. However, there may be other reasons for the loss of pacifist convictions in relation to broader identification with public policy makers. One of these reasons may actually be that what Koontz calls our "second language," the language of public policy, is corrupted by many people in power. Through the use of propaganda (such as the current talk about establishing a "democracy" in Iraq when apparently the major actors in the Bush Administration reject genuine democracy, as seen in their hostility to the leaders of potential U.S. allies such as Germany and Turkey, who listened responsively to their citizens who strongly opposed the U.S. war on Iraq), public policy actors often act in ways that actually contradict the stated values of the "second language" world itself.

Were leaders truly to act according to values such as democracy, humanitarianism, genuine national and global human interests, they would not lead the U.S. into the kinds of hegemonic violence that have often characterized U.S. foreign policy. It remains an interesting theoretical debate as to whether a nation-state is conceivable that does not use violence,[46] but surely all Anabaptists should welcome movements that seek to make the state *less* violent.

Many of the stated values of U.S. public policy are not inherently antithetical to Christian pacifism. The value system of public policy could support the thorough rejection of warfare.[47] However, the likelihood of that happening is lessened by the self-imposed inhibitions Koontz seems to call for, as they limit the involvement of voices that could support such a rejection.

If we do not have a clear sense for how our theologically based convictions *link* with pragmatically and humanistically grounded convictions we will be more likely to toss them aside when they are challenged. We all know stories of people who "lose their faith" when they encounter a wider

---

[46] See Gene Sharp's classic study on practical nonviolence, *Politics*, for evidence that nonviolence has practical legitimacy. Jonathan Schell, while stating that he is not a complete pacifist, argues in *Unconquerable* that war is becoming obsolete.

[47] See Schell, *Unconquerable*, for evidence supporting this assertion. Both Schell and Stout do explicitly deny that they themselves are pacifists. Part of what I seek to argue, though, is that for both, their perspectives would seem to welcome the participation of overt pacifists arguing in favor of pacifism in the public square.

world that their narrow "first language" has not prepared them to deal with.

Koontz argues we should cultivate our "first language" so we will still have grounds to oppose war even when we do not have strong "second language" bases, citing World War II as a case when "pragmatic and humanitarian considerations did not line up clearly in opposition to war."[48] However, we must ask how viable a Christian pacifism ultimately can be when it grants that there are not strong real-world reasons for opposing each war. Such an admission may lead to a kind of pacifism where our rejection of war becomes merely a "leap of faith."

In fact, many did oppose World War II on pragmatic and humanitarian grounds. To them it was clear even if they did not have Jesus' commands to fall back on.[49] Simply the fact that the war left fifty million people dead would legitimate strong humanitarian grounds for opposing it.

Koontz's point that we do not have strong "second language" reasons for opposing some wars may lead to Christian pacifism becoming primarily a "vocational" matter for people who agree that their core convictions are not normative for the wider world. This position will not be very attractive for those who do feel a strong sense of responsibility for positively influencing that wider world or who seek to integrate their Christian convictions with social life.

Fortunately, many outside of Koontz's "first language" circle have been doing excellent work over the past century in articulating and implementing convictions that point toward pacifism and have great relevance to the wider world we live in. We may, most obviously, cite Mohandas Gandhi and those influenced by his work. But many others have also been working at understanding the world in ways that are fully compatible with Christian pacifism, providing evidence that all wars are illegitimate on pragmatic and humanitarian grounds.

Koontz's argument implies that Christian pacifists should not seek to utilize to the full extent possible their call (and opportunity) to have an impact on public life as citizens of the United States. In his focus on the

---

[48] Koontz, "Thinking," 94–95.

[49] See, for example, Grimsrud, "Saying." Chapters four and five of that work consider two significant groups of COs who mostly grounded their opposition to the war in "second language" considerations: "resisters" who had the stereotypical unyielding conscience that forbade using violence and "transformers" who sought to effect social change toward a warless world. Such pacifists tended to be articulate and hence have left an extensive literature accounting for their convictions. A couple of representative books include Peck, *We*, and F. Zahn, *Deserter*.

integrity of our "first" language he seems to be echoing Hauerwas's focus on the "church being the church" as our main social responsibility.

Both Koontz and Hauerwas argue that we should hope to have an impact in our larger society on issues of war and peace; both would abhor the "two kingdom" notion that the wars of the world are of no concern for followers of Jesus. Yet they seem ambivalent about taking up Jeffrey Stout's implied challenge actively to enter the public square as Christian pacifists and to challenge American foreign policy head on—with the language of citizenship and democracy.

If we take seriously the distinction between the Empire Story and Democracy Story, and accept Stout's claim that the American democratic conversation *does* allow for us to remain fully committed to our faith convictions and to express those convictions openly without watering them down, then we may affirm full and active participation in public debate as Anabaptists.

Seeking the Welfare of the City

If we combine an overt commitment to Anabaptist convictions with boldness in fully participating in the democratic conversation of the American civic nation, joined with a special concern for resisting the supremacy of the Empire Story, what might we say and do?

Let us return to the four core sixteenth-century Anabaptist convictions: the church as free from state control, the refusal to fight in wars, the affirmation of upside-down social power and the commitment to an alternative economics.

Understanding the community of faith to be free from state control in the sixteenth century not only led to institutional independence. It also signified a different worldview, centered on a different set of values. The way of Jesus took precedence over the way of Caesar. Anabaptist tradition, however, has tended to draw some distorted applications from this principle.

Abraham's calling in the ancient Near East centered on the faith community being a light to the nations (Gen 12:3).[50] However, his faith descendants tended to see the security of election as the called people of God as being an end in itself rather than as being about their calling to be a light to the nations. In parallel fashion, the embrace of a free church approach is best understood as being a means for people of faith to have a more creative

---

[50] See Grimsrud, *God's,* for a popular-level presentation of an argument that this calling of Abraham serves as the best overall rubric for understanding the Bible as a whole.

and profound impact on their wider world ("the nations"), not as a warrant for withdrawal and separation.

As a free church we should be in a strong position to perceive the *difference* between the Empire Story and the Democracy Story. We should be in a position to discern how the best of the Democracy Story draws on the best of the biblical tradition and deserves our strong support. Likewise, we should also be in a position to offer penetrating critiques of the Empire Story and its inevitable commitment to the myth of redemptive violence.[51]

The same challenge applies to the rejection of participation in warfare. Certainly, as Koontz powerfully argues, we need to devote great energy and creativity to sustaining our Anabaptist peace position. However, our "treasure" may turn to dust if we are not testing it, strengthening it and applying it in the world around us. Our pacifism is not given to us merely so that our own children may remain safely behind when the servants of Mars send their children off to war. Rather, our pacifism should help us join the *public* discussion and help our neighbors better see how the Empire Story so powerfully subverts the Democracy Story we all affirm. I fear that focusing only on keeping the "first and second languages" distinct and on "the church being the church" may be selling the potential power of our pacifist witness far too short.[52]

The Anabaptists' convictions about upside-down social power pose a clear challenge to the top-down political and ecclesial patterns of domination that have characterized the modern era. As articulated by Jonathan Schell, perhaps the major global political dynamic in our postcolonial time is that people in countries throughout the world desire to be free from the domination of outside powers.[53] Anabaptists should support such movements, perceiving them as a sign of great hope that the Empire Story may be resisted.

---

[51] We should also offer critiques of the Democracy Story itself insofar as it sometimes allows for the use of violence. Such critiques, though, need not lead to a rejection of the Democracy Story. They are an inherent part of the give and take the Democracy Story affirms; it implicitly encourages us to make the case for a thoroughly nonviolent civic culture.

[52] I appreciate Koontz's story at the end of his essay about his own witness to his Christian pacifism in his lecture to a conference of public policy thinkers ("Thinking," 104–8). It strikes me, though, that his story illustrates why we are better off not to think of our "first language" as being "unintelligible or unacceptable to our neighbors and our policymakers" (94). Rather, it seems to illustrate that all humans speak the same basic language (which is why Jesus' style of teaching is so effective) and that the best thing we can do is articulate our pacifist convictions and their policy ramifications to any and all who will listen (as Stout would have us do).

[53] Schell, *Unconquerable*.

To be sure, we insist that these drives for self-determination dare not become merely new versions of the Empire Story. We may draw upon Anabaptist tradition to offer theological critique of violence and domination in all of its forms. However, we may also offer this critique in conjunction with affirmations of the Democracy Story by providing a vision for self-determination that is humane and life enhancing.[54]

Finally, our "alternative economics" may be seen as constructing an alternative community. We are called to live as a people of faith shaped by God's mercy whose common life embodies that mercy. This calling likely will lead people of faith to live differently from their wider culture. The Anabaptist commitment to share life together in practical ways as a means of sustaining a witness to the way of Jesus remains central to the possibilities of genuinely living faithfully. As present-day Anabaptists, we must not simply allow ourselves to acculturate and be absorbed in the broader American culture. However, I am trying to suggest that our task of fostering a sense of separation from the "world" (i.e., "domination system") is for the sake of a constructive engagement with the "world" (as the object of God's love—John 3:16).

Koontz captures an essential Anabaptist insight by challenging the church to devote energy to being clear about its distinctive beliefs, and to insist that those beliefs must *always* govern Christian social involvement. But he does not articulate clearly enough how this focus on a theologically-based social ethic serves our calling to be fruitful instruments of God's in helping to heal the nations and transform "the kings of the earth" (Revelation 21–22).

Jeffrey Stout has challenged Anabaptists. We may see continuity between the core convictions of the Anabaptists and our potential today in the United States creatively to contribute to making the world a more peaceable, humane place. We must take seriously the potential we have through our nation's democratic processes to resist Empire as a way of life.

Stout gives us hope that it is indeed possible (and necessary for our sake as Anabaptist Christians and for our sake as citizens of a powerful country) for us to enter America's public conversation boldly as citizens and as Anabaptist Christians—recognizing that we would not be faithful to either calling were we to separate them.

---

[54] On this point, engagement with liberation theology might be fruitful. For an earlier, quite interesting, beginning conversation see Schipani, ed., *Freedom*.

CHAPTER ELEVEN

Who is Part of the Conversation? "Neo-Mennonites" and Anabaptist Theology[1]

THE EARLY years of the twenty-first century are a time of challenge for Anabaptist faith. Anabaptist Christians are engaged in intense conversations concerning the meaning of Christianity in a tumultuous, rapidly changing world. A central issue in this conversation is simply whose voices will be heard. How will Anabaptists define their faith, order their communities, prepare their young people—and *who* will have voices in this defining?

This essay reflects on this issue of who partakes in Anabaptist conversations about the future of their faith. I believe our best approach is to affirm that *all* the voices within the current broad community of Anabaptists are to be respected parts of the conversation. To make such allowance requires an awareness of the identity of these voices.

I will summarize one set of voices often excluded, at least from more "official" discussions. My intention here is to surface this perspective, presenting it mostly descriptively. I am sympathetic with the perspective I describe, but my intention in this chapter is not to be presenting *my* views so much as representing an important set of voices in the broader Anabaptist conversation that deserves attention.

I will call these voices "neo-Mennonites." I am a bit unsure of the best shorthand term for the general perspective to which I am referring. I will use "neo-Mennonite" as a non-value laden term[2] for describing people who affirm many of the elements mentioned by Mennonite theologian Gordon Kaufman in his 1979 book *Nonresistance and Responsibility*:

---

[1] This essay is slightly revised from Ted Grimsrud, "Mennonite Theology and Historical Consciousness: A Pastoral Perspective" in Alain Epp Weaver, ed., *Mennonite Theology in Face of Modernity: Essays in Honor of Gordon D. Kaufman* (North Newton, KS: Bethel College, 1996), 137–53. Used with permission of Bethel College.

[2] Other terms I considered and discarded as too value-laden, too vague, or otherwise potentially misleading include: "Muppie," postmodern, universalist, professional, historically-conscious, urban, educated, critical, culturally-open, liberal, and progressive.

> Many persons—especially younger professional people, well-educated and living in settings quite far removed, at least culturally, from traditional rural Mennonite communities—feel the need for an interpretation of the Mennonite perspective which breathes more freely the atmosphere of the contemporary life and culture in which they are so deeply involved. They do not wish to give up some of the basic insights and convictions of the faith in which they were raised, but the only interpretations of that faith which are readily accessible do not seem to address the questions and problems they are facing.[3]

I believe "neo-Mennonites" should be legitimate parts of Anabaptist conversations on all levels. I mean to suggest that church-wide conversations on all aspects of church life should welcome the "neo-Mennonite" perspective as a legitimate part of the Anabaptist "circle."

I do not argue that the "neo-Mennonite" perspective should be *privileged*; simply that it be respected as part of the conversation. Our discernment will be most fruitful if all appropriate voices are heard. A big danger as we face our challenges is to ignore or silence voices from within our existing communities. The "neo-Mennonite" perspective exists now *within* the circle of the Anabaptist community. Even if not well understood, or even acknowledged by many in the churches, it is part of what the Anabaptist faith community has become. Rather than seen as an alien perspective, or one to be resisted, it should be seen as one voice in the Anabaptist choir.

To clarify the "neo-Mennonite" theological perspective in this essay, I reflect on some central theological themes and briefly summarize the perspectives of four "mainstream" Anabaptist theologians[4]—not intended to critique those perspectives but to illumine the distinctives of the "neo-Mennonite" perspective. I will conclude with a more straightforward summary of the "neo-Mennonite" perspective on these themes.

Since my intent is primarily to *introduce* the general "neo-Mennonite" perspective and to argue that it should be respected as part of the Anabaptist theological conversation, I will not be articulating a critique of "neo-Mennonites." Such critique certainly is fully appropriate—but not as an attempt to exclude "neo-Mennonites" from the conversation.

---

[3] Kaufman, *Nonresistance*, 7–8.

[4] By "mainstream Anabaptist theologians" I simply mean theologians who have been teaching at Anabaptist institutions and whose writings mostly have been published under Anabaptist auspices. I will be considering Thomas N. Finger, of Eastern Mennonite Seminary; A. James Reimer, of Conrad Grebel College; C. Norman Kraus, of Goshen College; and J. Denny Weaver, of Bluffton University.

I pastored a "neo-Mennonite" congregation in Eugene, Oregon, from 1987–1994. Based on my experience in Eugene and conversations over the years with "neo-Mennonites" throughout North America, I have become convinced that the neo-Mennonite perspective deserves to be taken seriously by all Anabaptists as part of the Anabaptist faith circle.

I am reflecting here on a way of thinking that *exists already* in the churches, not arguing that people *should* think in a certain way. My references to mainstream theologians focus primarily on how they might be read in "neo-Mennonite" congregations, more than on a general critique. If I am advocating anything, it is simply that mainstream Anabaptists should be aware of the ways of thinking characteristic of "neo-Mennonites."

Historical Consciousness

One important element of the contemporary world within which "neo-Mennonites" live and think is "historical consciousness." By this I mean the self-awareness that we are *all* always part of history, and that, consequently, our awareness of meaning, truth, values, and spirituality has a relative cast because we are unable to separate ourselves from this historicity.

Within Christian theology, the emergence of historical consciousness caused turmoil. Part of the dynamic has been an attempt by those who resist historical consciousness to continue to do theology as if the traditional "house of authority" of objective, even absolute, authorities such as scripture, church tradition, and church hierarchies still held sway.[5] Such theology seems inadequate for people who think self-consciously within the context of historical consciousness.

For people with eyes shaped by historical consciousness, the dogmatic method that bases its authority on absolute "facts" existing outside historical relativity has little value. For such people, these "facts" simply do not exist.

This immersion in the thought-world shaped by historical consciousness shapes "neo-Mennonite" congregations. I will mention three typical attitudes.

(1) Historical consciousness denies that outside, objective authorities (e.g., Edward Farley's three-pronged "house of authority": scripture, tradition, church hierarchies) determine belief and practice. "Neo-Mennonites" resist citing such authorities as a means of *ending* discussions. Such citations assume that the absolute "truth" cited resolves any possible disagreement.

---

[5] For a description and powerful critique of this three-pronged "house of authority" see Edward Farley, *Ecclesial*.

Such use of the "way of authority" has often occurred among Anabaptists. All three prongs are used, even in spite of our claim not to be a hierarchical tradition. Certainly *scripture* is cited authoritatively, in particular verses that are said once and for all time to proscribe certain behaviors. However, *tradition* is also a major authority, as in "the Church has always believed this." Perhaps even more surprisingly, current church pronouncements (what we could call, in a sense, *church hierarchies*) are also utilized to end discussion.

Farley argues that such use of authority is doing theology by citation, not inquiry.[6] Historical consciousness leaves many "neo-Mennonites" quite suspicious of such a method. If *everything* that comes into the heads of human beings is historically relative, then we have *no* authorities that we can simply cite as an end to theological and ethical conversation.

This hermeneutics of suspicion based on the principle of criticism is simply part of how many people think. Part of what makes many church controversies difficult is the lack of weight many "neo-Mennonites" give to citations that people still operating within the way of authority make. These authorities are cited as if they obviously will bring closure to the debate. However, to people dwelling *outside* the house of authority, they carry no such weight.

(2) Many "neo-Mennonite" congregations, influenced by historical consciousness, show more interest in spirituality and ethics than classical creeds and dogmas. They experience life concretely and practically—that is, *in history*. They see abstract theological constructs as having little practical relevance; such constructs mostly emerge from a way of thinking that tries to transcend historical being.

Contemporary uses of doctrines such as the Trinity, the deity of Christ, and the divine inspiration of the Bible do not emerge so much from practical historical life in the *present* as from *past* constructs that at one time emerged from practical life. For many shaped by historical consciousness, these have now become abstract, ahistorical intellectual constructs long disconnected from their original controversies and ways of life. These doctrines may be interesting to think about. And, with some work, they can be shown to relate to actual life. However, "neo-Mennonites" doubt the concrete relevance of these doctrines. That is not to say they reject them, so much as question their centrality and their use as boundary markers.

"Neo-Mennonites" find it difficult to see in actual life how belief in the Trinity has made a practical difference. Many Trinitarian Christians *support* imperialistic wars, nuclear weapons, economic exploitation, and sexism.

---

[6] Farley, *Ecclesial*, 109.

On the other hand, many non-Trinitarian Christians, Jews, agnostics, and atheists come much closer to following the teachings of Old Testament prophets and Jesus against violence and in favor of care and compassion for the poor and oppressed.

(3) For "neo-Mennonites," sensitivity to historical consciousness leads to openness to other expressions of faith. If one believes that Christian theological distinctives are historically conditioned; and if spirituality and ethics take priority over abstract, precise, doctrinal theology in determining our faith expression, then one will tend to be much more open to common ground with other expressions of faith.

"Neo-Mennonites" spend little energy defining how they differ from other religious or even non-religious people. Few "neo-Mennonites" concern themselves with converting others to their religion, though they always happily welcome people to walk with them should they so choose. They find common ground within their faith communities based on a sense of tolerance for different views, similar ethical ideals, an enjoyment of singing, and a respect for traditional Anabaptist emphases such as pacifism, service concerns, potlucks, and quilting projects.

"Neo-Mennonite" communities do facilitate a meaningful expression of faith. Historical consciousness does not lead to total relativism or individualism. These communities still come together; people show great commitment of resources to keep them going. Worship, a sense of community, encouragement for faithful living, do not require the house of authority.

"Neo-Mennonites" do tend to have difficulty articulating *positive* expressions of belief. Many people in such communities find the old way of authority to be untenable as a means to express their beliefs. They mourn this loss little. With all its tensions and even pain, Christian living within the modern thought-world is possible, even exhilarating. The question is not whether "neo-Mennonites" can be Christians outside the house of authority. "Neo-Mennonite" communities show that they can. But they do suffer from not having a widely articulated theological language that might help them better to make sense out of their Christian experience.

For people who live in the thought-world of historical consciousness, a moral-theological language based on the house of authority will not be viable. However, that does not mean that *no* language is possible. Nor does it make the construction of such a language less crucial.

Mainstream Perspectives

"Neo-Mennonite" communities, deeply influenced (consciously and unconsciously) by historical consciousness, must grapple with some key theological issues. A sampling: (1) How do we characterize life? More in terms of "abundance" or "scarcity"? (2) What is the nature of theology? More "construction" or "citation"? (3) How do we approach the Bible? More as a "dialogue partner" or as an "authority"?

I will briefly mention some perspectives of several contemporary mainstream Anabaptist theologians in relation to these questions. Then I will focus on how these contrast with "neo-Mennonite" perspectives and outline how "neo-Mennonites" may approach these issues.

A. James Reimer. (1) How do we characterize life? For Reimer, the present world is an unfriendly place for genuine Christianity. Two "phenomena combined—the conflicting diversity of theological options . . . and the absolutizing technological monolith" greatly hinder "any faith in and experience of that which is eternal and transcendent."[7] He denies that genuine meaning can emerge from historical relativities. "If humankind's knowledge is radically historical, how can one speak of truth and knowledge at all, how can one speak of universal norms by which the relativities of human history can be judged?"[8]

(2) What is the character of theology? Theology has to do with accurately representing the truthfulness revealed in the Bible and Creeds. Reimer rejects the idea of *our* constructing our theology in the modern world. "Rather than deliberately setting out to 'construct' a new concept of God on the basis of modern historicism, it seems that we ought to recover the profundity of the classical trinitarian view and put fresh meaning into it in the context of our age."[9]

Reimer emphasizes that the trinitarian conception of God corresponds with eternity, as does the deity of Christ. Because of this correspondence, these doctrines are not relativized by history, but remain objectively true. Hence, our job is, essentially, finding meaningful ways to cite these once-for-all, outside of time, truths. "A trinitarian understanding of God and his ways with the world is more than simply an approach; it is in some sense the content of truth itself."[10]

---

[7] Reimer, *Mennonites*, 235.

[8] Reimer, "Nature," 33.

[9] Reimer, "Nature," 34–35.

[10] Reimer, "Response," 73.

(3) How do we approach the Bible? Reimer is suspicious of attempts to synthesize the biblical materials with present-day life and thought. We need "jealously [to] guard the distance between the biblical world and the contemporary world."[11] Otherwise we will have no transcendent authority. "The underlying affirmations embedded in the church's confessions, doctrines, creeds, and dogmas assert something fundamental (call it ontological, metaphysical, whatever you like) about God."[12] Ultimately, these are truths before which we must submit.

Thomas N. Finger. (1) How do we characterize life? A central theme in Finger's theology is future-oriented eschatology. The present world is the location of continuing evil that is evidence that God's kingdom is not yet completed. "To me, evil is still appallingly real and active enough that I cannot see how Jesus' return can manifest the reality of his prior victory unless that evil is also somehow destroyed."[13] Finger's argument implies that when we compare the present, with its continued manifestation of evil, to the promised and assured completed kingdom, it will be seen as incomplete and characterized by scarcity.

Finger also resists historical consciousness. The New Testament, according to Finger, goes beyond history in establishing Jesus' identity. The transcendent/eternal realm, outside of history, ultimately more genuinely determines Jesus' identity. God resides in this eternal realm, and it is from this realm that absolute truths are revealed in the context of human history.[14]

(2) What is the nature of theology? Finger attempts to do systematic theology primarily as reporting on biblical truths. He certainly recognizes the need to communicate in the language of the modern world. However, Christian theology is essentially a matter of interpretation of past, once-for-all-time revealed truth. "Theology's critical and constructive norms cannot be derived simply from [the communities it represents], their histories and their practices, but only from truth claims which it believes transcend and critique all human communities whatsoever."[15]

(3) How do we approach the Bible? "The biblical writers express a unique perspective on reality—one that will undergo distortion if subordinated to, or reinterpreted in terms of, other language games."[16] Finger understands

---

[11] Reimer, *Mennonites*, 388–89.

[12] Reimer, *Mennonites*, 391.

[13] Finger, "Response," 163; see also Finger, *Christian*, 152.

[14] Finger, "Is," 46.

[15] Finger, "Response," 164.

[16] Finger, "Biblical," 4.

the Bible to be our absolute norm. Theology that speaks of ultimate reality and meets human needs requires such a norm. "To distinguish between the ephemeral and the permanent, between the misleading and the trustworthy in experience, theology requires a *norm* by which to test it. How can Jesus and the kingdom be apprehended so that we might test our implicit convictions and our contemporary language about them? To apprehend them with any concreteness, scripture is our only norm."[17]

C. Norman Kraus. (1) *How do we characterize life?* In his understanding of human nature, Kraus emphasizes the significance of our being created in God's image, creatures hence with the potential for relating personally with God. And, he asserts that we are unable in our present state fully to realize that potential. Kraus understands the present world to be both a place loved by God and a place in need of transformation.[18]

(2) *What is the character of theology?* Kraus strongly emphasizes the need to do theology *within* history. "A disciples' theology must have a specific location in time and space. . . . [We] should [not] expect our statements of truth to be timeless. This does not mean that ultimate reality changes, but only that our partial knowledge and experience of it changes."[19]

Theology, for Kraus, does not simply interpret past materials. Nor does it primarily abstractly speculate about the future. "Theology should describe and point to a *present reality* and not *present theory, past experience,* or *eschatological prediction.*"[20] Kraus has little interest in abstraction, opting instead for reflection that relates to communal Christian living. "Theology should be a functional discipline in the life of the congregation. There is little value, for example, in rational speculation about the essential nature of the Godhead."[21]

(3) *How do we approach the Bible?* Kraus sees the Bible as the core material for doing theology. He does emphasize the Bible *as interpreted* more than the Bible as an objective, outside-of-us absolute norm. "I consider systematic theology to be essentially a hermeneutical discipline, not a speculative one. This means that one begins with the biblical text as the basic document and attempts to transpose it into a new cultural context."[22] This centrality of the Bible as source remains true everywhere. "In cross-

---

[17] Finger, "Is," 46.
[18] Kraus, *God,* 102–30.
[19] Kraus, "Toward," 114–15.
[20] Kraus, "Toward," 114 (Kraus's italics).
[21] Kraus, "Toward," 114.
[22] Kraus, "Reply," 77–78.

ing cultures with the gospel we must adhere radically to the *sola Scriptura* principle."[23]

In placing highest priority on a pre-creedal reading of the Bible, Kraus places the strongest emphasis on the story of Jesus as the key for understanding the whole. "I think that theology as a hermeneutical discipline should begin with the definitive self-revelation of God in Christ as it has come to us in the biblical tradition."[24]

J. Denny Weaver. (1) How do we characterize life? Weaver emphasizes the possibilities of faithfulness to God's will in the *present*. Life in the here and now is the locus for fruitful living. "We should take seriously the world and its history as God's arena."[25] Yet, he also sees the here and now as the locus of a major confrontation between two worlds, that of God's mercy as expressed in Jesus and his followers, and that of the forces of hostility to God's mercy. "The church is a sign and a witness to the world that the kingdom of God is different from the world. The church lives with the goal of transforming all of society into the kingdom of God."[26]

(2) What is the character of theology? Weaver makes Jesus central more radically than the other three theologians. "It is the story of Jesus—and not the Bible or theocentrism or trinitarianism—which Christian faith claims as the particular point in history which reveals God's presence and will most fully."[27]

(3) How do we approach the Bible? For Weaver, the Bible very much plays the authoritative role, specifically the Bible as witness to Jesus. "Jesus or the Jesus story is the regulative principle for a Mennonite systematic theology. . . . To be Christian is to take Jesus . . . as the norm and the beginning point for theology."[28] The Bible retains central significance for contemporary theology, and contemporary theology faces the challenge of interpreting the biblical message anew in the context of our modern world.

> The Bible . . . contains the narratives with which any christology must begin and with which any christology must be compatible, and it also has a number of examples of the development of christologies. It is thus indispensable. At the same time, awareness of the worldviews depicted in it means that no modern theology can limit its vocabulary or its images to the biblical language and images.

---

[23] Kraus, "Response," 209.
[24] Kraus, "Reply," 78.
[25] Weaver, "Perspectives," 194.
[26] Weaver, "Response," 30.
[27] Weaver, "Mennonites," 127.
[28] Weaver, "Mennonite," 55.

Even less can theological language and images begin with or be limited to or require compatibility with the fourth and fifth century creedal formulations.[29]

Points of Contrast

Reimer and Finger most strongly express theological perspectives that contrast with emphases of "neo-Mennonite" perspectives self-consciously affirming historical consciousness. However, Kraus and Weaver also contrast with such perspectives in key ways.

(1) How do we characterize life? These four theologians tend to see life in the here-and-now world as essentially characterized by scarcity more than abundance.

We see this most clearly in their negative language about "the world." Reimer articulates this the most strongly.[30] He seems to accept an Augustinian/Hobbesian notion of the nature of human reality being dog-eat-dog. We compete to prove the truth.

"Neo-Mennonites" question this portrayal. Do we need to arbitrate *between* competing systems as if they were mutually exclusive? Might we not better learn from all and working together to learn better? Might not attitudes of competition actually *undercut* spiritual growth?[31]

Reimer's negative perspective also finds expression in his antipathy toward what he calls "historicism," an antipathy shared by Finger. They understand God's ultimate reality to be located *outside* history. They thus see the here-and-now as secondary, transient, suspect. They do not find genuine abundance in everyday human life but believe it must come from the outside, where the divine realm is located.

Reimer's negative attitude toward the human reality also finds expression in his perceiving in God a dark, wrathful, judgmental side. Finger, in emphasizing the centrality of evil in the present in contrast to the future, eschatological paradise, also reflects a negative attitude toward present human reality. Finger's eschatological focus implicitly minimizes the *present* possibility for human experience of abundance.

Kraus and Weaver, in positing discipleship as more central in their theology reflect more optimism about the possibilities of present life. We may also see this in each expressing a much more positive view of the *his-*

---

[29] Weaver, "Perspectives," 198–99.
[30] Reimer, *Mennonites*, 391.
[31] See Kohn, *No Contest* and *Brighter*.

torical locus of God's salvific work. Nonetheless, both qualify their positive attitudes toward present life in significant ways.

Kraus emphasizes our need for Jesus' intervention in order for us to live in God's presence. "He accomplished for us what we could not do for ourselves."[32] Weaver uses the language of church versus world as a way to minimize present possibilities for abundance and points toward the *future* for the full manifestation of human possibilities.

These emphases on the need for *outside* intervention; on the need for *future*, eschatological fulfillment of God's purposes; on a clear categorization of the "world" as *not* the place of God's expressions of abundance, all reflect a more negative attitude toward *present* life than many "neo-Mennonites" have.

A perspective affirmative of historical consciousness tends *not* to understand God to be outside human history, tends *not* to think of an apocalyptic future as the locus of human possibilities, and tends *not* to divide present human existence between a place called "world" and another place distinct from "world."

(2) What is the character of theology? For all four theologians, again recognizing different emphases, theology often has more the character of citation than construction. The main content for theology comes from the past, and the present-day theologian has the job of interpreting, perhaps even translating, that ancient body of material into present-day usefulness. Reimer especially emphasizes the early church's creeds and confessions, Finger the entire biblical corpus, and Kraus and Weaver the accounts of Jesus.

All would agree, though, in understanding theology to be "essentially a hermeneutical discipline" in which classical texts are interpreted for the present.[33] They understand theology's task being to interpret pre-existing truths more than constructing *new* understandings.

The approach essentially is deductive, not inductive. Farley's characterization fits, by and large, the approach of all four theologians. "Theological judgments (and contents) themselves are established not by demonstration but by citation, by appeal to authority . . . Classical theological thinking occurs not in the mode of science but in the mode of authority . . . The theologian relates to the location of divine-human identity not by *inquiry* but by *exposition*."[34]

---

[32] Kraus, "Jesus," 184.
[33] Kraus, "Reply," 77.
[34] Farley, *Ecclesial*, 116, 117, 112 (Farley's italics).

Theology by citation places the issue of normativity at the center. However, "neo-Mennonites" understand part of the problem with telling people what they *should* believe (especially if this belief requires anachronistic or foreign thought-forms) to be that even when they assent to the "should," *mystification* (making affirmations which are not fully understood and often do not connect with life) and *ressentiment* (internalizing extrinsic values resulting in deep-seated antipathy toward actual reality)[35] likely result.

Even though Finger and, especially, Reimer, align their theological construct with "classical Christianity," in actuality they seem, for "neo-Mennonites," to be claiming special authority for what is every bit as much a contemporary formulation as the "relativistic historicisms" of a "neo-Mennonite" theologian such as Gordon Kaufman. For "neo-Mennonite" theology, *no* formulation of theology can help but be a contemporary construct no matter how much old language is used. *None* of us can transcend *our* location in *our* day and age.

A desire to avoid "anthropocentrism" lies behind much of the desire to find outside authorities on which to base theology. However, a "neo-Mennonite" perspective argues that because we are limited to *human* language in articulating our theology, our theology is in some sense *by definition* anthropocentric. The question is not how can we escape this but how do we think *within* our limits, which relativize *all* theological constructs. Then, we must ask what values our constructs are serving—those that enhance humaneness and creativity or those that enhance hierarchies and the status quo.

(3) Bible as authority, not dialogue partner. Finger asserts the need for "truth claims which transcend and critique all human communities."[36] Reimer also sees absolutes that tell us which truth claim is correct as crucial.

In contrast to these appeals to outside authority, Daniel Liechty (a "neo-Mennonite" theologian) speaks from a point of view within historical consciousness when he speaks of authority. In introducing his book, *Theology in Postliberal Perspective*, he writes, "the question of authority in theological writing is with me at every point in this presentation. Authority, authorship, the author. I have finally come to the conclusion that authority must reside with the author."[37] The central authority we may appeal to is

---

[35] See James Breech's penetrating discussion of *ressentiment* in *Silence*, utilizing insights of Friedrich Nietzsche and Max Scheler.

[36] Finger, "Response," 164.

[37] Liechty, *Theology*, ix. For a revised edition of this book with commentary from a number

that of our own argument, not something outside of us that provides coercive force to buttress our assertions.

This contrasts with Reimer's claim that his view of God is more than "an approach", but corresponds with Reality.[38] One who thinks in terms of historical consciousness finds this latter view incomprehensible. For historical consciousness, all reality is filtered through human perspectives to such a degree that we simply cannot speak of reality as Reality.

Kraus and Weaver do not make quite the same exalted claims regarding biblical authority. They both clearly argue for seeing the biblical materials as *historical*. However, the way they privilege the Jesus story reflects a viewpoint that appeals to a transcendent authority more than many "neo-Mennonites" are comfortable with.

Sketching a "Neo-Mennonite" Perspective

As I understand key aspects of "neo-Mennonite" thinking, this is how I believe a "neo-Mennonite" alternative might begin in constructing a different approach to theology.

(1) World as abundant.[39] An attitude of trust toward life in the concrete world as created by God characterizes theology that affirms the reality of historical consciousness. This theology can refer to God without positing "classical" notions of Transcendence and Eternity. "Neo-Mennonites" make a choice for one understanding of present *particular* "metaphysics" over

---

of theologians, see: *Reflecting*.

[38] He writes: "A trinitarian understanding of God and his ways with the world is more than simply an approach; it is in some sense the content of truth itself," Reimer, "Response," 74.

[39] I use the term "abundant" of the world here based in part on the distinction between "abundance" and "scarcity" made by Palmer, *Active*, 124–25: "The quality of our active lives depends heavily on whether we assume a world of scarcity or a world of abundance. Do we inhabit a universe where the basic things that people need from food and shelter to a sense of competence and of being loved are ample in nature? Or is this a universe where such goods are in short supply, available only to those who have the power to beat everyone else to the store? The nature of our action will be heavily conditioned by the way we answer those bedrock questions. In a universe of scarcity, only people who know the arts of competing, even of making war, will be able to survive. But in a universe of abundance, acts of generosity and community become not only possible but fruitful as well."

By "world," I mean the realm of creation, our present historical existence. In this sense, "world" has *positive* moral connotations: that which is loved by God, which is the place where human beings encounter God. This is not to deny that there is also a sense in which "world" can appropriately be used with negative moral connotations: that realm of existence that is in rebellion against God. The Gospel of John reflects both usages: John 3:16 in the positive sense and John 1:10 in the negative sense.

other possible *particular* "metaphysics," including those such as Reimer's that claim Authority.

"Neo-Mennonites" understand the central criterion for one's *own* theology to be that it be meaningful for the theologians' communities, addressing *their* reality in terms they understand and can relate to. Scripture and creeds must serve *this* criterion or one engages in mystification.

They would say that the best "governor" for theology is *not* some external authority—even the "Bible" or "God." These do not prevent differences. Investing those differences with "absolute" certainty often leads to violence. The best "governor," rather, is the on-going, ever-evolving quest for *truth*. If one seeks truth, one will be open to the validity of arguments and will be willing to adjust one's viewpoint accordingly. Doing theology then becomes a process of working *together* better to understand rather than working *against* each other to win arguments. Seeking truth fits well with a trust in God that does not need us to coerce others on God's behalf.

Does one believe God (and, hence, life) to be trustworthy or not? If one does, then one will not feel the anxiety to "change the world"/"protect the truth" that seems, at times, to characterize "mainstream" Anabaptist theologians.

This all relates to our views of human beings. "Neo-Mennonites" suggest that violence *results from* negative anthropology, not provides *evidence for* such a view. A positive anthropology is based on (1) a doctrine of creation as good; (2) a doctrine of providence, including concrete expressions of God's involvement in human history; and (3) an awareness of human responsiveness to love.

Martin Buber articulates an anthropological perspective quite close to "neo-Mennonites." He affirms the human being, and he affirms the world in which we live as where we will encounter God.

> I know nothing of a 'world' and of 'worldly life' that separate us from God. What is designated that way is life with an alienated It-world, the world of experience and use. Whoever goes forth in truth to the world, goes forth to God. Only he that believes in the world achieves contact with it; and if he commits himself he cannot remain godless. Let us love that actual world that never wishes to be annulled, but love it in all its terror, but dare to embrace it with our spirit's arms—and our hands encounter the hands that hold it.[40]

(2) Theology as Construction. We best see "neo-Mennonites'" theology as *inductive* theology, flowing out of their experience, expressed in their

---

[40] Buber, *I*, 143.

language.[41] They would say we all do this anyhow. Attempts to do theology deductively often result in mystification due to the gap between archaic religious language and one's actual experience of meaning in life.

"Neo-Mennonite" theology is committed to Anabaptist distinctives. "Neo-Mennonites" believe many of these distinctives fit better with this approach to theology. They include a *positive attitude toward the world*, consistent with pacifism (it is possible to live consistently in non-coercive love) and adult baptism (infants are not born condemned to Hell). This theology is *dialogical*, consistent with the Anabaptist emphasis on community. It is *concrete in* history, consistent with Anabaptist low-church worship patterns that emphasize immediacy more than sacramentalism.

This construction takes place in conversation with the Bible. Each affirmation can and should utilize biblical images because the Bible has genuine authority for Christians due to its connecting with life and providing a common language for Christians. However, the Bible works best as a conversation partner that shapes *our* construction. The Bible is not authoritarian but the key source of language that must always merge with our horizon in ever-evolving ways.

For "neo-Mennonites," to say our theology must be done in terms of our thought-forms is mostly a *descriptive* statement. We cannot do theology otherwise. "Neo-Mennonites" call for honesty and self-awareness about what we in actuality cannot help but do. To think Classically (Reimer) and biblically (Weaver, Kraus, Finger) is just finding sources (creeds and confessions, Bible, story of Jesus) that provide language and ideas that we use to make sense of our world.

When these sources become an alternative to paying attention to life in the present instead of a means to help us be attentive to life in the present, they primarily heighten one's lack of perception of God's presence in the world.

(3) "Authorities" are Dialogue Partners. "Neo-Mennonites" believe the mainstream theologians claim too much for the Bible. This over-claim contributes to many thoughtful "neo-Mennonites" distancing themselves from the Bible altogether. They have been taught authoritarian hermeneutics as the only approach. When that approach proves unhelpful, they jettison the Bible itself. "Neo-Mennonites" need a constructive, non-authoritarian

---

[41] This kind of theology is not objective, authoritarian, or foundational. However, it is also not relativ*istic*. It hopes to speak to something that is real and exists outside individual whims and subjectivities. Many modern-day philosophers and theologians have struggled with finding a way that goes "beyond objectivism and relativism." One of the more successful has been Richard J. Bernstein, in *Beyond*. See Grimsrud, "Pacifism," for an argument that John Howard Yoder's theology also goes *beyond* objectivism and relativism.

biblical hermeneutic that allows them to utilize the Bible in ways that connect with their lives.

"Neo-Mennonite" theology rejects fearfulness toward the actual world. A theology that will be genuinely "congregational" has a great deal to gain by turning back to the Jesus story as a central source, reading it and its broader biblical context non-fearfully and non-foundationally. In that story we find useful content: God's compassion, the "divinity" of everyday life, the rejection of conventional wisdom and power politics, abundance over scarcity, etc. We need to return to the Bible via historical consciousness.

Reading the Bible together as a witness of openness to God and life provides a way to converse together. Is the biblical story, especially regarding Jesus, in itself authoritative enough or do we need external claims to buttress that authority (e.g., doctrines of inspiration; an absolute, transcendent God; church hierarchy)? Do we best connect with the Bible through our experience of life/self-awareness or through submission to external authorities/doctrines/creeds that tell us what the Bible must be?

Jesus and Paul (and Old Testament prophets) themselves embody the power of immediate awareness of God. They challenged the conventional wisdom and the received theological method of their own times, giving priority to God's word spoken directly to them in the context of their own world. They modeled creativity in how they respected and worked within the faith as passed on by their forebears while also responding in new and at times iconoclastic ways. Through their honesty and courage, they became channels for new, life-giving gifts of God's Spirit. They serve as models for "neo-Mennonites"—and all other Christians.

Certainly the "neo-Mennonite" perspective should be critiqued. My comments in the previous four paragraphs point to a criticism concerning "neo-Mennonites" distancing themselves from the Bible. However, my intent with this essay has been to attend sympathetically to the "neo-Mennonite" perspective. I do so with hope that the broader Anabaptist community would learn better to understand and respect the possible contribution "neo-Mennonites" might make to contemporary Anabaptist faith communities.

PART FIVE: Vision

In the theological method articulated in this book, a fourth source is joined to the three fairly standard sources (Bible, tradition, and experience). This fourth source, here named as "vision," does not necessary provide new content so much as provide the basis for *ordering* the content of theology. "Vision" is roughly synonymous with "eschatology"—not primarily in the sense of predictions about future as much as purpose, ultimate meaning, and direction.

Chapter twelve, "Why Are We Here? Two Meditations on an Ethical Eschatology," contains a pair of sermons that reflect on how Christian eschatology has more to do with "end" as in purpose and direction than with "end" as specifying future events. The "purpose" of people of faith, according to the biblical story, is most of all to work together to bring healing to a hurting world.

Chapter thirteen, "Theological Basics: A Contemporary Anabaptist Proposal," sketches an outline of a systematic theology. Each of seven themes or doctrines is discussed, all in light of the true "purpose" (or vision) of Christian faith.

CHAPTER TWELVE

Why Are We Here? Two Meditations on an Ethical Eschatology

AT VARIOUS times since 1525, groups of Anabaptists have gained notoriety for their eschatological views, particularly the Anabaptists who gained control of the city of Münster in 1534–5, proclaiming it to be the New Jerusalem. As a rule, though, the Anabaptist tradition has been characterized by caution concerning views of the "last things."

Anabaptist convictions, at their heart, have focused on faithfulness in this present life much more than on speculation concerning the future. Implicit in such a focus, we may see a sense of trust in God. As we follow the way of Jesus we may be confident that the God who remained faithful to Jesus will also remain faithful to Jesus' followers.

What follows are two meditations on these convictions concerning importance of the call to discipleship for viewing the doctrine of eschatology.

The End of the World[1]

At the turn of the millennium, many Christian bookstores and the Christian airwaves included an extra large number of "end times" types of writings and sermons. Reflecting on "the end of the world" is called "eschatology," the doctrine concerned with the end of the world. However, what follows here more accurately could be seen as "*anti*-eschatology," or, at least, a different kind of eschatology than that found on the Christian airwaves.

This is my main point: In the Bible, and I want to propose, for us today, the point in talking about the "end of the world" is *not* so much to focus on what is going to happen to the world in the future. Rather, to talk about the "end of the world" biblically points us to the *purpose* of the world. Or, more directly, our purpose in living in the world.

---

[1] Adapted from a sermon preached at Shalom Mennonite Congregation, Harrisonburg, Virginia, January 16, 2000. A version was published as "The End of the World," *The Mennonite* 5.15 (August 6, 2002), 12–13. Used with permission.

The word "end," of course, can have two very different meanings. One is, "the last part, final point, finish, conclusion." In this sense, "the end of the world" is something future and has to do with the world ceasing to exist. The other meaning, though, is "what is desired or hoped for; purpose; intention." "End of the world," in this sense, is, we could say, what God *intends* the world to be for. Why is the world here and why are we here and what are we to be about?

In the years right after I became a Christian as a teenager, I thought of the "end of the world" strictly in terms of the future and how things will conclude. I looked for the soon return of Christ—and would have been shocked to be still living in the twenty-first century. When I was in college in the mid-1970s, I quite seriously contemplated dropping out. Why should I work at preparing for the future when the future wasn't going to come?

In those days, I basically welcomed the development of nuclear weapons, the conflicts in the Middle East, the likelihood of war with the Soviet Union and possibly also China. I welcomed wars and rumors of wars. These all meant that the second coming was at hand. The "end of the world" was coming soon, and in that I rejoiced.

At some point, though, I realized with a start that I welcomed, actually, incredible human suffering and the destruction of nature, unprecedented death and bloodshed. I welcomed, in a word, extreme *evil*. And, I understood *God* to be the agent of this evil. In this view, God's purposes could only be worked out, I realized, by God killing human beings and all other living creatures on an unimaginable level.

When the scales fell from my eyes (which is how I see it now), I recoiled at my old worldview. But it has taken many years since then to think through these issues more, and to decide that I don't need to reject the *Bible's* understanding of the "end of the world", but I need to reject the lenses I had been given as a young Christian for reading the Bible.

I do not fully understand how this view of the "end of the world" as the destruction of the world came to dominate Christian thinking. However, as with many problems in the so-called Christian worldview (such as seeing God as punitive, such as supporting so-called just wars, such as viewing human beings as corrupted by original sin), I suspect that the "Doctor of the Church," Augustine of Hippo, had something to do with it.

Augustine's great fifth-century book, *The City of God*, grafts Greek philosophy onto biblical theology and comes up with a notion of heaven (the "city of God") as something outside of time and history and future. This city, "heaven," is sharply distinguished from the world we live in, from historical life in the here and now (the "city of man"). For Augustine, life in history is characterized by brutality, sinfulness, and the struggle for power.

This disjunction between heaven and life in the present led to focusing Christian hope, in effect, on the destruction of this world. Genuine salvation requires an escape from this life to heaven and eternity and something totally different and separate.

Life on earth is nasty, brutish, and short. The end of the world is coming (thank God), and the sooner the better. It is tragically ironic that the worldview that looks to the future for salvation and achievement of heaven, in the present tends to justify violence and punishment and domination—and uses the Bible for support. This worldview fosters self-fulfilling prophecy. Since we believe that life here and now is nasty, brutish, violent, and short, we act to make it so. We see these actions in Augustine and so many other Christians since supporting death-dealing violence toward heretics, pagans, and criminals.

What if, to borrow my friend Howard Zehr's metaphor,[2] we change our lenses? What if we look at the Bible and at the world differently? I found a typo a while ago that, in a published bibliography, switched the name of Howard's book from "Changing Lenses" to "Changing Lanes." I think that image also works. Let's push the metaphor. What if we changed lanes and exited this six lane interstate of the Western, anti-creation worldview? What if we got on a local road where we could see the world more how it actually is and realize that our key question is not about the future destruction of the world but about our purpose in the here and now?

I believe that the biblical worldview was corrupted by the fusion of Greek philosophy and the Bible. This worldview has much more in common not with our modern western worldview but with the worldview of the very cultures western civilization has sought to stamp out.

This other worldview has been identified by recent writers as "primal", "aboriginal", and "indigenous." In the primal worldview, the world has purpose, full of the grandeur of God. We don't need a future destruction of the world to experience God's presence, to know the beauty of creation, to be in harmony with the creator. What we need is a new awareness of God in the here and now, a new awareness of the purpose of the world. This world is where the action is.

Should we look at the Bible with new eyes, looking for what it tells us about the purpose of the world rather than looking for what it tells us about the future destruction of the world, what might we see? To illustrate, I will briefly mention three biblical texts.

[2] Zehr, *Changing*.

First, Mark 2:23–8 tells us of Jesus' encounter with opponents who challenge his laxness in allowing his followers to feed themselves on the Sabbath, ignoring God's law, acting as if the earth is friendly. Jesus responds: the law is to serve human well-being, not human beings to serve the letter of the law. The purpose of the law, of the world, of life is to flourish right now. The purpose of the law is to enhance peace, wholeness, well being in this life.

In Jesus' entire ministry, he makes it clear that the law is something to be welcomed as a means to the end of abundant life. Jesus utterly rejects the notion that life is bad, nasty, brutish, and short and that we need the coercive restraint (of legalistic law and its human enforcers) to keep us in line until we go to heaven. No. For Jesus the law reflects the God behind the law. It guides us into the fullness of life in the present and into harmony with the rest of creation.

A second text comes from Revelation 21:1–4. As often interpreted, Revelation provides a challenge to my proposal. Is Revelation not about the future destruction of the world? Well . . . it is precisely through studying Revelation that I have developed my understanding of the biblical notion of the end of the world.[3] The message of the Bible challenges us to find the *purpose* of life in the here and now, not in some otherworldly future.

The Book of Revelation is highly symbolic. We need to take seriously the opening words of the book—this is a revelation of *Jesus Christ*. We are shown with symbolic imagery the meaning of Jesus' message. We have here a revelation of a different way of seeing the world; different from power politics, from nationalism, from the worship of wealth. The revelation of Jesus Christ is simply that the purpose of the world is found in love, in mercy, in peaceableness, in faithfulness to the Lamb's way. The world is where singing and celebration and joy happen—here and now, if we but have eyes to see and ears to hear.

A key world-affirming vision in Revelation comes in chapter four, where we see the one on the throne being worshiped by all creation. Chapter five follows with joyful singing of uncounted voices from heaven and earth and under the earth. So, when we get to the end of the book and the vision of the New Jerusalem we realize that we are not seeing something from the future and outside of history coming into being after the destruction of this world. Rather, we see a revelation of what reality is right now. We need but change our lenses to see the holy in the firm, the presence of the spirit of God here and now, the reality that creation is good and is to be embraced.

---

[3] See Grimsrud, *Triumph*.

Finally, the following words from Micah have become well known precisely because they contain such a precise but comprehensive message of the end of human life—our *purpose*. These words could, I imagine, come from any number of primal or aboriginal cultures: "What does the Lord require of you but to do justice, and to love kindness, and to walk humbly with your God?" (6:8).

"Do justice." In the Bible, and in aboriginal justice as well, this means seek wholeness and the restoration of relationships; seek to bring healing when there is harm. "Love kindness." Treat people, all people, with respect, with friendliness and hospitality, with compassion. Be gentle. Listen. Enjoy. "Walk humbly with God." Know your place in the cosmos. Remember and accept your finitude. Remember your responsibility to your children and your children's children and on and on. Trust in God - don't grasp for power and control and dominance.

The "end of the world", then, remains the same even as we change millennia. The world is the good creation of a good God. Our end, our purpose, is to seek harmony and wholeness in relationship with one another and this good world.

Revealing a New World[4]

I find it understandable that people who seek peace and justice in our world and advocate for the vulnerable, would want to stay away from the Bible. As Desmond Tutu famously said, in reaction to most every movement for social justice in the past two centuries, Christians have used the Bible to defend the status quo, often violently. "Bible-thumper" is usually used of a person who thumps the Bible while making a strong point. In reality we could also say a "Bible-thumper" is someone who uses the Bible to thump the peace and justice advocate.

I am thankful I didn't grow up in a Bible-thumping family. I was lucky enough to be able, in time and without too much emotional trauma, to begin asking after what the Bible actually says rather than simply accept the authority of those who use it to oppress.

I now believe the emperor has no clothes. The "Bible thumpers" do *not* reflect the central teachings of the Bible. People justify capitalism in the name of what they call biblical Christianity when, in fact, the Bible has a term of condemnation for what capitalists do—*usury*. People assert that government leaders come straight from God and, as citizens we are simply

---

[4] Adapted from a sermon preached at Shalom Mennonite Congregation, February 20, 2005.

to obey, not to question why but simply to ask how high when we are ordered to jump. In fact, from the start to the end, the Bible itself teaches suspicion of and takes quite a critical stance toward kings. The typical sentiment in the Bible is not, "obey the government." The typical sentiment is, "we must obey God not human beings." Human beings who lord it over others are singled out by Jesus as being exactly what his followers are not to be like or to be impressed with.

As Americans, we live in a time of Bible thumpers in high places. Now, perhaps more than ever, people who read the Bible as the story of God's incredible love and care for vulnerable victims of power politics and for the people who resist the unjust status quo need to recover and spread abroad the actual content of this book.

The story of God's promise to Abraham and Sarah in Genesis twelve has long been one of my favorites. We have in a nutshell the basic message: God brings life out of barrenness (Sarah was unable to have children, a terrible tragedy; she and Abraham had no future). God gave life as pure mercy. That is what God is like. But the point is not simply to give Abraham and Sarah children and future descendants. There is a bigger point for this gift. God has an agenda. Through Abraham and Sarah's descendants God will bless all the families of the earth.

As Christians, we consider ourselves to be children of Abraham. We live in light of this promise and have been blessed as a consequence of the promise. With this blessing, though, comes a calling. Be channels of blessing to all the families of the earth. Jesus repeated this calling. His final words call his followers to go to the nations, take the message of God's love, teach the nations to follow Jesus' commands (see Matt 28:18–20).

The last book in the Bible, Revelation, tells of the fulfillment of the promise. The world is transformed, the New Jerusalem comes down, and within this renewed world we find leaves from the tree of life that are for the healing of all the nations. The blessing is carried out.

The promise to Abraham and Sarah sets the agenda for the rest of the Bible, actually, for the rest of history. Live as a channel of blessing for all the families of the earth. This promise, in a real sense, conveys a worldview, an understanding of what matters most. As human beings, we are meant to be in communities of wholeness and healing. We are meant to know God and to know each other as children of God.

The context of the promise, the context for the rest of the Bible and for the rest of history, is that we all need healing. Abraham and Sarah are broken and without hope. They need healing. The nations need healing.

And this is how God brings healing. God forms a people who know love and who share this love.

As we know, Jesus lived directly out of the promise. He ended up coming face to face with powers of brokenness and being broken. The conclusion to that story is the basis for hope that the promise remains. But God raising Jesus from the dead does not gloss over the reality of the brokenness, though it does inspire us to continue to trust in the promise as God's way.

However, the brokenness continues. The worldview centered on the promise remains contested. It is not the only option in our world, not even the dominant option. People in our world have other worldviews in which to trust. Some of these, though, instead of fostering wholeness foster barrenness and alienation. A buzzword today is "globalization." Globalization often refers to a worldview that I would suggest is a major rival to the worldview of the promise to Abraham and Sarah.

Globalization, in one definition, refers to neo-liberal economics that increasingly dominant all four corners of the globe, transforming everything in its path, treating everything (and everybody) as a commodity fit to be exploited for the sake of profit. This globalization stands dead set against the promise.

One expression of globalization may be seen in the incredible growth of urban slums throughout the world. I quote from the beginning of an article called "Slum Politics" by James Westcott posted on the AlterNet website on February 18, 2005.

> In the last three months, the Bombay Municipal Corporation has demolished eighty thousand shanties in a city where three million people are slum dwellers. The local government recently granted legal status to homes built before 1995, and bulldozed everything else. The devastation is "tsunami-like" according to the Indian Inter Press news agency. Three hundred and fifty thousand people have been made homeless but only fifty thousand new apartments have been provided. The program is part of Bombay's plan to re-model itself on the ruthlessly prosperous Shanghai, which has tried to eradicate its slums.
>
> But Shanghai's slums remain, as they do in other cities, as part of an inexorable global trend: two hundred thousand people a day are carrot-and-sticked from the countryside to cities that then refuse to accommodate them. In Bombay they end up in shacks by the road, on the railway tracks and next to the airport—embarrassingly visible from landing planes. In Lagos, two-thirds of which is made up of slums, a shantytown has sprouted up on an enormous, slowly

burning garbage dump. In Kibera, the slum surrounding Nairobi, raw sewage flows over the few water pipes, and latrines are so scarce that people simply defecate in plastic bags and then throw them as far away from their dwelling as possible—a phenomenon called "flying toilets." Eighty-five percent of the developing world's urban population now lives in slums, and forty percent of slum dwellers in Africa live in what the UN calls 'life-threatening' poverty.

We ask, why this proliferation of slums? Probably the main factor is the dispossession of masses of the world's people. The economics of globalization have driven people from the land. The ages-old farm economies are being devastated. The rural populations have become utterly expendable. So they end up in urban areas in hopes of scraping some kind of livelihood together—where they tragically remain expendable.

This is how sociologist Mike Davis describes the situation in his book, *Planet of Slums*: "The labor-power of a billion people has been expelled from the world system, and who can imagine any plausible scenario, under neo-liberal auspices, that would reintegrate them as productive workers or mass consumers?"[5]

Does biblical faith provide resources for responding to these developments?

It is tragic that so many Christians have capitulated to the worldview of globalization. This capitulation has been accompanied by neutering probably the most powerful sets of images in the Bible that could help Christians resist, the so-called apocalyptic writings of the Bible.

Modern interpreters of the Bible tend to read biblical apocalyptic as irrelevant to present life. They see apocalyptic as speaking of the future final outcome of history, the destruction of this world, the catastrophic intervention of God to use brute power to obliterate and rebuild. On the one side are the future-prophetic interpreters (such as the writers of the *Left Behind* books) who take this as literal prediction of the future. Biblical apocalyptic then becomes actually a buttress for the status quo. Its concern is not the here and now but the by-and-by.

On the other side we find the scholars and mainstream interpreters. They tend to assert that the early Christians (including Jesus himself) believed this world-ending catastrophe would happen in their lifetimes. Of course the early Christians were wrong (plus, such world-ending supernatural acts are unbelievable for modern scholars), so these early Christian visions end up having nothing to say for our lives in the here and now.

---

[5] Davis, *Planet*, 199.

However, a closer look at biblical apocalyptic, reading it on its own terms in the context of the entire Bible, without the blinders of either the future-prophetic or the failed-expectation views, reveals a worldview that directly speaks to us and can help us resist globalization.

We start the rethinking by considering the word "apocalypse" itself. This is the beginning word in the Book of Revelation: "the *apocalypse* of Jesus Christ." This term is translated in English, of course, as "revelation"—"the *revelation* of Jesus Christ." The Book of Revelation is about envisioning the world in light of Jesus Christ. The visions given in Revelation address the need for fresh insight into the meaning of history.

However, what is the actual content of this revelation? What is the author of Revelation trying to convey? John, in reality, gives a concrete message about life in *this* world. The focus of the book is on John's pastoral message to the churches of Asia Minor (see Revelation 2–3). John gives this basic exhortation: stand strong in the face of the "globalizing worldview" of the day. Stand strong in the face of the civil religion of the Roman Empire that treats people as commodities, stand strong in the face of Rome shedding the blood of the prophets and seeking to separate people from God's love by requiring them to trust in the Empire's supremacy.

Revelation concludes with a clear and direct contrast between two kinds of community—the community of Babylon (the community of empire, of exploitation and oppression) and the community of the New Jerusalem (the community where people worship together, where the Lamb is followed in the paths of persevering love, where even the kings of the earth find healing). The reader is given the choice. Which community will you be part of?

If we stick with this motif of "revelation," using the Greek term "apocalypse," we may see that Paul's writings, say especially Romans, are also apocalyptic. At several key points in Romans the term "apocalypse" is used, again translated "revelation" or "revealed." At the beginning, Paul's thesis statement: "I am not ashamed of the gospel; it is the power of God for salvation to everyone who has faith, to the Jew first and also to the Greek. For in it the righteousness of God is *revealed* through faith to faith"—or we could say, the righteousness of God is "apocalypsed" through faith (1:16–7). The gospel *reveals* the true will and saving character of God. And God's will is revealed for the purpose of bringing together Jew and Gentile in a new community to carry out the promise to Abraham.

The other key moment of "revelation" in Romans is at the end of Paul's long and careful argument about the need all people have for God's mercy: The righteousness of God has been revealed ("apocalypsed") apart from the law in the message of Jesus Christ (3:21). We misunderstand this "apart from the law" if we read this as a rejection of Judaism. Rather, it is the opposite. Paul is saying that the true message of the promise is the unification of Jews and Gentiles in one community of faith. The exclusiveness centered on a misuse of the law is abolished through Jesus' death and resurrection.

The result, again, of the "apocalypse" of God through Jesus is something that transforms life in the here and now—a new community that knows peace due to the breaking down of walls of enmity. Remember that the letter to the Romans was written to Christians in the belly of the beast, the capital of the Empire. This community of faith directly challenges the oppression of Empire, as we see in Paul's litany of various "Gentile" injustices in Romans chapter one.

So, in these two apocalyptic texts—Revelation and Romans—what we see is not a promise about the end of the world but a promise about the transformation of life in this world. As God's answer to Rome's injustices, Rome's version of globalization, the apocalyptic message focuses on the formation of communities of resistance. These communities embody the worldview of the promise and make it known to the nations.

A third passage reflecting these same dynamics comes is the foundational revelation of the entire ancient Hebrew story, God's involvement in freeing the people from slavery in the exodus. Again, God acts in opposition to the world's "globalizing" empire, in this case Egypt. Egypt also treated people as commodities, breaking their backs in exploitation (Exodus 1:13–4).

God intervenes with saving work—a revelation ("apocalypse," even if the actual word is not used in the book of Exodus) with the same consequence as in Revelation and Romans. God's intervention results in the formation of a community of resistance, a community formed out of the ashes of the exploitation and enmity, to be characterized by transformative justice.

So, biblical apocalyptic speaks directly to our present world crisis. We see in the apocalyptic imagery of the Bible a direct clash of worldviews. On the one hand, we see the worldview of promise, of healing community, of valuing each human being. On the other hand, we see the worldview of forced labor, of hard work in mortar and brick, of the trafficking in human souls spoken of in Revelation, of the manifold injustices mentioned in Romans one.

The Bibles resolves this clash of worldviews not by a history-ending catastrophe. The Bible's message does not give hope for escape from life on earth. Rather, the Bible's resolution may be found in witnessing to genuine life in history, in banding together in communities of resistance to say no to the idolatry of violence and the so-called progress that creates a planet of slums—and to say yes to ways of life that are sustainable and equitable and joyful.

CHAPTER THIRTEEN

Theological Basics: A Contemporary Anabaptist Proposal

ANABAPTISTS POSITION themselves theologically pretty much in the Protestant mainstream when it comes to many theological doctrines. Core elements of Anabaptist theology, though, reflect a commitment to integrate faith and practice—as I tried to describe above in chapter eight.

The outline I will follow in this chapter condenses several of my lectures from the "Introduction to Theology" class I teach at Eastern Mennonite University.[1] I will present in an abbreviated form a proposal for a constructive theology from one Anabaptist's perspective, using little argumentation. These are concise responses to basic theological questions.

An important issue before we start looking at the various doctrines is how we order them. Following Norman Kraus, I will begin with Christology. All of the other doctrines look different when we look at them most of all in relation to what we believe about Jesus' life and message. In this approach, I believe I echo sixteenth-century Anabaptist assumptions.

Jesus Christ

What about Jesus convinces Christians to call him the normative expression of God? What in his life is crucial for our understanding his significance? What do we know about his identity? What titles have been used of him? What do they mean?

Mine is "christology from below," based first of all on the evidence we have from Jesus' life. The conclusions we draw about Jesus' significance follow from the gospel accounts of his life, in the same way that they did for the early followers of Jesus. So, the basis for the Christian confession of Jesus as the normative expression of God stems foundationally from his life. Jesus was goodness, mercy, and love incarnated. He fulfilled the true

---

[1] My outline is the same as the one used by Anabaptist theologian C. Norman Kraus in his one-volume systematic theology, *God*. As will be clear to anyone familiar with Kraus's work, I am indebted to him for more than just this outline.

meaning of the Law, and he embodied as no one else the message of the prophets.

The following are only some of the ways Jesus did this. He performed miracles of healing. He taught with authority of the meaning of the Kingdom (or reign) of God. He included marginalized people as full members of God's community. He confronted unjust structures, challenging oppressive and exclusive legalism, hierarchical religion, and cynical politics. He practiced nonviolence, even in the face of his own arrest and impending death. He manifested deep trust in God, from the time of his initial temptations in the wilderness to his execution.

The confession of Jesus as normative expression of God also stems from the claims that he made for himself and the claims made about him by others. These claims found expression in titles that were used of Jesus. Among other titles, key ones included calling him God's Son, the Messiah or Christ, the Savior, and the Son of Man. All of these titles had Old Testament roots. Son of God was a term used of King David, as was Messiah ("Anointed One"). A Hebrew term for "Savior" was "Joshua" (or, in Greek, "Jesus")—the liberator who led the Hebrews into the Promised Land. "Son of Man" is an apocalyptic figure in the Book of Daniel.

The content of these central titles used of Jesus has its basis in the Old Testament. Because of this, we appropriately may speak of the titles indicating that Jesus fulfilled prophecy. However, these prophecies were mostly understood in retrospect. That is, *after* Jesus' resurrection, his followers re-read the Old Testament and then perceived the connection with Jesus.

Ultimately, all of these titles must be understood in relation to Jesus' life. For example, only due to Jesus' life was "Messiah" redefined in terms of the "suffering servant" of Isaiah fifty-three. Those two concepts had never been linked until after Jesus' life, death and resurrection.

Only *after* God raised Jesus from the dead were his life and his claims fully understood and integrated. The resurrection was crucial most of all because it displayed God's power in a way that made it incontrovertible the Jesus was and is God's Son, that Jesus' way equals God's way.

What does Jesus tell us about God? What does it mean to say that God is the "Father"[2] of Jesus Christ? How does Jesus shape our view of God as "Father"?

To confess Jesus as "divine" (affirming titles such as "Son of God," "God Incarnate," and the "Word" who is God) means defining God in terms of Jesus' way. A theology from below in relation to Jesus as the revela-

---

[2] To avoid awkwardness and undesired controversy I am using this gender-specific term. However, I enclose it in quotes in order to remind us that God is not a male deity.

tion of God focuses on the content of Jesus life as essential data for assembling content for understanding God, the "Father." This contrasts with a theology from above that would that would begin with abstract concepts of God's attributes (e.g., omniscience, omnipotence, impassibility) and either try to conform content from Jesus' life to those attributes or ignore Jesus' life as a resource in spelling out what we can say about God.

If we start with God as revealed in the life of Jesus, what might we then say about the character of God? God is peaceable, exercises upside-down power, expresses unconditional mercy as the main means for reconciliation and atonement, redefines justice as restoration of relationships, is characterized by suffering love, transcends national and ethnic boundaries, is radically inclusive of sinners and outcasts, and is opposed to human power-over practices and narrow religiosity that ignores the "weightier matters of the law."

What does Jesus reveal to us about human nature and destiny?

Jesus shows us that the proper human/divine relationship is characterized by total trust in God on the part of the human being. In contrast to Adam and Eve, Jesus lived constantly with an acceptance of his human limitations, not grasping for power and autonomy. Jesus shows us that human beings are capable of living lives of consistent peaceableness. Mercy, compassion, respect, openness, forgiveness may indeed be central to human existence.

Jesus shows us that human wholeness is more important than the letter of the law. He shows us that human beings flourish best when compassion takes priority over legalism. The fundamental law God gives to order human life is that we must love God and neighbor.

How does Jesus bring about salvation? What is the human problem? What causes the rift—the alienation in human/God, human/human, and human/nature relationships? How does Jesus Christ heal this rift?

The problem is a human problem. The "rift" is due to human action and inaction, not because of God being alienated. This dynamic is illustrated from the first story of alienation—Genesis three. Here, God enters the Garden of Eden to fellowship as always with Adam and Eve. But the first humans had eaten the forbidden fruit and they hide. That is, the humans running from God broke the fellowship, not God refusing to come to them.

The "logic of salvation" has remained the same from the time of this first alienation, this first break in the relationship. God in many ways has displayed to people that they do not need to be "afraid" of God. God is a God of love, healing, and restorative justice. God has shown saving love throughout the biblical account, from the giving of the rainbow after the Flood, the unmerited calling of Abram and Sarah and giving them life (descendents) in a miraculous way, the initiative to free the Hebrews from slavery in Egypt, the giving of the law to order life in harmony with God, the giving of the Promise Land, the sending of the prophetic word (most notably, in Isaiah forty and the chapters that follow, the message of God's continued love for the Hebrews). All of these are expressions of God simply acting to restore wholeness with unearned mercy.

In each case, God simply wants human beings to turn. Repent, turn toward God, trust in God's saving mercy. I desire mercy and not sacrifice (Hosea). I desire justice and not religious rituals (Amos). I require kindness, justice, and humility, not sacrifices (Micah). Jesus' message echoes this same theme. Jesus enters the stage in Mark with a statement summarizing his entire ministry. "The Kingdom of God is at hand. Repent and believe the Good News" (Mk 1:15). God is here offering you mercy. Simply turn to God. Trust that this is true.

When John the Baptist had a follower approach Jesus and ask if Jesus is the Coming One, Jesus responds with a summary of his saving work. The sick are healed. Good news is preached to the poor, and the blind see (Lk 7:18–23). Jesus as Savior is one who brings healing to those who need it and cannot in any way earn it or even deserve it. It is pure mercy, the same as God liberating the enslaved Hebrews from Egypt. Jesus brings salvation by revealing the nature of God's love. Jesus reveals God as Abba, in contrast to God as wrathful avenger.

In revealing God's love as he did, though, Jesus also revealed the un-love of human culture, religion, and politics. Jesus revealed the choice we each have to make. We must choose between love and un-love, peace or un-peace, Christ or anti-Christ, God or Satan.

Jesus' execution reveals just how incredibly misdirected human culture, religion, and politics are. They conspired to put to death the very son of God. His resurrection reveals how powerful God's love is and that choosing God's love is the way to true life.

Jesus conquers Satan by revealing once and for all Satan's lies for what they are. Jesus reveals that the basic institutions of human culture tend to value order over love. These structures cannot stand unmediated, all-inclusive love. In this way, the structures (no matter how they present themselves) serve Satan and not God. In revealing this, for those with eyes to see, Jesus breaks the bondage such structures have. When God raised Jesus from the dead, God made it clear through Jesus that the only power Satan has is the power of deception. Satan was impotent to stop God from bringing Jesus back to the world of the living.

Jesus conquers sin by living free from its control and revealing that we all may do so as well. As we live following Jesus' model of profound trust in God and God's mercy, and not in our own self-righteousness, we too may be free from the power of sin. Jesus reveals God's attitude toward us as an attitude of forgiveness and mercy, not anger and retribution—should we simply turn to God in trust.

Revelation

How does God communicate with humans? What forms do God's self-disclosure take?

Christians see God in all aspects of the created universe, from the immensity of outer space to the mysteries of the atoms. The Psalms team with allusions to the beauty and majesty of the natural world, and draw from this beauty and majesty a sense of worship and gratitude to Israel's Creator God.

Christians confess that life itself comes from God. Consequently, any birth, the renewal of nature each spring, anything that enhances life, discloses God. Christians also believe that human rationality, the ability to reason and to solve problems, expresses characteristics of the One in whose image human beings have been created.

As well, human relationality, our ability to love others, to live in friendship, and the devastation of isolation and loneliness, also reflect being created in the image of a social, relational God ("male and female we created them").

Another way that God is disclosed in human life is in the reality of facing consequences when we trust in ultimate realities other than God. That is, in biblical language, idolatry carries with it intrinsic consequences that reflect the nature of the created universe. This is not so much punishment for its own sake as more directly simply disharmony caused by traveling "off the track," so to speak, of the universe.

God is also disclosed in acts of liberation and salvation. Events such as the calling of Abraham and Sarah, the exodus out of slavery in Egypt, the life, death, and resurrection of Jesus have revealed God in liberating acts. Similar acts since the time of Jesus wherein oppressed people gain liberty, where healing communities are formed and sustained, where the way of Jesus is embodied in real life, are all in continuity with these formative acts and therefore also disclosures of God.

These formative acts, and many other stories of God's involvement in communities of faith, were written down along with teachings that reflect the messages these communities received from God. These writings, gathered in the Christian "scriptures," provide the "master stories" that give the Christian community direction for its beliefs and practices.

The Bible, this collection of the master stories, serves as the basis for the community's discernment concerning other disclosures from God. The content of these other revelations is measured against the content of the Bible. While Christian's understand God to disclose God's self in many ways, they give a privileged status to the Bible. God communicates in various ways, but the test of the authenticity of these communications ultimately can be understood in terms of how well the alleged disclosure coheres with the disclosure of God in scripture.

Other forms of God's self-disclosure include personal ways of communication such as dreams, visions, prayer, meditation, and special insights. These are all subservient to God's self-disclosure in scripture and are evaluated in relation to scripture. The on-going discernment of the community of faith ("tradition") is also understood to be a form of revelation subject to scripture.

Why should Christians give the Bible authority?

Christians confess that the Bible is inspired by the Holy Spirit. God was directly involved in the writing, preservation, and interpretation of the Bible. The God who created the universe and acted in history in ways that have fostered healing relationships between human beings and God, also guided the writings that were collected into the book Christian confess to be scripture.

The Bible is authoritative for Christians most of all because from the Bible we learn of God's entry into human history in a particular human being whose life and teaching reveal, more than anything else, the character of God, the will of God for human beings, and the approach God takes in providing salvation for all who trust in God. The rest of the Bible provides the context (Old Testament and New Testament) we need properly to understand God's revelation in Jesus.

In giving us the story of Jesus, and the broader setting in which the Jesus story makes sense, the Bible provides us with the "master story" we need for an orienting framework to understand everything else about human existence. As the master story, the Bible provides direction, clarity, norms, and standards for what is true, for what constitutes God's will for human life, for the needed direction for the common life of God's people.

How does the Bible's authority function?

The identity of the Bible as authoritative scripture follows from the confession Christians make concerning its status. The authoritative element of the content of the Bible takes the form of an on-going story that is persuasive, relational, and evocative of faith for those who confess it to be revelation from God. The authority of the Bible, then, is not so much coercive and "outside-of-us" as it is trust-based, the consequence of a freely made choice to accept its normativity.

The authority of the Bible takes the form of a story that we are invited (not forced) to join, to identify as our own. As such a story (Christians confess the foundational story), the Bible is not so much a blueprint believers follow out of fear and in a spirit of legalism as it is a friend and guide whose power stems from its trustworthiness as a basis for healthy living and belief.

The authority of the Bible is of the kind that the truthfulness of its message is appropriated only as we live with it, following its directives. That is, the Bible's truth is not so much objective, clear to all eyes, outside-of-us, scientific verifiable "truth" as it is "personal truth" becoming operative as we assent to it, trust in it, live in relationship with it.

The story of Jesus provides the "angle" for interpreting the broad variety of materials included in the Bible. In other words, as believers accept Jesus' authority as their savior, teacher, and guide, they will recognize the authority of the source of our understanding of Jesus—and understand the materials in that source in light of the message of Jesus.

What problems do we face in using the Bible; how do we respond?

(1) A major challenge in understanding the Bible is that it comes to us from great distance. It was written thousands of years ago, in languages and cultures very different from ours. Nonetheless, we are able to assume significant common ground between ourselves and the biblical people. We are all human beings with similar questions and more commonalities than differences. The kinds of issues that were alive for the biblical writers remain alive in our world.

We have translators who build upon long, careful scholarship. While we must recognize the lack of perfect understanding of all the language of the original writings of the Bible (not to mention that we, of course, do not have the original writings but only copies dating to much later times than their original composition), we may with a great deal of confidence trust that we are able to approach with a pretty high level of accuracy the intentions of the biblical writers.

However, the various distances do remind us that the truths of the Bible are most reliable in their broad articulation. The authoritative content of the Bible begins with its general themes of God's love and the people's response to that love over time. Many of the more specific statements in the Bible are difficult to apply directly (e.g., the commands for parents to execute rebellious children and the commands for women to be silent in the church) because we cannot be certain of their precise context and their specific intent. However, we may with great confidence apply the more general thematic truths that tell us of God's character and human struggles. What matters most as a source for our beliefs and practices is that the Bible witnesses to the reality of Jesus' message.

(2) Another problem for many people in relation to the Bible is the existence of what seem to be many internal inconsistencies and historical inaccuracies.

Key to dealing with this problem is to recognize the nature of the biblical materials. The Bible is not a history book in a modern, scientific sense. It collects stories and exhortations written according to the standards of ancient expressions of faith, not modern historical research. Readers of the Bible should not read it expecting perfection of facts and details.

The Bible itself emphasizes that heroes of faith are human, but still serve as channels of God's truth. "We have this treasure in earthen vessels," Paul wrote. The principle here applies to the Bible itself as well. The value of the "treasure" is measured by its capability to connect people with God and to provide clear direction for faithful living.

Overall, the historical accuracy of the Bible is remarkable; the biblical stories, as near as we can ascertain, are believable on historical grounds to a surprising degree. Yet, we must also remember that the biblical writers told stories to buttress faith and challenge life practices; the writers are preachers, proclaiming the "good news" of God's saving love. It is as a confession of faith, not a conclusion based on irrefutable facts, that the Bible succeeds in its intent.

(3) A third type of problem with the Bible is that it seems to contain numerous ethically problem problematic emphases. Three prime examples are the seemingly positive portrayals of sexism, military violence, and slavery.

The presence of these emphases is too prominent to be denied. However, the Bible is to be read directionally. Jesus provides the center to the Bible, and the rest of the Bible outside of the immediate stories related to Jesus are to be read as pointing toward the core message of Jesus.

For example, let's consider the sexism of the Bible. Reading the Bible as centered on the message of Jesus helps us to see the remarkable ways that Jesus overturned the sexism of his day—and that his message clearly points toward the equality of the sexes in God's eyes. With Jesus' message in mind, we then look at the Old Testament in a way that especially notices hints that point ahead to Jesus (under the assumption that Jesus understood himself as being compatible with the basic thrust of the Old Testament on this issue).

We will notice, for example, that the creation story in Genesis states that both male and female constitute the image of God. At times women play a surprisingly important part in the story, prophets and judges such as Sarah, Miriam, and Deborah. There are stories such as Judah and Tamar, the Levite and his concubine, and David and Bathsheba that perhaps point toward implicit critiques of sexual violence and exploitation. The special emphasis prophets make on the responsibility of Israel to care for widows also reflects an implicit critique of oppressive patriarchy that left these women in particularly vulnerable positions.

God

In formulating our doctrine of God, what material do we need to take into account? What are our criteria for determining what is the "true God"?

Basically, we take into account *all* the forms of God's self-disclosure: creation (nature); human rationality (science); human relationality; past experiences of God (and "non-God") from scripture, history, tradition; experience (community and personal awareness).

The fundamental criterion for discerning God is the enhancing of life. The "true God" creates life out of love and seeks to bring life and healing where there is death and brokenness. That is, the true God is discerned in God's actions more than in God's being.

The Bible, our "master story," portrays such a God. The biblical portrayal of God as life-giver is confirmed by our own experience (and the experiences of others) and by the experiences of those who have gone before us. Because of the need for our experiences to be confirmed by others, we need to be part of communities that seek God.

The logic of the Bible's portrayal of this loving, life-enhancing God culminates with Jesus' life, teaching, death, and resurrection (the "Christ event"). As a consequence, Jesus is our fundamental criterion in determining what is the "true God"—because of what Jesus did.

What are the central aspects of our *beliefs about God (recognizing that God always remains* beyond *our description)? Which aspects are the ones we draw upon the most?*

(1) God is loving. God is Jesus' "Abba" who loves unconditionally, upon whom we can turn in trust and security. God initiates healing action toward God's enemies, always desiring the best for all of God's creation. God's love includes holiness and justice. That is, as a just God, God desires to heal that which is broken. As a holy God, God desires to clean up that which is dirty. God does not heal or clean up as a means of making people loveable; God initiates the healing and cleaning up because God loves already (even while we are broken and dirty).

Brokenness that refuses to respond to love perceives the love as harsh. God's love also includes "wrath." "Wrath" may be understood as the allowance of consequences for refusing love. These consequences are not best understood so much in terms of punishment, but more as aspects of God's work to bring long-term healing to creation.

(2) God is personal. God has (or, we could say, is) personality and is relational. God cares for specific people, not only people in general. God is emotional (especially the emotions of grief and joy), self-conscious, and rational. However, God is not a "person" like we are. Because God is not a person, God cannot be reduced to a particular gender. God is both he and she and neither. Because God is not a person, it is not helpful to speak of God "existing." God does not exist like a person, with the implication that God could not exist. Rather, God "is."

(3) God is powerful, rather than "omnipotent" (all-powerful). God is able to accomplish God's purposes. God is not defeated by sin and evil. God endures over all time and is always present (that is, there is no "sacred"/"secular" split). The best analogies for God's power are persistence, persuasion, awareness, and consistency. God's power is like the power of water gradually making a path for itself. This understanding of power contrasts with the notions of power as coercive, arbitrary, overwhelming, and like a bulldozer.

(4) God is knowledgeable, rather than "omniscient" (all-knowing). God's knowledge is personal. God knows me and you and all people, our relationships, needs, and sorrows. God's knowledge is not so much knowledge of "facts" as of people. God is more like the wise, deeply loving matriarch in a close-knit community than like an infinite computer. God hears all and remembers all more than foresees all. God knows that love wins out, but not precisely how. God does not override our freedom and responsibility. To speak of God having a "plan" for our lives is not so much that God

has prepared a detailed blueprint for each of us. Rather, it is that God has created life in such a way that faithfulness to God leads to happiness, contentment, and joy.

(5) God is steadfast, rather than "impassible" (unchanging). God's will is consistent, dependable, always seeking healing. This will of God is steadfast, never changing—it cannot change. God is responsive and changeable in "tactics" in relation to human beings because human consciousness of God does (must) change. God's "plan" has more to do with God's will to love and heal than with predetermining events and never wavering from this detailed "script."

What is "Christian" about our concept of God?

The central element of the Christian concept of God is that God is most clearly revealed in Jesus. Jesus saw God as compassionate, empathetic, forgiving ("be merciful as God is merciful," the parable of the Prodigal Son), caring, saving, and liberating. God may be seen in Jesus' way of life—peaceable, indiscriminatingly loving, subversive of human power structures, and steadfast in face of resistance. We may also speak of creation itself reflecting consistency with God as revealed in Jesus. Jesus was with God in creation. We might infer from this that creation itself reflects the same characteristics of God that Jesus' life and teaching reflect.

God is "Trinity." Trinitarian doctrine needs to be understood as part of confessing God as one. It recognizes that the one God relates to the world in various ways. God relates to the world in three distinct ways. (1) God as creator and sustainer (God, the "father"). (2) God as incarnated in Jesus, who embodied God's will for human life completely (God, the "son"). (3) God as immanent, all-pervasive presence (God, the "spirit").

Christians must not to let their reflections on God as Trinitarian diminish their awareness of God as one ("*mono*theism"). Each expression of God is all God. There is no differentiation in will or strategy or concern. God is always the God of Jesus Christ. The Holy Spirit is always the spirit of Jesus Christ.

God, as portrayed by Jesus (see the Prodigal Son story) waits for us to turn to God (i.e., to "repent"). God continually shows us love; all we must do is turn and accept that love (with the concomitant self-consciousness that we depend on that love alone for our being). Part of God's "waiting" is God's respect for our limits, our finitude, our sinfulness. God shows perseverance in God's love, patiently bearing with our fearfulness until we do turn to God in trust.

What is the opposite of belief in God?

The main challenge to faith in the true God is faith in other pseudo- or penultimate gods. All people are religious in the sense that we all trust in something, offer something our ultimate allegiance. In this sense, "atheism" is impossible. Such ultimate allegiance, when misplaced, is made known by its fruits. That is, violence, alienation, oppression, exploitation of people and nature are always indicators that something other than God is being trusted in. Whenever such are present, there is "unbelief" in relation to the true God, and "belief" in some other god. Examples of large-scale "idols" that foster such brokenness when they become object of ultimate allegiance include the Market, the Nation, the Self, Wealth, Science, Technology, and Power.

Trust in love as the core value of life is closer to trust in the true God than doctrinally correct "religion" in the context of misplaced trust (making "God" subordinate to the Market, Wealth, Science, et al). Amos focused on precisely this point when he condemned the Israelites for disregarding inter-personal justice in their quest for Wealth, while at the same time flocking to the religious rituals and "worship" of Israel's God. This "worship," according to Amos, was proven to be false worship because it co-existed with the most heinous kinds of injustice.

Holy Spirit

How do we understand the Holy Spirit in the context of our doctrine of God, that is, as part of the Trinity?

Christians think of the Holy Spirit in terms of God as presence. They link the Holy Spirit with the internal witness of God in the believer's life. Christians also speak of the Holy Spirit as the interconnectedness among human beings. Insofar as we understand God as always everywhere, we think in terms of God as Holy Spirit.

Christians use the term "Spirit of Christ" to underscore the close connection between God's expressions in Jesus and in the Holy Spirit. The Holy Spirit filled Jesus, empowering him to live the life he lived, walking the paths of love and compassion even in the face of hostility and violence. Likewise, the Holy Spirit fills followers of Jesus, empowering them too to follow Jesus' path. In this sense, the Holy Spirit makes Jesus present in an on-going way.

God as Holy Spirit provides strength, encouragement, and guidance for the person of faith and for the community of faith. The Holy Spirit gives gifts of insight, hopefulness, joy, and peace of mind. The Holy Spirit enables us to connect with others, to give and receive love and encouragement. The Spirit is the spirit of reconciliation, empowering those who depend upon it to restore broken relationships, to forgive and to accept forgiveness.

For the Holy Spirit to be part of the Trinity means there is complete continuity among the three members. "God" the creative force is the "Father of Jesus Christ," the "Holy Spirit" as the on-going divine presence is the "Spirit of Jesus Christ." Jesus, God incarnated as a human being, filled with the Spirit, embodied God and God's ways.

What is the continuity between the human spirit and the Holy Spirit?

The Holy Spirit may be understood as God as life force. Genesis two tells of the creation of human beings, the final act being that God "breathes" life into the earth-creature. This "breath" of God may also be called the Spirit of God. In this sense, all human life comes from God and expresses God as enlivening Spirit.

The Holy Spirit witnesses to the human spirit of God and is the connecting point between human beings as creatures of flesh and blood and God as a being of spirit.

How do we understand the Holy Spirit in relation to creation, to "the world"—physical and social? How do we understand the Holy Spirit in relation to other religions?

The Holy Spirit is always everywhere. There is no sacred/secular split whatsoever; there is no realm of life that is Spirit-less. Wherever there is life the Spirit is present. Wherever there is goodness, peace, and justice they are the work of the Holy Spirit. Consequently, insofar as religions other than Christianity foster goodness, peace, and justice in the world, they are expressions of the Spirit. That in them that enhances life can be attributed to the Holy Spirit.

If we understand salvation having initially to do with trusting in God's mercy, it does seem possible that religions other than Christianity also may foster such trust. It is the work of the Holy Spirit to elicit this trust, and to guide the person of faith toward fuller understanding. This Spirit-led guidance toward fuller understanding is growth toward Jesus—though not necessarily toward Christianity as a religion. Two twentieth-century examples of well-known people of faith who exhibited growth toward Jesus but did not become Christians are Mohandas Gandhi, who remained a Hindu, and Martin Buber, who remained a Jew.

What is the role of the Holy Spirit in salvation? In sanctification?

The Holy Spirit is gently persuasive and enlightening. It clarifies as we go through life and always waits for our openness. It walks the fine line between coercion and passivity, neither forcing a person to trust in God nor simply leaving us totally to our own devices. As we open to God, the loving persistence of the Spirit moves in our hearts. However, the Spirit is only as powerful in our lives as we let it be. A good analogy for the Spirit's work in the lives of the believer, perhaps, is a road map. We need the map to know where to go, but we do the driving.

The Holy Spirit transforms our lives as we let it, moving us toward sanctification and wholeness. The Spirit gives us gradual awareness, flashes of insight, moments of joy, comfort in sorrow, courage to step out, a sense of connection with others, the ability to love and be loved.

Human Beings

What characterizes human beings as "human"?

We may start with Jesus' great commandment: "You shall love the Lord your God with all your heart and all your soul, and you shall love your neighbor as yourself." This statement by Jesus tells us: (1) The core meaning of life is love, trust and mutuality. We are valued. (2) We find ourselves insofar as we are oriented toward God, the God of love. We find ourselves insofar as we say yes to God, and to life. Life is characterized by abundance and not scarcity. (3) We find ourselves insofar as we are oriented toward other people. We are social creatures with a need and ability for friendship; we wither without it.

As human beings we are worshiping (i.e., trusting) creatures. We become like that which we worship. When we genuinely worship the true God, we become like God—loving, merciful, just, peaceable, kind. When we are unloving, judgmental, unjust, violent, and unkind, we are worshiping something other than the true God.

Our mixture of attributes fosters a sense of tension. We are limited, finite, and dependent on God and other human beings; yet, we also are imaginative, spiritual, and creative. We are limited by our earthiness, yet also able to imagine not being limited. We are material creatures with a sense of life beyond the material.

As well, we are language users. We communicate with one another through our use of language. We communicate across time through the language people in others times and places have used. Being language users means that we are linked with traditions, uses from the past. We are communal, communicating with others via language. We are rational, using language to reason and solve problems. We are symbolic. Our language tells about reality but is also removed from the reality it describes. Our words are perspectival and limited; they capture only incompletely that of which they speak. We gain our essential humanness in relation to God, yet, as language-users, we are not capable fully of describing God or our experiences.

Scripture presents human beings as having been created good. This "goodness" is not the same as perfection. It is an attribute assigned by God and means, essentially, that we are created as God wants us to be. We remain good in this sense—loved by God, created as God wants us to be. As God's good creatures, we are of intrinsic value. We are created good also in the sense that this means that we are able to be responsive to God, able to live in relationship with God.

What is the "image of God" in humans?

Based on Genesis one, we link the "image" with the exercise of creative power. Human beings, like God, are given the ability to shape our environment. In Genesis one, the basic dynamic is God's "kingly" power in creating what is. As sharing in this power, human beings are given the vocation of exercising responsible stewardship in relation to God's creation. Also, as beings created in God's image, we are male and female. Inferred here, human beings created in God's image are relational creatures. We are created to relate with God and with one another.

Jesus is spoken of as being the "image" of God. Jesus' way of being human is normative for all of us. We are created in God's image, and Jesus reveals the core characteristics of that image. In Jesus' case, his way of being human found expression in his being loving, just, willing to suffer, intimate with God, in partnership with others, inclusive of outcastes, in general showing upside-down kingliness in relation to the sense of "kingship" of his day and age.

Jesus as King (Messiah, Christ) also shares central characteristics with God as King in Genesis one. In particular, the use of creative, non-coercive power and the giving of human beings the vocation to "be fruitful and multiply"/"go into all the world and make disciples."

How do we incorporate our understanding of Jesus into our theological anthropology?

In Jesus we see two key aspects of the calling of human beings. The first is the calling to live responsibly. That is, human beings are called to take responsibility to follow God's will, to live with trust in God, to care for other people and creation, to be creative, and to respect others. Secondly, human beings are called to love. Jesus showed this love in his "Abba relationship" with God and with his openness to all sorts of people.

The Christian confession that in Jesus God was incarnated in human flesh is also a confession of God's endorsement of and commitment to humanness. With Jesus, we also have an eschatological dimension. Jesus shows what all humans might become, with at least some sense of promise that he shows what all humans will become.

What is "sin"? How does it affect humanness?

Sin is a relational (more than legal) concept. It involves alienation in the relationships of human beings with God first of all. Sin also involves alienation in the relationships with other human beings, with one's own self, and with the natural world. Sin finds expression in harmful activities and in the lack of good activities. It leads to brokenness among human beings, characterized by violence, exploitation, objectification, exclusion, and avoidance.

Sin is connected with lack of trust in God, with false worship (given that we are "worshiping creatures"), with building walls of separation, and with fearfulness. The story of Adam and Eve in Genesis two and three captures this connection between sin and fearfulness in a powerful way. After they disobey God, God approaches them as before for fellowship. However, this time the human beings hide from God, fearfully. In so doing, they set in motion a terrible spiral of fearfulness leading to violence leading to alienation.

Human false-worship is interrelated with the structures of human social life (the "principalities and powers" referred to in the New Testament). When created things (including institutions and ideologies) are "worshiped" they take on a power outside of individual consciousness. This power fosters idolatry, sin, and evil—that is, trust in things other than God. These empowered "idols" epitomize the demonic realm. They take on a will autonomously from God's will and seek to separate human beings from God.

Sin corrupts humanness. Human beings under the power of sin fail to achieve their potential as God's creature. However, even as living under the power of sin, human beings remain "good" ("good" defined as that which is loved by God). As "good" creatures, all human beings retain their value in God's eyes and retain the capability of responding in faith toward God. The "Fall" does not change human nature from good to evil. Human beings remain good. We remain loved by God, creative, powerful, and capable of loving God and others.

We best think of sin in "public health" terms, considering it not in order to condemn, punish, eradicate and avoid, but rather to find healing. Just as public health officials seek to understand the causes of the disorder and find ways to treat the problem, so too Christians think of sin. We hope to foster honesty about the sins, objectivity about their causes and consequences, seeking to undo the harm caused by the sins, and to find healing and restoration for all involved.

Human beings must continually trust. Healing is an on-going process even after we turn. There are lasting consequences to sin. However, we always have the option to turn back; God never cuts us off. Beyond the simple act of turning, there is nothing human beings need to do to gain God's mercy. We simply must accept it. God is the one who overcomes sin by offering forgiveness, healing, and restoration. Our role is simply to trust in God's mercy.

The Church

What is the church?

We may talk about the church in three senses: the structural church, the visible church, and the invisible church.

The "structural church" refers to the church's existence as an organized group of Christians with a recognized (usually ordained) leadership, membership, regular rituals (most commonly baptism and communion), a regular meeting place and regular meeting times. The church in this sense serves as the location for weddings and funerals with designated officiants. Here also is where we talk about official beliefs (such as confessions and creeds), legal status as incorporated entities, regional conferences, and denominations.

The "visible church" is the church as the concrete fellowship of followers of Jesus who form a community, meet regularly, worship together (usually involving singing, prayer, and preaching), study scripture together, offer one another encouragement, organize for service, social action, and witness, and share in rituals such as baptism and communion.

The structural and visible aspects of the church overlap. The distinction may be seen in an analogy with language—vocabulary and rules of grammar provide the structure, but the actual face-to-face interaction of human beings using the words is what makes the language alive.

The "invisible church" is the mystical "communion of the saints" made up of all those who trust in Jesus Christ. The church in this sense exists throughout time and all over the world. It is made up of all who have received salvation.

The second sense, the "visible church," takes precedence over the first and third. The "structural church" and the "invisible church" only exist in relation to the "visible church." There is no "invisible church" apart from many visible congregations. Without authentic, face-to-face discipleship, the "structural church" is only a calcified human institution.

What is significant with saying that it is "the church of Jesus Christ"? How does this affirmation shape the church's mission?

The church gains its direction from the life and teaching of Jesus. That it does so means that the church should be characterized by Christ-like love, openness, peacemaking, opposition to the powers of death, willingness to suffer for the sake of the truth, suspicion of institutions and human self-aggrandizement, and adherence to the prophetic faith of the ancient Hebrews.

The church exists to witness to God's love to all the earth, as Jesus challenged his followers just before he left them in Acts 1:8. The church so witnesses (1) by manifesting in the present, in its common life, the reality of God's promised kingdom; (2) by finding ways to communicate this reality to the wider world as invitation; and (3) by confronting the powers of death through exposing those powers for what they are and fostering disbelief in them.

The church, by definition, is "political" (political meaning how we order our common life). However, the church lives in the tension of ambivalence toward the "world" ("world" being defined both as that which God created and loved [Jn 3:16] and as that which opposes God [Jn 1:10]). There is no part of the world in which Christians should not bear witness. At the same time, *all* parts of the world (including within the church) may manifest opposition to God and hence may seduce Christians. The key criterion for discernment for when the world opposes God is its adherence to the peaceable way of Jesus.

How does the church become "the church as it is meant to be"?

The focus of the church should be positive. It seeks to understand and live out its mission of witnessing to God's love. Christian existence is based on God's mercy, not human strictness and purity. The key metaphor for the aspiration of the church is "health." Health is found through self-awareness and identity security.

Church discipline should primarily be a matter of members living with openness and integrity. The church best sustains its health by being a community from which those who do not want to live with openness and integrity will choose to excuse themselves. The center of the church is faithfulness to Jesus' way, not doctrinal formulations or legalistic purity. The focus is on the center, sustaining the community's core identity—not on the boundaries, striving to separate insiders from outsiders.

Our End

What is "Christian" about Christian eschatology?

Eschatology is best understood as the study of the ultimate nature of things. This study includes both where we have come from and where we are going. The distinctively Christian element of Christian eschatology is to be seen in it being centered on Jesus' life and teaching.

Christian eschatology asserts that history is best understood in terms of Jesus' way of love, compassion, openness, critique of power politics, and obedience to God. Christians understand the way of Jesus to be the purpose of human life. Our understanding of the future is in continuity with our understanding of the past. We understand the meaning of deep reality by considering God's revelation in Jesus. Christians confess that God is fully revealed in Jesus in that there will be no new revelation that is in tension with God as revealed in Jesus.

Wherein lies our hope?

Christian eschatology is "realized eschatology" in the sense that the Christ-event has manifested God's victory. In Jesus' way of life, in Jesus' faithfulness even to the death, and in God raising Jesus from the dead, God has revealed to the world God's will for human life and God's love as more powerful even than death.

Our hope is founded on what God has done, on who God has already been revealed to be. This point about the ultimacy of what God has already done is reflected in Jesus story of the rich man and Lazarus. Jesus responds to the plea of the rich man that God send his brothers new revelation to turn them from their unbelief. Jesus responds with a statement of realized eschatology, "they have Moses and the prophets." As Christians, we would say "we have Jesus" and that that is all we need. There will be no new bases for hope.

When Revelation portrays the final "battle" between Jesus and the forces of evil, it turns out not actually to be a future battle. In an image not always noticed by modern-day interpreters, Jesus rides forth to battle in Revelation nineteen having already shed his blood. There is no further battle. Jesus simply captures his enemies and throws them into the Lake of Fire. The only "battle" that Jesus ever fought in came during the final days of his life when his faithfulness to the death led to his being raised, victorious, the winner of the battle of the ages.

Our hope is based on our trust that Jesus is the revelation of God and that in raising Jesus from the death, God insured that life and love continue victorious over death and evil.

What is biblical prophecy about?

Primarily, prophecy in the Bible portrays the prophet receiving a message from God that provides insight into the present of the prophet. When biblical prophets refer to the future, they do not predict so much as issue warnings that challenge their listeners in the present toward faithfulness. In general, these warnings take two forms. (1) They warn of negative consequences should the people not change their ways and turn from their unfaithfulness. (2) They promise of healing to come while implicitly warning that those who do not seek God will miss the healing.

The one element of prophetic proclamation that the Bible presents as having predictive-type prophecies are occasions when Old Testament writings are understood as predicting Jesus. In these instances, however, the specific predictive elements of the prophecies are understood as such only after the fact. Only after Jesus' resurrection did his followers discover passages in the Old Testament that seemed to predict what happened with Jesus. However, notably, these prophecies were not understood as such before Jesus came onto the scene.

The writer of Revelation identifies his treatise as "prophecy." When read carefully, Revelation prophesies in the sense of challenging people of its own time to faithful living. For example, Revelation challenges its readers to follow the Lamb wherever he goes and not to conform to the values of the Roman Empire. Revelation is not best understood as prophecy in the sense of predicting the future in a way that would not have made sense to its first readers.

The Bible's prophetic message contains eschatological content in the sense of portraying the ultimate meaning of reality. Jesus is Lord. We are to follow his way no matter what. Death cannot defeat those who trust in the Risen One. The eschatological message of the Bible affirms that God's faithfulness to God's ways of mercy and justice will continue. We can stake our lives on this. We do not know the time or day for the completion of God's healing work. We never will know this ahead of time. Our call simply is to be faithful all the time.

The content of biblical prophecy does "reveal" to us insights into the nature of reality. It helps us to discern our idolatries. It challenges us to make Jesus Lord in all areas of life. That is to say, biblical prophecy reveals to us that Jesus' way must shape all of our commitments.

How do we best understand "heaven," "hell," and "judgment"?

"Heaven," biblically, is best understood as the spiritual element of the world where God is known to be present. It is an element of historical reality, part of this world. Heaven is not atemporal; it is not the realm of "eternity" in contrast to the finitude of everyday life.

As part of this world, heaven, for the time being, does contain evil. This is reflected in various stories that portray Satan in God's presence (e.g., the book of Job). Heaven is the spiritual element of life, both for good and evil. Revelation teaches that heaven will be transformed just as the rest of reality will be ("the new heaven and the new earth"). The spiritual forces of evil abiding in heaven now will be destroyed according to Revelation. When they are thrown into the Lake of Fire, the unity of heaven and earth will be fully seen.

"Heavenly awareness" is the opposite of "otherworldliness." Heavenly awareness means spiritual sensitivity concerning our present, historical existence. Heavenly awareness is seeing the unity of all life, the presence of God in everything—that there is nowhere that God is not.

"Hell" is to be understood as existence apart from God. Hell is total alienation from the goodness of life. It is emptiness and lifelessness. As is heaven, hell is historical, the experience in life of deadness and separation from God. According to the vision in Revelation, the coming of the New Heaven and Earth brings a newness that is the full revelation of reality as it is meant to be, without the alienation and brokenness that leads to hell on earth. Revelation twenty looks to when "death and Hades and the Dragon, the Beast, and the False Prophet will be no more."

"Judgment" is part of the experience of human beings with God in the world. God loves everyone and desires that each person be with God. According to Revelation 21–22, the way to joining with God remains open ("the gates to the New Jerusalem are always open"). However, the Bible also clearly portrays this joining with God as something human beings must choose. The existence of hell is a necessary consequence of human beings having the power to make such a choice as a genuine choice. That is, human beings must have the power to choose "no."

What happens when the New Jerusalem "comes" and temporal hell is "destroyed"? Logically, it would appear that those who have chosen against God would also be destroyed. However, many Christians doubt that an all-loving God whose main power is persevering love would giving up on particular human beings. Can human obstinacy outlast God's love? Is there a way to be a universalist without negating human freedom? Can God be loving toward a person and then destroy that person?

The practical issue for present-day Christians is that our message must be one of God's love, not one of fear of God's anger. Life with God is based on our "yes" to God, our trust, our turning from sinfulness and toward God, our acceptance of Jesus' way. Along with this affirmation also comes the awareness that there are natural consequences to saying "no".

PART SIX: Church

Throughout this book, the theme of the community of faith, or church, has been closely connected to each of the themes we have considered. In this final section, we will conclude with two chapters that overtly consider issues related to the Anabaptist understanding of the community of faith.

Chapter fourteen, "Rethinking the 'Church-Sect' Typology," looks critically at the foundational treatment of "sectarianism" in the historical theology of Ernst Troeltsch and seeks to articulate a different perspective on faith communities such as those Troeltsch called "sectarian." These communities are seen as much more socially "responsible" and "transformative" than allowed for in Troeltsch's analysis.

Chapter fifteen, "Anabaptist Theologians as Servants of the Church," draws upon Anabaptist understandings of the faith community as a crucial context for spiritual discernment in order to argue both that Anabaptist academic theologians should be supported in their creative work and that such theologians should oriented their work toward building up the faith community.

CHAPTER FOURTEEN

Rethinking the "Church-Sect" Typology[1]

MOST DISCUSSIONS of the relationship between Anabaptists and the wider world over the past several generations have been profoundly shaped by the work of Ernst Troeltsch, a German theologian and politician who died in 1920. In particular, Troeltsch's magisterial work, *The Social Teaching of the Christian Churches,* set forth the definitive church/sect typology that has influenced all subsequent analyses of Christianity and culture.

Now, about a century after the first publication of *The Social Teaching*, Troeltsch's analysis still provides the starting point for thinking about church and culture issues. I argue in what follows that, perceptive as Troeltsch was, his influence has left us with a barrier that must be overcome for more fruitful thinking about the Anabaptist tradition and culture.

"Sectarianism" in the *Social Teaching*

Ernst Troeltsch attempts through historical reconstruction to understand interrelationships between Christianity and the wider world, and thereby to help Christians know better how to relate to current social problems. He does this by identifying the basic religious impulse of Christianity and tracing its interaction with "secular" or "social" institutions such as the economy, the family, and the state through the various eras of the past 1900 years.

Troeltsch sees the basic Christian "idea" as independent of these social institutions. It is not totally determined by these institutions, nor is it unaffected by them. The history of Christianity is a history of constant interaction between the religious impulse and secular institutions. Troeltsch sees this interaction as the story of the continual compromise of the pure religious impulse in the churches' efforts to influence the world, coupled with

---

[1] The first draft of this chapter was written at the Graduate Theological Union, Berkeley, CA, 1986.

215

continual rebellions against these compromises. "Sectarianism" emerges from these rebellions against compromise.

1. The Early Church. The early church was not a sect per se because sectarianism as a type was not possible until the church-type fully emerged many centuries later. The early church was founded on the "religious idea," with its inner dynamic independent of social and historical forces.[2] Jesus founded a *new* religion based on a "purely religious" message. His first followers leaned toward comparatively simple conditions of living and saw the community of faith as a united whole independent of the state (in contrast to the rest of the ancient world). They regarded the "world" as evil, made the ethic of love central, articulated strong eschatological expectations, and emphasized a non-sacramental and purely ethical gospel.[3]

Not surprisingly, later manifestations of "sectarianism" pointed back to the early church as their ideal since the core characteristics began then. In Troeltsch's view, though, from early on—at least from the time of the Apostle Paul—the sectarian impulse was joined by a church-type impulse.[4] The early church was never purely sectarian. So the church-type can also point back to early developments indicating its authenticity as well.

The seeds of the church-type can be found in Paulinism. Troeltsch sees the movement of the early sect-like church to the church-type as inevitable. The early naive vital religious content very early on began to fuse with the religious forces of the surrounding intellectual milieu.[5]

Early Catholicism implemented a key characteristic of the church-type by centralizing salvation, making it unattainable outside of the sacraments that required a duly ordained priest.[6] As time went on the church became increasingly urbanized and lost its expectation of a soon end to history. It became more conservative and drew ever closer to the state.[7]

The pure "religious idea" did not (perhaps, in Troeltsch's view, could not) die out. It lived on, even in the church, with the ideal of sanctification and brotherly love that, though bound up with sacramental ideas, remained nonetheless always capable of a vital release.[8] The main em-

---

[2] Troeltsch, *Social*, 48.

[3] Troeltsch, *Social*, 44, 86, 97, 101.

[4] Some of the church-type impulses in Paul, according to Troeltsch, included: (1) objective salvation, (2) submission to the state, (3) rich people welcomed into the church, (4) urban location.

[5] Troeltsch, *Social*, 68.

[6] Troeltsch, *Social*, 95–96.

[7] Troeltsch, *Social*, 186.

[8] Troeltsch, *Social*, 161.

bodiment of the sect-type, standing close to the pure "religious idea," was found in monasticism. As the church-type became solidified, monasticism increasingly served as a "safety valve" for the power of the sectarian impulse. Monasticism arose as the church found rapprochement with Roman society and ultimately took charge of all genuine Christian social work maintaining close identification with the love ethic of the gospel.[9]

2. *Medieval Christianity.* The full-fledged church-type found its embodiment in the reign of Pope Gregory VII in the eleventh century and its fullest intellectual articulation in the theology of Thomas Aquinas in the thirteenth century. Here we have Troeltsch's "unity of civilization," where the church dominates the entire social order.

Concomitant with the establishment of the mature church-type came the first emergence of the more-or-less pure sect type, the eleventh-century Cathari, who shared many characteristics with movements that were to follow:

> Free lay-preaching, the criticism of the Church by the laity, the intimate fellowship of the scattered members, the practical example of poverty, indifference towards the state and the ruling classes, the rejection of the official church and of its priesthood, the refusal to swear in a court of law, or to have anything to do with the administration of justice, or with force, the abrogation of duties and tithes, the independent study of the Bible, and the habit of testing everything in church life by the standard of the primitive church.[10]

Various movements followed the Cathari over the next few centuries. These included Waldensians and Franciscans of the thirteenth century (the latter being assimilated into the Catholic church and soon losing its sect status), Lollards in England in the fourteenth century, and the Hussites in central Europe in the fifteenth century. This latter movement split into two groups embodying two types of sectarianism, the Taborites and the Czech Brethren. The former were an "aggressive sect," arguing for and practicing violent revolution. The latter were a "passive sect," favoring withdrawal and pacifism. Troeltsch asserts that the sixteenth-century Anabaptists constituted the last "pure" manifestation of the sect-type.[11]

---

[9] Troeltsch, *Social,* 329.
[10] Troeltsch, *Social,* 209.
[11] Troeltsch, *Social,* 366–67.

Characteristics of "Sectarianism"

In the *Social Teaching* Troeltsch follows the stream of history, describing and analyzing as he goes along. Numerous times he lists the characteristics of "sectarianism," and the lists are not always the same. His first and most extended discussion comes up in chapter nine of the larger section "Medieval Catholicism" entitled "The Absolute Law of God and of Nature, and the Sect."[12] Here Troeltsch focuses on the early sectarian groups, especially the Cathari, Waldensians, and early Franciscans. The various characteristics listed by Troeltsch here become definitive of what he means by "sectarianism." The central ones include:

(1) Indifference and even hostility toward the world and toward secular social institutions and toward the authority of the state and ruling classes.

(2) Made up of comparatively small groups, often appearing in the form of love communism. The sects rejected the idea of dominating the masses but gathered a select group of the elect. They expected that all of the people in these small groups would follow the radical demands of the gospel.

(3) Membership is strictly voluntary.

(4) Connected with the lower classes.

(5) Contact with God not mediated through sacraments or church hierarchy. Members are referred directly to the supernatural aim of life. Essentially lay movements. Critical of the official spiritual guides and theologians of the church. The office of the ministry is based on religious service and can therefore rest entirely upon lay people.

(6) All members expected to be ascetic, not so much in rejecting the sense life and normal day-to-day life like monks, but in the sense of general detachment from the world expressed in the refusal to use the law, swear in court, own property, or take part in war.

(7) The appeal is made to the early church and New Testament. "Scripture history and the history of the primitive church are permanent ideals to be accepted in their literal sense and not the starting-point, historically limited and defined, for the development of the church."[13]

(8) Subjective holiness is emphasized, not objective grace. Spiritual progress depends not on the objective impartation of grace through the sacrament but on individual personal effort.

---

[12] Troeltsch, *Social,* 329–47.

[13] Troeltsch, *Social,* 336.

(9) There is no conception of relative elements and gradual evolution of society—absolute contrasts alone existed.

(10) The idea of law is substituted for the idea of the church as the organ of grace and redemption.

In his conclusion to this section, Troeltsch again summarizes the characteristics of "sectarianism": it makes central the principle of subjective truth and unity, and of the evangelical standards without compromise. It renounces universalism. In the sect the individual puts the gospel into practice. The sect is more mobile and subjective. Sectarianism is the truer and more inward principle, because it is at the same time more exclusive and more powerful, and it is firmly based upon the literal interpretation of the gospel.[14]

Another summary comes in the discussion of Protestantism; Troeltsch focuses on four attributes: (1) the Christian character of the social ideal of the gospel should be proved by the group's internal unity and the practical behavior of the members, not by objective institutional guarantees; (2) because secular institutions, groups, and values are sinful, sects radically reject secular life and its works, seeking to create a social order based purely upon the principle of the gospel; (3) the sect-type rejects the idea of nature as the "complement" of grace and the corresponding goal of dominating the masses, confining its influence to small circles of the committed and rejecting "fallen nature" altogether as something which could not possibly be harmonized with grace at all; (4) Christ is seen as the law-giver, divine example, and source of all immediate influence and activity.[15]

Troeltsch sees Anabaptists as the quintessential sect. His summary of their views closely parallels his more lengthy summary of the Medieval sects: adult baptism, implying the voluntary principle; church discipline and "a pure church;" the Lord's supper as a festival of Christian fellowship; detachment from the state; endurance of persecution; mutual aid; the impossibility of carrying out the law of Christ in the world; Sermon on the Mount; rejection of the oath, war, law, and the state's authority; equality of all church members; selection of church leaders by congregations; and in general the whole movement springing from the lower classes.[16]

The sect, in Troeltsch's view, separates individuals from the world by its conscious hostility to "worldliness" and by its ethical severity, binding them together in a voluntary fellowship, established upon mutual control and penitential discipline, laying upon individuals the obligation to follow

---

[14] Troeltsch, *Social*, 381.
[15] Troeltsch, *Social*, 461–63.
[16] Troeltsch, *Social*, 695–96, 703.

the example and submit to the authority of Christ, increasing individualism by placing it within the mutual influence of group-fellowship and worship.[17]

Troeltsch sees the sect-type as being in close touch with the basic "religious idea" that was responsible for Christianity to begin with. Thus it is important as a source of dynamism and life for the church-type, which all too easily sinks into mere conformism with the wider world. However, because the mission of the church in the modern world, as it was in the medieval world, is that of being a "political and civilizing agency,"[18] the church-type is superior to the sect-type in terms of Christianity's responsibilities for the real world.

> The church-type preserves inviolate the religious elements of grace and redemption; it makes it possible to differentiate between divine grace and human effort; it is able to include the most varied degrees of Christian attainment and maturity, and therefore it alone is capable of fostering a popular religion which inevitably involves a great variety in its membership.[19]

Troeltsch's Method

Troeltsch attempted a more or less inductive historical study, claiming that the results of his study "are genuine results which have been gained from the process of research, not theses which the book was written to support."[20] Nevertheless, he has methodological assumptions with which he approaches the material and that he uses to interpret his data. Three assumptions seem to have particular significance for his discussion of "sectarianism" and for discussions following in his wake. These three are his use of ideal types, the centrality in his discussion of his concept of the "religious idea," and his posing many of his perceived problems in dialectical form.

1. Ideal Typology. The "ideal type" method is obviously very important for the study of "sectarianism." Troeltsch uses this method to explain and characterize various ways Christians have related the basic Christian religious impulse, or "idea," with the social structures of the secular world. Troeltsch comes up with a typology that provides a model that is able to order and explain the church-world issue throughout the history of Christianity.

---

[17] Troeltsch, *Social*, 743.
[18] Troeltsch, *Social*, 222.
[19] Troeltsch, *Social*, 1007.
[20] Troeltsch, *Social*, 20.

To a large degree Troeltsch's types grow out of the historical reality of medieval Christendom. When the defining characteristics are applied to later eras the danger of a reification of the types arises. Troeltsch's own historical descriptions throw into question the applicability of "sect-type" to phenomena as diverse as, for example, the Cathari and Methodists.

What seems to happen with Troeltsch's treatment of "sectarianism" is that the ideal type "sect" comes to be perceived as an independent unit, despite the fact that it is a contextual synthesis. Varying characteristics are selected as the significant ones, depending on the context in which the type is being used. Since "sect" does not have to correspond with any particular historical reality, there are fewer checks against it being used in a manner conforming with pre-existing biases—whether the sociologist is overtly trying to be normative or not.

2. *The "Religious Idea."* The "religious idea" is an important assumption of Troeltsch's that greatly affects his method. He argues that religion grows out of the autonomy of mind or "spirit" over against nature. Religion must, primarily, be considered to have a validity of its own. It cannot be explained in terms of some other human phenomenon. It must be understood in its own right, in terms of what is essential to religion as such.

Duane Friesen points out that Troeltsch was influenced by Kantian epistemology in his attempt to abstract from reality the *a priori* principles of religion.[21] The attempt to construct a rationally valid truth content for religion presupposes that there is an essential core of religion that can be referred to in abstraction from the socio-cultural context of experience. The religious "idea" relates to a transcendental realm that must then be related to culture. The religious "idea" of Christianity, being at first purely religious and in opposition to culture, must then be synthesized with culture. By definition the core or heart of religion is "beyond" or "different" from culture. The distinction between the *a priori* and the actual is thus the basis for a fundamental duality that distinguishes religion from culture.

One implication of this perspective is that anyone who has a radical commitment to religion is thus *by definition* "beyond" or opposed to culture. This assumption regarding the total disjunction between radical religious commitment and human culture is central in just about all treatments of "sectarianism" from Troeltsch on.

The special problem for Christianity, as Troeltsch sees it, is how to relate the religious goal of Christianity, by definition a goal oriented "beyond" history, to the basic values and goals inherent within the cultural

---

[21] Friesen, "Relationship," 39–40. I am indebted to Friesen for my entire discussion of Troeltsch's methodology. Friesen has updated his critique of Troeltsch in "Critical."

process itself. He sees the problem of church and world as the problem of relating the absolute to the relative. The purity of the religious idea is defined in relationship to the absolute, a realm of being beyond culture. This establishes a fundamental duality between religion and culture that can only be overcome through compromise.[22]

Though always expressed in culture, a structure of religious consciousness exists beyond culture that itself is not immersed within the historical world. Religion both is set over against culture and at the same time must be expressed within culture or synthesized with culture.

Troeltsch, disagreeing with church historian Adolf Harnack, asserts that in the original form alone we do not find the essence of Christianity. His notion of the religious idea with regard to Christianity is not that of an unchangeable idea established for all times that continues to develop in a variety of manifestations. In Troeltsch's view, the core of Christianity is a spiritual principle that evolves. Its continuity lies in its spiritual power expressed in various ways.[23] For Troeltsch, Christianity's essence may be found in the integration of the spiritual and driving impulse of the Christian idea with the present cultural situation.

Troeltsch's religious idea concept shapes his view of the relationship of Christianity and history, Christianity and culture, and thus his typology of the main ways this relationship has been expressed. Friesen argues that Troeltsch's sharp opposition between the Christian idea and history and culture does not allow for an "ethics of redemption." This "ethics of redemption" rejects Troeltsch's view of God's kingdom as a realm of absolute ideals beyond history. Rather, this other view sees the kingdom in relation to a redemptive process happening within history already in part being realized in Jesus, in the church, in the church's prophetic witness in the world, and in the partial expressions of authentic existence in institutions other than the church.[24]

This definitional assumption regarding the sharp disjunction between the Christian idea and culture has the effect of making it also definitional that those closely identified with the "pure" Christian idea (i.e., "sectarians") are necessarily totally opposed to secular culture. This assumption remains central in the social scientific study of "sectarianism."

3. Dialectical Thinking. The third methodological consideration is Troeltsch's use of dialectical thinking. Troeltsch expresses the heart of his thought in polarities or tensions that must be related to each other. The

---

[22] Friesen, "Relationship," 40–41.
[23] Friesen, "Relationship," 137.
[24] Friesen, "Relationship," 312.

major questions behind all of his research in the *Social Teaching* are posed as issues in which opposing principles must be related.

He posits a three-part typology (church, sect, and mysticism) that can be seen as a reflection of this mode of reasoning that defines groups in terms of a radical dualism, two extremes with a position in the middle. The sect-type and mystic-type express primarily one-sided values whereas the church-type usually synthesizes the one-sided values expressed in either of the other types with some other value.

The *Social Teaching* seeks to discover the way that the church has been able in the past to harmonize with the basic non-religious forces of the world and achieve a unity of civilization. This historical analysis is necessary in order to solve the normative problem for the modern world. Thus the concepts "compromise," "unity of civilization," and "harmonization" are all terms Troeltsch uses to describe the way that the conflicting value structures of religious institutions and secular institutions have been bridged in the past and how they can be and *ought* to be bridged in the future.

Troeltsch formulates the church/world problem as an opposition that must then be synthesized in various ways by various groups. It is the interplay of religious and cultural values that produce great syntheses of church history.

This process may be seen as a process of thesis (the Christian idea)—antithesis (history/culture)—synthesis (compromise between the two) that is the only way the Christian idea can survive in history. After the synthesis comes a reaction fed by the pure Christian idea leading to "sectarianism." Troeltsch writes that the kingdom of God is "an ideal which cannot be realized within this world apart from compromise. Therefore, the history of the Christian ethos becomes the story of a constantly renewed search for this compromise, and of fresh opposition to this spirit of compromise."[25]

In its basic religious idea the sect-type revives the radical religious spirit over against the compromises of the church. The pure religious perspective orients humankind toward an objective value beyond the world, leading to an attitude of indifference toward the world. The radical ideal of the sects then either draws them out of the world or involves them in programs of radical reform to transform the world according to their ideal. Thus it asserts religious ideals over against secular ideals, and is not interested in compromising these values with each other.

Troeltsch inevitably tends to value the highest those religious views most adequately relating the polarities he sees in human existence. The "inadequate" religious views are the one-sided ones that fail to bring together

---

[25] Troeltsch, *Social*, 999.

the polarities. The more adequate religious views must assert the radical transcendence of the religious idea (toward the absolute), but only in order to again synthesize with culture (toward the relative). For Troeltsch, the sect-type asserts transcendence without synthesizing with culture, whereas the church-type more adequately relates both with the absolute and historicality.

Friesen argues that this polarity-oriented perspective blinds Troeltsch to the possibility that "sectarianism" is best seen in its discriminating ethic. Sometimes "sectarians" argue that full cooperation with an aspect of secular culture is legitimate, at other times they opposed a certain practice. Troeltsch's "either-or" dualism cannot allow for a discriminating position.[26]

Sociologists' Critique of Sect Typologizing

Many sociologists have expressed criticisms of the sect-typlogizing of Troeltsch and his successors largely on methodological grounds. I will focus on three general criticisms.

1. Ideal Typology. Critics see great danger of distortion in the use of ideal typology. The ideal types are often formulated with regard to one particular set of data and then applied as is to other *different* data. Paul Gustafson makes this charge specifically with regard to Troeltsch.

> The very near proximity of type and "reality" becomes the stumbling block for Troeltsch. The types become readily reified. The new forms of post-Reformation Christianity must be churches or sects. When it becomes impossible to fit them into either category, and this happens easily because as realities the new forms vary from the many logically interrelated characteristics of the church and sect, new categories are created. These categories are not consistently related to the original one because they are ad hoc creations, without attention to the originally accentuated characteristics first used.[27]

Gustafson argues that those who have followed after Troeltsch in using ideal-typology of churches and sects share the same problem. The Troeltsch typology was constructed with reference to a particular time in the history of Christianity. But that typology has tended to be universalized, even though formulated with regard to particular historical realities. When this universalized type does not directly fit a new particular historical reality, new categories are created. Over time the number of categories proliferates,

---

[26] Friesen, "Relationship," 311.

[27] P. Gustafson, "Church," 144–45.

the original particular historical realities that gave rise to the type are left far behind, and confusion reigns.[28]

2. Normativeness. Troeltsch and his follower H. Richard Niebuhr are accused of being too concerned with what the appropriate relationship between Christianity and the world should be to allow them to be adequately scientific and objective in describing the types.

Allan W. Eister makes a clear distinction between Troeltsch studying the churches as a theologian and Max Weber studying them as a social scientist.

> Whereas Weber wrote from the perspective of the sociologist, first and last, Troeltsch was *primarily* concerned with Christian ethics—and this has a *very* important bearing on the latter's conceptions of church and sect. Whereas Weber distinguished sect from church on the ground that the former was an elective association of adults—exclusive in terms of some selective principle, belief, or practice, while the church was *inclusive*—Troeltsch chose to emphasize, as the central characteristic of the church, its "acceptance" of the secular order, at least "to a certain extent . . . in order to dominate the masses." And he implied that this is what the church *desired*—and intended to do. By stressing the "accommodative" character of the church (and the non-accommodative character of the sect)—and by tying these to "compromise" (or non-compromise) of the Christian ethic, Troeltsch introduced what is in effect an open invitation, if not a demand, for subjective, value-laden definitions. For what is "compromise" of an ethic to one believer—or even to a non-believer—is *not* compromise to another.[29]

Eister is concerned that Troeltsch and his followers use concepts in which judgments regarding notions such as "compromise" are implicit. These can be built into definitions themselves on the basis of procedures that do not readily lend themselves to explicit specifications. Thus, many scholars may at times be guilty of making value judgments unwittingly and, hence, necessarily also uncritically.[30]

This uncritical use of value-laden concepts in the service of normative evaluations of the relationship of Christianity and the world distorts the very definitions of the types.

---

[28] P. Gustafson, "Church," 147.
[29] Eister, "Toward," 87.
[30] Eister, in Glock and Hammond, eds., *Beyond*, 367.

3. Not Testable. Critics also argue that Troeltsch and his followers assert too many variant characteristics of "sectarianism" for the concept "sectarianism" to be empirically tested.

According to Eister, surveying what is said about "sectarianism" as an analytic concept reveals a list of dozens of separate characteristics that are combined in a variety of ways and presented as "defining traits" of "sectarianism." Frequently the same author utilizes different definitions within the space of a single article, giving the impression that the writer him- or herself is not clear as to what conception has been settled for.[31]

In sociology of religion, in Gustafson's view, the frame used in the discussion of church and sect varies from person to person, resulting in two problems: (1) the use of the same terms for differing concepts which in the overlap of observable characteristics have frequently been assumed to be identical; and (2) a proliferation of sub-types when the types "church" and "sect" are seen as inadequate to apply to the variety of phenomena. But due to differences in frames, these groups of subtypes vary greatly one from another.[32] Such diversity of definition and application makes commonly accepted empirical testing and verification virtually impossible.

Sociology of religion simply has not been able to determine a widely agreed-upon definition of the church-sect typology. Thus it also has been unable to establish what the *empirical* correlates of "sectness" are.[33]

Without empirical testability and testing, the concepts "church" and "sect" are said to lose their potential for illumination. For example, the assumption of a direct correlation between low socio-economic status and "sectarianism" is so widely held that it is difficult to find social scientists who have given this proposition a searching critical examination. Without such testing, this proposition stands in danger of being erected into a self-perpetuating stereotype that reveals only what the observer is conceptually prepared to "see."[34]

These criticisms reveal problems that lead Erich Goode to this conclusion:

> Too often because of a respectable ancestry, certain concepts and theories have been used, re-used, and have been perpetuated long after their usefulness has come to an end. Church-sect is very much in danger of being in that position. As it stands today, it is a hodgepodge of definition and empirical correlates and empirical non-cor-

---

[31] Eister, "Radical," 86.
[32] P. Gustafson, "UO-US-PS-PO," 68.
[33] Goode, "Some," 76.
[34] Eister, "H. Richard Niebuhr," 397–98.

relates. It has no power to explain or elucidate. Unless it undergoes a radical revision which is universally accepted by researchers and theorists in the field, church-sect must be seen as a dead concept, obsolete, sterile, and archaic.[35]

Critics of Troeltsch from Minority Traditions

Several writers who are themselves part of what could be called "sectarian" groups tend to be much more sympathetic and favorable toward this "minority" tradition that Troeltsch calls "sectarian." They tend, to a large degree, to avoid the term "sectarianism." A term a number use instead is "believers church," highlighting one of the positive distinguishing characteristics of Troeltschian sects—"membership is strictly voluntary."

Most of these writers would agree that at least two significant problems exist with an unqualified use of "sectarianism" as a label for these groups. One is that throughout church history, "sectarian" has been an epithet used from majority churches for dissenting movements that have been alienated from the established churches. Such pejorative connotations remain in the air, and despite claims by sociologists to be non-normative in their use of "sectarianism," the term is more often than not used in a depreciating way by them—not to mention the openly judgmental use by some church-related scholars.[36]

A second problem is that "sectarianism" carries the implication that these groups are best understood in terms of what they are not, in terms of what it is they reject. One of the major theses of the "insiders" is that the "believers church tradition" has an independent, positive orientation and is best understood on its own terms and not as a protest movement merely splintering off the "real" church.

Troeltsch himself used the term "sectarianism" with the claim that it was to be neutral and descriptive of an independent movement. At best, he was only partially successful in holding to that usage in the *Social Teaching*. Most who have come after him have been even more value-laden in their usage, claims for "scientific neutrality" notwithstanding.

---

[35] Goode, "Critical," 77.

[36] For an example of how this language has not yet been discarded, see J. Gustafson, "Sectarian."

Characteristics of the Believers Church Tradition

Writers in the believers church tradition argue for a view of church and culture that differs quite strongly from many Troeltschian assumptions. What follows synthesizes their arguments.

1. Discriminatory Toward the Wider World. These "sympathizers" challenge the notion that the believers church tradition is intrinsically rejectionist toward the wider world. The basic thrust of this tradition's orientation toward the wider world is one of discrimination. They accept as legitimate things that do not contradict their understanding of Jesus Christ's will, seeing these as "subsumed in his lordship."[37] They do not see "culture" as totally evil and off limits. But they do reject elements of the wider culture that they believe contradict Jesus Christ's will. Thus the relative involvement in the wider society by these Christians will vary depending on the characteristics of each particular society.

The believers church tradition fosters critical distance from the wider culture. This distance can facilitate freedom of thought and action and an ability creatively to address human reality. These Christians may be better able to discern the possibility that people's minds can be "darkened" by a quite subtle and dangerous temptation, that of being unable to see the truth because of a total involvement in the temporary order.[38] In particular, they can be aware of the encroachments of statist and nationalist ideologies on Christians' worldviews and a concomitant inability to discern God's will from the values and self-interests of their society.

With this critical distance, believers church Christians have the possibility of influencing wider society through a kind of social pressure more critical, more flexible, less conformist, and less patient than the "responsible involvement" advocated by majority traditions. In their concern for the wider society, believers church Christians assume, at least implicitly, that their best potential for doing good is realized in faithful witness to the love and power of God in their common life—manifested in their community of love open to all comers, their acts of service, their active concern for the poor and needy, and in their refusal to join in nationalistic campaigns of violence. However, these are tactical choices focusing on what is possible for minority, relatively powerless groups to do. They do not reflect in any way a general rejection of the wider world.[39]

---

[37] Yoder, *Priestly*, 11.

[38] Redekop, *Free*, 83.

[39] Yoder, *Priestly*, 11–12.

"Culture" may be understood too narrowly, and things such as the use of the sword and capitalistic economics identified as definitive of "culture" (with the implication that a rejection of the sword and capitalistic economics has meant a rejection of "culture"). Believers church Christians have always utilized and affirmed various types of governance and economics; they have always seen that Christian obedience takes place in this world and hinges on issues such as how people use their money and order their lives together.[40]

Historically the main cause of alienation between believers churches and the wider world has been the world's rejection of these Christians, not vice versa.[41] The core characteristic of this tradition is not rejectionist toward culture but rather is discriminatory—accepting parts and rejecting parts. This takes on a more rejectionist hue only when the particular culture the believers churches find themselves in will not accept their lack of total allegiance to it.

A strictly "phenomenological" view that defines these groups only by specific historical manifestations of alienation between the group and wider society greatly distorts the character of those groups. Such an approach has the tendency to make one historical slice definitive for all time and to make one manifestation of a discriminatory ethic into a principled ethic of rejection.

2. Mission and Service Mindedness. Rather than being intrinsically otherworldly, the believers church tradition shows deep concern for the world, manifested in its pioneering efforts in Christian mission and social service. The sixteenth-century Anabaptists were mission-minded at a time when both Catholics and state-church Protestants saw nothing illogical in dividing up Christendom by political agreement.[42] The Quakers in the seventeenth century spearheaded the first truly inter-cultural mission efforts and became well known for their concern for social service.

Missionary witness is structurally incompatible with the sociological and political posture of the established church, since everyone in a given country is already within that church, and in any other state everyone, by the same token, is the responsibility of some other state-church.[43] Hence, at least in terms of missionary concern, the believers churches have displayed more commitment to more of the world than have established churches.

---

[40] Redekop, *Free*, 120.
[41] Yoder, *Priestly*, 34.
[42] Littell, *Free*, 132.
[43] Yoder, in Garrett, ed., *Concept*, 267.

Whenever they have not been pushed into withdrawal by persecution, believers churches have been extremely active with works of social service such as relief, education, health care, and third-world development in more recent years. These types of concerns reflect a strong commitment to being in the world and an assertion that Christian obedience means obedience within present history as a witness to a new order manifested, in part, amidst the old.

3. Service and "Pilot Plants." Their relative freedom vis-à-vis secular culture allows believers churches to be innovative with regard to ministry to the world in ways established churches cannot. This freedom to innovate has transformative potential. These groups may undertake pilot programs to meet unmet needs. Popular education and hospitals were first experienced in believers church Christianity.[44]

The power of these groups follows from their relative freedom of action vis-à-vis their societies' dominant ideologies. Voluntary commitment to a community distinct from the total society provides important resources for practical moral reasoning.[45]

Combined with their freedom is the strength of mutual support in these communities. They provide power for change because people banding together in common dissidence affect a kind of social leverage that is not provided by any other social form. The believers church community may provide economic and social as well as moral support to individuals standing with it against the stream who could not stand alone.[46]

Believers churches have the possibility and responsibility to remember and create utopian visions that in turn provide the best hope for long-term social change.[47] There is no genuine hope for society, without an awareness of transcendence. Transcendence is kept alive not on the grounds of logical proof to the effect that there is a cosmos with a hereafter, but by the vitality of communities in which a different way of being keeps breaking in here and now.

4. Concerned with Christian Unity. These groups did not set out to cause schism but rather to renew existing churches and bring Christians together. The basic impetus for church division has come from the established church side that, with a few exceptions, has rejected these renewal impulses and given these groups no choice but either to continue their existence as separated groups or to give up on their new insights and vitality.

---

[44] Yoder, *Priestly*, 92.
[45] Yoder, *Priestly*, 91.
[46] Yoder, *Priestly*, 91.
[47] Yoder, *Priestly*, 94.

These minority groups have called all Christians to the ethic to which they see themselves called. They have not seen their position as only for heroes or those who would withdraw from wider society. They have not separated themselves from the church at large, but rather called the church to the quality of commitment that would in effect lead them all to be separated from sinful elements in the world once again in order to be appropriately in mission to the world.[48]

One element of this radical ethic that has actually facilitated international ecumenism is the rejection of the territorial or state church. The notion that the Christian church is an independent—and, for Christians, more fundamental—entity in relation to any and all nations is an indispensable perspective for there to be any hope for worldwide Christian unity.

5. Social Ethics for the "Average Person." Far from being elitist, this tradition relates to common people. It counters what is the actual elitist notion of an established church viewpoint that ethics should be approached from the perspective of people in power.

History has come to be told as the history of people in power. The ruler, not the average person or the powerless person, is the model for ethical deliberations. A moral statement on the rightness of truth telling or the wrongness of killing is tested first by whether a ruler can meet such standards. "Social ethics" comes to mean not what everyone should think and do about social questions, but what people in power should be told to do with their power.[49]

In contrast to this, believers churches have sought to articulate an ethic for all Christians.[50] They have asked, as their most basic question, how ought people live in obedience to Jesus Christ in the everyday. They have assumed that Jesus' will is knowable to all sincere people, it does not need the mediation of a priest, and that it is do-able.

These groups do not envision the faithful Christian as some super-human hero or a monk-like recluse who must escape the world, but a sincere common person who lives day-to-day as part of a community of faith and seeks mundanely to live as Jesus would have him or her live.

Conclusions

Troeltsch's *Social Teaching* remains a key text due to his insights and the influence of his typology and due to the sheer magnitude of his efforts.

---

[48] Yoder, *Priestly*, 85.
[49] Yoder, *Priestly*, 138.
[50] Durnbaugh, *Believers*, 43.

As H. R. Niebuhr wrote in his introduction to the English translation to the *Social Teaching,* though "every part can be legitimately criticized by specialists, none has the ability to put all the corrected pieces together in any similar, synoptic view of the whole, nor to stimulate equally the labors of scholars and the exercise of responsible churchmanship and statesmanship."[51]

I see Troeltsch's general approach of closely and objectively examining history in dialogue with pressing present-day concerns as exemplary. The stimulus for his writing the book was a critique he gave of a contemporary book on social ethics that he saw as miserably unhistorical. He insisted that to understand and act appropriately in the present we must understand the past. Likewise, his concern with the past was fueled and shaped by his concern with the present. History is only meaningful when it is studied with present questions in mind. Troeltsch's historical reconstruction, while certainly open to criticism and correction with regard to many specifics, is remarkable in its sensitivity to the data.

Any attempt to come to grips with what Troeltsch called "sectarianism" must follow in his footsteps, rigorously and objectively doing close historical work while always keeping the present in mind. This approach seems preferable to that of the "neutral" social scientists, whose masking of their own values only makes them uncritical propagators of those values. It is also preferable to ahistorical theology that accepts the types as self-evident and almost transcendent over history in their applicability. Troeltsch himself borders on this kind of ahistorical approach in the conclusion to the *Social Teaching*.

My biggest problems with Troelstch's discussion in the *Social Teaching* have to do with his inability to transcend totally his intellectual milieu (which admittedly no one can do completely; Troeltsch certainly did better than many others) and what one could call his "chastened Constantianism."

The particular aspect of Troeltsch's milieu I have in mind is his concept of the "religious idea." He modifies Adolf Harnack's ahistorical "essence of Christianity," insisting that this essence should be seen as a "developing spiritual principle." But he still sets it up as being *by definition* the opposite pole from history and culture. Thus those seen to be especially close to the "religious idea" (the sects) are *by definition* opposed to "culture." This assumption distorts reality; more recent work on the sociology of knowledge and the social setting of early Christianity recognizes the problem.

There has never been a "Christian idea" or any other kind of "idea" that is not socially embedded and not itself thereby a part of "culture." Thus

---

[51] Niebuhr, "Introduction," 11.

the "compromise" is not the Christian idea compromising with "culture," but rather a process of discernment as to which parts of one's wider culture cohere with one's Christian worldview, which itself is a "cultural" entity. "Sectarians" are not "Christ against culture" but Christians discerning their place in culture—like all other types of Christians, though at times with different answers.

By "chastened Constantinianism" I am referring to Troeltsch's assumptions regarding Christians' responsibility to "run the world." It is "chastened" in that he does not actually seem to be sure that this is possible any more. But he remains a person thinking of ethics for the ruling classes. He still thought within Christendom. To the degree Troeltsch's contemporary Friedrich Nietzsche was correct to herald the end of Christendom (which is a large degree), Troeltsch's Constantinian assumptions diminish in significance and helpfulness. And certainly in places in the non-Western world where Christians have always been minorities, Constantinian assumptions have very little relevance.

I propose that the term "sectarianism" be eliminated from serious social scientific, ethical, and theological language. The term is too vague and slippery; all too often "sectarianism" is used either to speak of something held to be self-evident (which in fact is not) or to condemn someone its user does not like.

This is not to say that what these people have studied under the rubric of "sectarianism" does not exist. A variety of movements similar to what Troeltsch and the others have called "sects" and the "insiders" have called "free churches" and "believers churches" has indeed existed. But these movements fit into several distinct categories and are best not grouped under a single rubric unless that rubric is very general.

One useful quite general rubric may simply be the term "minority traditions." This would recognize what is probably the only characteristic all these groups share in common—that they are small groups, distinct from mainline, majoritarian groups. This term is mostly a descriptive, non-value-laden characterization. It would also recognize that these groups are not merely (or even primarily) deviant, aberrant manifestations of protest. They constitute genuine "traditions" with a positive history of their own.

More specifically for Anabaptists, new thinking continues to be needed, integrating Troeltsch's best insights with a positive appreciation for how the Anabaptist tradition has in various ways actually manifested creative and *responsible* engagement with culture.[52]

---

[52] See Friesen, *Artists* and McClendon, *Witness* for two theologically rigorous attempts to engage culture from believers church perspectives.

CHAPTER FIFTEEN

Anabaptist Theologians as Members of the Community of Faith[1]

THEOLOGIANS[2] WHO work for Anabaptist colleges and seminaries do so, I am convinced, due to a sense of calling to serve God and the churches with their gifts and abilities. For example, Eastern Mennonite University, where I teach, states explicitly its mission to be seeking to answer Christ's call to lives of nonviolence, service, witness, and peacebuilding. Such a mission provides an enormously challenging and exciting program for scholarship and teaching.

However, pursuing this mission amidst the institutional concerns characteristic of churches and colleges in our contemporary culture poses challenges. Is our responsibility as Anabaptist scholars primarily to fulfill such a mission as stated above by seeking to understand and follow the truth of the gospel of peace wherever it may lead? Or is it primarily to make sure our work serves the economic viability of our institutions—recognizing that for the sake of what may be perceived as the institutions' best interests, we may at times want to avoid addressing certain issues or sharing the fruit of our scholarship?

Numerous issues arise when we reflect on the relationship between Anabaptist-school scholars and the wider Anabaptist world in North America. Anabaptists have traditionally socialized their people to consider the faith community as central to their lives. Individuals are to subordinate their personal inclinations to the community's values. What implications follow from privileging the collective in this way, particularly in relation to the inherently personal work of theological scholarship? Is the Anabaptist world ready to validate as essential to the wider community the boundary-stretching dynamics of vital theological scholarship?

---

[1] A version of this essay was published as "The Responsibility of Anabaptists Scholars" *DreamSeeker Magazine* 2.1 (Autumn 2001). Used with permission.

[2] I am using the term "theologian" in a broad sense here to include scholars working in disciplines such as biblical studies, theology, ethics, ministry, spiritual formation, and Christian history.

Do we agree that it is the best perspective to accept the notion of the wider faith community as inherently conservative? Is the faith community always being faithful when it seeks to sustain past understandings and resist innovation?

The Anabaptist tradition includes at its heart a powerful tension at this point. On the one hand, the sixteenth-century Anabaptist movement arose as an innovative change-agent in Western European, earning the name *Radical* Reformation. Yet, as the movement evolved, it has been characteristically resistant to change. The general impact of being part of the modern Anabaptist faith community has surely been one of imposed restraint on Anabaptist theologians in the modern, pro-education era in North America beginning in the late nineteenth century.[3]

The tension between Anabaptist "radicalism" and present-day caution can be seen clearly in the mid-twentieth-century efforts to "recover the Anabaptist vision." As articulated by Harold Bender in his influential 1943 paper, "The Anabaptist Vision," the Anabaptist movement had a radical core—pacifist, resistant to state domination, centered on discipleship to that first-century revolutionary rabbi, Jesus of Nazarath.

However, Bender's "recovery" was not actually intended to be a full-scale opening of the Anabaptist world to a free-flowing appropriation of the theological ferment of the sixteenth century. He advocated a normative Anabaptism that excluded theologically "unorthodox" Anabaptists. Bender's hope, it would appear, was cautiously to revitalize existing structures, not open the doors to an entire spectrum of perspectives.[4]

Since Bender's time, a key dynamic in the world of Anabaptist higher education has been extraordinary growth in the expense and complexity of operating our schools. For example, at the turn of the twenty-first century, the four Mennonite Church USA four-year colleges each were engaged in major building projects with combined costs of well over sixty million dollars.

So, part of the tension in reflecting on the role of theological scholarship in the Anabaptist community surely is theological, part surely is cultural, but as well we have the tension that is institutional. With schools getting bigger and more dependent on more financial resources, sensitivity toward the sensibilities of potential donors enters the picture. Should our schools welcome theological reflection that might be offensive to moneyed interests in the Anabaptist community or the broader culture? Maybe even

---

[3] For accounts of theological tensions in Anabaptist colleges in the first half of the twentieth century, see Keim, *Bender* and Bush, *Dancing*.

[4] Keim, *Bender*, 306–31.

more complicated is the dependence of Anabaptist schools on tuition income and the concern that theological innovativeness might keep some prospective students away.

Another aspect of the tension arises from Anabaptist schools being part of the broader community of higher education in secular North America. North American higher education has established fairly strict principles of "academic freedom." Anabaptist schools must accept at least some of the implications of "academic freedom" in order to participate in this broader academic community. Yet, clearly, some of the principles underlying "academic freedom" in the broader North American culture stand in tension with the Anabaptist ethos. The importance of free speech, of the inviolable rights of individual conscience, and of the free marketplace of ideas are not necessarily central Anabaptist values.

Most problematic, perhaps, "academic freedom" proponents and church-related "conservatives" who are deeply suspicious of academic theology seem to agree in assuming an inherent conflict between the academic endeavor and the life of the wider faith community. To base an affirmation of open theological inquiry on North American notions of "academic freedom" risks driving an unnecessary and mutually damaging wedge between theology as an academic discipline in Anabaptist schools and the spiritual and intellectual vitality of the community of faith.

The trend in North American higher education for generations has been ever-increasing separation between academia and church communities. In my experience, this separation has gained impetus from both sides. Rather than fostering a vital, we're-in-this-together and we-need-each-other relationship, church leaders and academic theologians alike have all too often happily avoided each other's company. Church leaders are fearful of theologian's creativity. Theologians are fearful of church leaders' resistance to creativity.

I suggest that rather than being suspicious of and resistant to open theological inquiry in Anabaptist schools, the faith community should welcome the work of academic theologians as an essential component of the on-going discernment task of the followers of Jesus. Rather than either seeking independence from faith communities or avoiding speaking on controversial issues, theologians should gain direction from the needs of the faith communities and understand their work as being in service to these communities.

All too often, points of tension between the community of faith and academic theologians have led to silence and avoidance in the Anabaptist world—or to a severing of relationships. At precisely these points of tension we find the core of the community's responsibility to utilize the gifts of its theologians and theologians' responsibility to exercise their gifts.

The category of "spiritual gifts" provides my context for reflecting on the issue of open theological expression. I believe that because of the gifts theologians have been given, have nurtured, and are hired to exercise, open expression is something our schools should encourage.

This is my central proposal: Anabaptist churches, colleges, and seminaries must respect the giftedness of their theologians. They should expect those theologians to be honest and open in the responsible expression of their gifts in teaching and scholarship.

In other words, the priority for theologians should be to serve Jesus and his followers, seeking the truth at all times and speaking directly to the issues of our day. Our responsibilities to our institutions are genuine and important, but the institutions (including the churches) lose their reason for existence if mere institutional viability becomes the ultimate value.

I do believe Anabaptist churches and schools should expect their theologians to be active members in Anabaptist congregations. I believe Anabaptist theologians should understand their vocation as being to serve their broader Anabaptist faith community (as well as the broader Christian community and the world itself).

This membership and vocation should not, however, be constraining. Rather, they are precisely the factors that give theologians the responsibility to speak freely and forcefully, to articulate openly the fruits of our research. Like all members of the church, we are to boldly speak the truth as we discern it.

I joined the Mennonite Church in 1981. I was first licensed as a minister in 1982 and ordained in 1991. On each occasion, I vowed to be part of the process within the church of giving and receiving counsel.

I have always understood this vow to be a commitment to exercise my gifts as a trained theologian for the sake of the church's discerning work. In seeing theologians, first of all, as gifted members of the broader church, I understand our called-out work not to be in tension with the broader church's mission but an essential part of it. We are not more important than other members with other gifts, but we do have an authentic role to play.

I well remember a conversation I had in the mid-1980s with Willard Swartley of Associated Mennonite Biblical Seminary that has continued to inspire me. Willard spoke of being moved to tears as he researched Mennonite writing on war and peace. He cited the unflagging efforts of Guy Hershberger, longtime professor at Goshen College. Guy sought to minister to the church by his writing, especially through popular-level articles in such denominational periodicals as the *Gospel Herald* and *The Mennonite*.

I vowed then that I would try to follow that model. So I am proud of the twenty-plus articles I have had published in the *Gospel Herald* and *The Mennonite* since then. Theologians are called to be ministers in the church.

I resist moves that on the one hand seek to protect faith communities from the academy or, on the other hand, seek to protect the academy from faith communities. Faith communities need the work of academic theologians as they seek to be faithful to the way of Jesus. For theologians to raise new questions, to challenge superficial understandings, and to foster care in our use of language should not be seen as a threat to the broader church's mission. Rather, these tasks of the theologian actually play a central role in this mission.

Our theology of the church (ecclesiology) asserts that we all are to share in the church's work of discernment. All voices within the fellowship must be heard. Faith communities must not censor or squelch those within the fellowship (including theologians) who raise questions and suggest new directions.

At the same time, all members within the fellowship (including theologians) are called to do their work in service of God through a relationship of mutual accountability with the broader community, not as autonomous individuals.

The work of articulating a living faith, using language that is meaningful and authentic in the present while also faithful to the message of the Bible, is the responsibility of Anabaptist theologians. We are being irresponsible if we shrink from this task.

Even when our work is not welcomed, as members of our broader faith communities we have made a commitment to offer our counsel to our brothers and sisters. We theologians must not be ruled by fear or timidity. We have an authentic role to play in our faith communities—for their own good.

Bibliography

Alterman, Eric. *What Liberal Media? The Truth About Bias and the News.* 2d ed. New York: Basic, 2004.
Assman, Hugo. *Theology for a Nomad Church.* Maryknoll, NY: Orbis, 1975.
Bacevich, Andrew J. *The New American Militarism: How Americans Are Seduced by War.* New York: Oxford University, 2005.
Bakke, Willem. *Calvin and the Anabaptist Radicals.* Grand Rapids, MI: Eerdmans, 1982.
Ballard, Bruce W. "The Death Penalty: God's Timeless Standard for the Nations?" *Journal of the Evangelical Theological Society* 43 (2000) 471–87.
Bellah, Robert, et al. *Habits of the Heart: Individualism and Commitment in American Life.* Berkeley: University of California, 1985.
Bender, Harold S. "The Anabaptist Vision." 1944. Reprinted in *The Recovery of the Anabaptist Vision*, edited by Guy F. Hershberger, 29–54. Scottdale, PA: Herald, 1957.
Bernstein, Richard J. *Beyond Objectivism and Relativism: Science, Hermeneutics, and Praxis.* Philadelphia: University of Pennsylvania, 1983.
Biesecker-Mast, Gerald. *Separation and the Sword in Anabaptist Persuasion: Radical Confessional Rhetoric from Schleitheim to Dordrecht.* Telford, PA: Cascadia, 2006.
Blunt, Sheryl Henderson. "The Unflappable Condi Rice." *Christianity Today.* 47.9 (September 2003) 42–48.
Breech, James. *The Silence of Jesus: The Authentic Voice of the Historical Man.* Philadelphia: Fortress, 1983.
Brock, Peter. *Pacifism in the United States: From the Colonial Era to the First World War.* Princeton, NJ: Princeton University, 1968.
Bruns, Gerald L. *Inventions: Writing, Textuality, and Understanding in Literary History.* New Haven, CT: Yale University, 1982.
Buber, Martin. *I and Thou.* Translated by Walter Kauffmann. New York: Scribners, 1970.
Bush, Perry. *Dancing with the Kozbar: Bluffton College and Mennonites Higher Education.* Telford, PA: Pandora, 2000.
———. *Two Kingdoms, Two Loyalties: Mennonite Pacifism in Modern America.* Baltimore: Johns Hopkins University, 1998.
"Campers Speak at Conferences." *Pike View News* 1.11 (Feb. 7, 1942) 1.
Carnes, Tony. "Bush's Defining Moment." *Christianity Today* 45.11 (November 12, 2001) 19–21.
———. "The Bush Doctrine." *Christianity Today* 47.5 (May 2003) 38–40.
Chomsky, Noam. *Hegemony or Survival: America's Quest for Global Dominance.* New York: Metropolitan, 2003.
———. *Understanding Power: The Indispensable Chomsky.* New York: Free, 2002.
Confession of Faith in a Mennonite Perspective. Scottdale, PA: Herald, 1995.
Cox, Harvey. "The Market as God." *The Atlantic Monthly* (March 1999) 18–23.
Crowley, Michael. "James Dobson: The Religious Right's New Kingmaker." *Slate* (November 12, 2004), http://www.slate.com/id/2109621/.
Davis, Mike. *Planet of Slums.* New York: Verso, 2006.

Driedger, Leo and Donald Kraybill. *Mennonite Peacemaking: From Quietism to Activism.* Scottdale, PA: Herald, 1994.

Driedger, Leo, and Leland Harder, eds. *Anabaptist-Mennonite Identities in Ferment.* Elkhart: Institute of Mennonite Studies, 1990.

Driver, John. *Radical Faith: An Alternative History of the Christian Church.* Kitchener, Ont.: Pandora, 1999.

Durnbaugh, Donald. *The Believers Church: The History and Character of Radical Protestantism.* New York: Macmillan, 1968.

Dyck, C. J. *Introduction to Mennonite History.* 3d ed. Scottdale, PA: Herald, 1993.

Ediger, Elmer. "Is It Right to Accept CPS?" *The Snowline* 3.4 (April 1945) 2.

Eister, Allan W. "H. Richard Niebuhr and the Paradox of Religious Organization: A Radical Critique." In *Beyond the Classics? Essays in the Scientific Study of Religion*, edited by Charles Y. Glock and Phillip E. Hammon, 355–408. New York: Harper and Row, 1973.

———. "Toward a Radical Critique of Church-Sect Typologizing." *Journal for the Scientific Study of Religion* 6 (1967) 85–90.

Enns, Fernando, et al, eds. *Seeking Cultures of Peace: A Peace Church Conversation.* Telford, PA: Cascadia, 2004.

Farley, Edward. *Ecclesial Reflection: An Anatomy of Theological Method.* Philadelphia: Fortress, 1982.

Finger, Thomas N. *A Contemporary Anabaptist Theology: Biblical, Historical, Constructive.* Downers Grove, IL: InterVarsity, 2004.

———. "Biblical and Systematic Theology in Interaction: A Case Study on Atonement." In *So Wide a Sea: Essays on Biblical and Systematic Theology,* edited by Ben C. Ollenburger, 1–17. Elkhart: Institute of Mennonite Studies, 1991.

———. *Christian Theology: An Eschatological Approach.* Vol. 1. Nashville: Thomas Nelson, 1985.

———. "Confessions of Faith in the Anabaptist/Mennonite Tradition." *Mennonite Quarterly Review* 76 (2002) 277–98.

———. "Is 'Systematic Theology' Possible from a Mennonite Perspective?" In *Explorations of Systematic Theology: From Mennonite Perspectives,* edited by Willard M. Swartley, 37–55. Elkhart, IN: Institute of Mennonite Studies, 1984.

———. "Response to J. Denny Weaver." *Conrad Grebel Review* 6 (1988) 161–4.

———. *Self, Earth, and Society.* Downers Grove, IL: InterVarsity, 1997.

Fiorenza, Elisabeth Schüssler. *Bread not Stone: The Challenge of Feminist Biblical Interpretation.* Boston: Beacon, 1984.

Forster, Walter. "The Place is Here and the Time is Now!" *Camp Walhalla News* 1.4 (Dec, 1942) 7.

Frank, Thomas. *What's the Matter with Kansas? How Conservatives Won the Heart of America.* New York: Metropolitan, 2004.

Friesen, Duane K. "A Critical Assessment of Troeltsch's Typology of Religious Association." In *Studies in the Theological Ethics of Ernst Troeltsch,* edited by Max A. Myers and Michael R. LaChat, 73–118. Lewiston, NY: Edward Mellen, 1991.

———. *Artists, Citizens, Philosophers: Seeking the Peace of the City.* Scottdale, PA: Herald, 2000.

———. "The Relationship Between Ernst Troeltsch's Theory of Religion and His Typology of Religious Association." Th.D. diss., Harvard University, 1972.

Friesen, John, ed., *Mennonites in Russia, 1788–1988.* Winnipeg, Man: CMBC, 1989.

Gadamer, Hans-Georg. *Truth and Method.* 2d ed. Translated by Joel Weinsheimer and Donald G. Marshall. New York: Crossroad, 1989.

Gara, Larry, and Lenna Mae Gara, eds. *A Few Small Candles: War Resisters of World War II Tell Their Stories.* Kent, OH: Kent State University, 1999.

Gingerich, Ray C. "The Mission Impulse of Early Swiss and South German-Austrian Anabaptism." Ph.D. diss., Vanderbilt University, 1980

———. "Theological Foundations for an Ethic of Nonviolence: Was Yoder's God a Warrior?" *Mennonite Quarterly Review* 77 (2003) 417–35.

Gingerich, Ray and Ted Grimsrud, eds. *Transforming the Powers: Peace, Justice, and the Domination System.* Minneapolis: Fortress, 2006.

Gish, Arthur G. *The New Left and Christian Radicalism.* Grand Rapids, MI: Eerdmans, 1970.

Goertz, Hans-Jürgen. *The Anabaptists.* 2d ed. Translated by Trevor Johnson. New York: Routledge, 1996.

Goode, Erich. "Some Critical Observations on the Church-Sect Dimension." *Journal for the Scientific Study of Religion* 6 (1967) 69–77.

Gorringe, Timothy. *God's Just Vengeance: Crime Violence and the Rhetoric of Salvation.* New York: Cambridge University, 1996.

Grimsrud, Ted. *God's Healing Strategy: An Introduction to the Main Themes of the Bible.* Telford, PA: Cascadia, 2000.

———. "Negotiating Democracy: Mennonite Reflections." *Conrad Grebel Review* 23 (2005) 94–103.

———. "Pacifism and Knowing: Truth in the Theological Ethics of John Howard Yoder." *Mennonite Quarterly Review* 77 (2003) 403–16.

———. "Saying No to the 'Good' War: An Ethical Analysis of Conscientious Objection to World War II." Ph.D. diss., Graduate Theological Union, 1988.

———. *Triumph of the Lamb: A Self-Study Guide to the Book of Revelation.* Scottdale, PA: Herald, 1987.

———. "Violence as a 'Theological' Problem." *Justice Reflections* Issue #10 (December 2005) 1–25.

Grimsrud, Ted and Howard Zehr. "Rethinking God, Justice, and the Treatment of Offenders." *Journal of Offender Rehabilitation* 35 (2002) 253–79.

Gustafson, James. "The Sectarian Temptation: Reflections on Theology, the Church, and the University." *Proceedings of the Catholic Theological Society* 40 (1985) 83–94.

Gustafson, Paul. "Church and Sect or Church and Ascetic Protestantism?" *Encounter* 30 (1969) 142–7.

———. "UO-US-PS-PO: A Restatement of Troeltsch's Church-Sect Typlogy." *Journal for the Scientific Study of Religion* 6 (1967) 64–8.

Gutierrez, Gustavo. *A Theology of Liberation: History, Politics, and Salvation.* Maryknoll, NY: Orbis, 1973.

Hauerwas, Stanley. *After Christendom? How the Church is to Behave if Freedom, Justice, and a Christian Nation are Bad Ideas.* Nashville: Abingdon, 1991.

———. "Confessions of a Mennonite Camp Follower." In *Engaging Anabaptism: Conversations with a Radical Tradition,* edited by John D. Roth, 25–39. Scottdale, Pa.: Herald, 2001.

———. *Performing the Faith: Bonhoeffer and the Practice of Nonviolence.* Grand Rapids, MI: Brazos, 2004.

Hauerwas, Stanley and William Willimon. *Resident Aliens: Life in the Christian Colony.* Nashville: Abingdon, 1989.

Bibliography

Heilke, Thomas. "Theological and Secular Meta-Narratives of Politics: Anabaptist Origins Revisited (Again)." *Modern Theology* 13 (1997) 227–52.

Hershberger, Guy F. *War, Peace, and Nonresistance.* Scottdale, PA: Herald, 1944.

Herzog, William. *Jesus, Justice, and the Reign of God: A Ministry of Liberation.* Louisville: Westminster John Knox, 2000.

Holland, Scott. "The Gospel of Peace and the Violence of God." In *Seeking Cultures of Peace: A Peace Church Conversation,* edited by Fernando Enns, et al, 132–46. Telford, PA: Cascadia, 2004.

Homan, Gerlof D. *American Mennonites and the Great War, 1914–1918.* Scottdale, PA: Herald, 1994.

Horst, Samuel L. *Mennonites in the Confederacy: A Study in Civil War Pacifism.* Scottdale, PA: Herald, 1967.

Hunsberger, Willard. *The Franconia Mennonites and War.* Franconia: PA: Franconia Mennonite Conference, 1951.

Hunter, Richard C. "From the Inside Out." In *If We Can Love: The Mennonite Mental Health Story,* edited by Vernon Neufeld, 295–300. Newton, KS: Faith and Life, 1983.

Janzen, Waldemar. "A Canonical Rethinking of the Anabaptist-Mennonite New Testament Orientation." In *The Church as Theological Community: Essays in Honour of David Schroeder,* edited by Harry Huebner, 90–112. Winnipeg: CMBC, 1990.

Jeschke, Marlin. *Discipling the Brother.* 3d ed. Scottdale, PA: Herald, 1988.

Johnson, Chalmers. *Sorrows of Empire: Militarism, Secrecy, and the End of the Republic.* New York: Metropolitan, 2004.

Juhnke, James C. *Vision, Doctrine, War: Mennonite Identity and Organization in America, 1890–1930.* Scottdale, PA: Herald, 1989.

Karp, Walter. *Buried Alive: Essays on Our Endangered Republic.* New York: Franklin Square, 1992.

———. *The Politics of War: The Story of Two Wars Which Altered Forever the Political Life of the American Republic, 1890–1920.* 1979. Reprinted, New York: Franklin Square, 2003.

Kaufman, Gordon. *An Essay on Theological Method.* 3d ed. New York: Oxford University, 1995.

———. *In Face of Mystery: A Constructive Theology.* Cambridge, MA: Harvard University, 1993.

———. *Nonresistance and Responsibility and Other Mennonite Essays.* Newton, KS: Faith and Life, 1979.

———. "The Mennonite Roots of My Theological Perspective." In *Mennonite Theology in Face of Modernity,* edited by Alain Epp Weaver, 1–19. North Newton, KS: Bethel College, 1996.

———. *Theology for a Nuclear Age.* Philadelphia: Westminster, 1985.

Keeney, William. "Experiences in Mental Hospitals in World War II." *Mennonite Quarterly Review* 56 (1982) 7–17.

Keim, Albert N. *Harold S. Bender, 1897–1962.* Scottdale, PA: Herald, 1998.

———. *The CPS Story: An Illustrated History of Civilian Public Service.* Intercourse, PA: Good, 1990.

Keim, Albert N. and Grant M. Stoltzfus. *The Politics of Conscience: The Historic Peace Churches and America at War, 1917–1955.* Scottdale, PA: Herald, 1988.

Kelly, Michael. "Pacifist Claptrap." *Washington Post,* September 26, 2001.

Klaassen, Walter. *Anabaptism: Neither Catholic Nor Protestant.* 2d ed. Waterloo, Ont.: Conrad, 1981; 3d ed. Kitchener, Ont: Pandora, 2001.

———. "Who can be called Anabaptist?" *Mennonite Weekly Review* (October 17, 2005) 6.

Klaassen, Walter, ed. *Anabaptism Revisited*. Scottdale, PA: Herald, 1992.

Kniss, Fred. *Disquiet in the Land: Cultural Conflict in American Mennonite Communities*. New Brunswick, NJ: Rutgers University, 1997.

Kohn, Alfie. *No Contest: The Case Against Competition*. Boston: Houghton-Mifflin, 1986.

———. *The Brighter Side of Human Nature: Altruism and Empathy in Everyday Life*. New York: Basic, 1990.

Koontz, Ted. "Thinking Theologically About War Against Iraq." *Mennonite Quarterly Review* 77 (2003) 93–108.

Koop, Karl. *Anabaptist-Mennonite Confessions of Faith: The Development of a Tradition*. Kitchener, ON: Pandora, 2004.

Kraus, C. Norman. "American Mennonites and the Bible, 1750–1950." In *Essays on Biblical Interpretation: Anabaptist-Mennonite Perspectives*, edited by Willard M. Swartley, 131–50. Elkhart, IN: Institute of Mennonite Studies, 1984.

———. *God Our Savior: Theology in a Christological Mode*. Scottdale, PA: Herald, 1991.

———. *Jesus Christ Our Lord: Christology from a Disciple's Perspective*. Scottdale, PA: Herald, 1987.

———. "Jesus Christ, the Servant-King." In *Mennonite World Handbook: Mennonites in Global Witness*, edited by Dieter Götz Lichdi, 179–85. Carol Stream, IL: Mennonite World Conference, 1990.

———. "Reply to Interpretations and Criticisms." In *A Disciple's Christology: Appraisals of Kraus's Jesus Christ Our Lord*, edited by Richard A. Kauffman, 77–93. Elkhart: Institute of Mennonite Studies, 1989.

———. "Response to Thomas N. Finger." *Conrad Grebel Review* 9 (1990) 209–11.

———. "Toward a Theology for the Disciple Community." In *Kingdom, Cross, and Community*, edited by J. R. Burkholder and Calvin Redekop, 103–17. Scottdale, PA: Herald, 1976.

Liechty, Daniel. *Reflecting on Faith in a Post-Christian Time*. Telford, PA: Cascadia, 2003.

———. *Theology in Postliberal Perspective*. Philadelphia: Trinity Press International, 1990.

Lind, Millard C. "Reflections on Biblical Hermeneutics." In *Essays on Biblical Interpretation: Anabaptist-Mennonite Perspectives*, edited by Willard M. Swartley, 151–64. Elkhart, IN: Institute of Mennonite Studies, 1984.

Littell, Franklin. *The Free Church*. Boston: Starr King, 1957.

Loewen, Howard John. *One Lord, One Church, One Hope: Mennonite Confessions of Faith*. Elkhart, IN: Institute of Mennonite Studies, 1985.

Loy, David. "The Religion of the Market," *Journal of the American Academy of Religion* 65 (1997) 275–90.

MacMaster, Richard K. *Land, Piety, and Peoplehood: The Establishment of Mennonite Communities in America, 1683–1790*. Scottdale, PA: Herald, 1985.

———, et al, *Conscience and Crisis: Mennonites and Other Peace Churches in America, 1739–1789*. Scottdale, PA: Herald, 1979.

MacQuarrie, Brian. "Dobson's spiritual empire wields political clout." *Boston Globe* (October 9, 2005).

Marshall, Christopher. *Beyond Retribution: A New Testament Vision for Justice, Crime, and Punishment*. Grand Rapids, MI: Eerdmans, 2001.

Martin, J. Mark. "That's Why!" *The Turnpike Echo* 1.13 (Aug. 17, 1942) 5.

McClendon, James Wm., Jr. *Ethics: Systematic Theology*. Vol. 1. Nashville: Abingdon, 1986.

———. "The Radical Road One Baptist Took." In *Engaging Anabaptism: Conversations with a Radical Tradition*, edited by John D. Roth, 15–24. Scottdale, PA: Herald Press, 2001.

———. *Witness: Systematic Theology*. Vol. 3. Nashville: Abingdon, 2000.

McClendon, James Wm., Jr. and James M. Smith. *Convictions: Diffusing Religious Relativism*. Harrisburg, PA: Trinity Press International, 1994.

McNair, David. "War is not an accident: A profile of radical pacifist A.J. Muste," *Oldspeak: An Online Journal Devoted to Intellectual Freedom* (October 21, 2002) http://www.rutherford.org/oldspeak/articles/politics/oldspeak_muste.asp.

Miguez-Bonino, José. *Doing Theology in a Revolutionary Situation*. Philadelphia: Fortress, 1975.

Montagu, Ashley. *The Nature of Human Aggression*. New York: Oxford University, 1976.

Murray, Stuart. *Biblical Interpretation in the Anabaptist Tradition*. Kitchener, Ont.: Pandora, 2000.

Nelson, Richard, et al. *Patriotism and the American Land*. Great Barrington, MA: The Orion Society, 2002.

Neufeld, Vernon, ed. *If We Can Love: The Mennonite Mental Health Story*. Newton, KS: Faith and Life, 1983.

Niebuhr, H. Richard, "Introduction." In Ernst Troeltsch, *The Social Teaching of the Christian Churches*. Translated by Olive Wyon, 7–12. New York: Harper, 1960.

Ollenburger, Ben C. "The Hermeneutics of Obedience: Reflections on Anabaptist Hermeneutics." In *Essays on Biblical Interpretation: Anabaptist-Mennonite Perspectives*, edited by Willard M. Swartley, 45–61. Elkhart, IN: Institute of Mennonite Studies, 1984.

Olson, Roger E. *The Westminster Handbook to Evangelical Theology*. Louisville: Westminster John Knox, 2004.

Palmer, Parker J. *The Active Life: Wisdom for Work, Creativity, and Caring*. San Francisco: HarperCollins, 1990.

Pannabecker, Samuel Floyd. *Open Doors: A History of the General Conference Mennonite Church*. Newton, KS: Faith and Life, 1975

Pavlischek, Keith J. "Can the Vital Center Hold? A Critique of the Evangelical Pacifist Left." *The Brandywine Review of Faith & International Affairs* 31 (2005) 31–37.

Peck, James. *We Would Not Kill*. New York: Lyle Stuart, 1958.

Pipkin, H. Wayne, ed. *Essays in Anabaptist Theology*. Elkhart, IN: Institute of Mennonite Studies, 1994.

Redekop, Calvin W. "Power in the Anabaptist Community." In *Power, Authority, and the Anabaptist Tradition*, edited by Benjamin W. Redekop and Calvin W. Redekop, 174–92. Baltimore: Johns Hopkins University, 2001.

———. *The Free Church and Seductive Culture*. Scottdale, PA: Herald, 1970.

Reimer, A. James. *Mennonites and Classical Theology: Dogmatic Foundations for Christian Ethics*. Kitchener, Ont.: Pandora, 2001.

———. "Response to Glenn Brubacher." *Conrad Grebel Review* 5 (1987) 71–5.

———. "The Nature and Possibility of a Mennonite Theology." *Conrad Grebel Review* 1 (1983) 33–55.

Robinson, Mitchell Lee. "Civilian Public Service During World War II: The Dilemmas of Conscience in a Free Society." Ph.D. diss., Cornell University, 1990.

Roth, John D. "Called to One Peace: Christian Faith and Political Witness in a Divided Culture." *Mennonite Life* 60.2 (June 2005) http://www.bethelks.edu/mennonitelife/2005June/.

———, ed. *Engaging Anabaptism: Conversations with a Radical Tradition*. Scottdale, PA: Herald, 2001.

———. "Recent Currents in the Historiography of the Radical Reformation." *Church History* 71 (2002) 523–35.

Roy, Arundati. "Seize the Time." *In These Times* 27 (July 7, 2003) 17–8.

Sampson, Cynthia and John Paul Lederach, eds. *From the Ground Up: Mennonite Contributions to International Peacebuilding*. New York: Oxford University, 2000.

Sawatsky, Walter. "Historical Roots of a Post-Gulag Theology for Russian Mennonites." *Mennonite Quarterly Review* 76 (2002) 149–80.

Schell, Jonathan. *The Unconquerable World: Power, Nonviolence, and the Will of the People*. New York: Metropolitan, 2003.

Schipani, Daniel, ed. *Freedom and Discipleship: Liberation Theology in an Anabaptist Perspective*. Maryknoll, NY: Orbis, 1989.

Schlabach, Theron F. *Gospel Versus Gospel: Mission and the Mennonite Church, 1863–1944*. Scottdale, PA: Herald, 1980.

———. *Peace, Faith, Nation: Mennonites and Amish in Nineteenth-Century America*. Scottdale, PA: Herald, 1988.

Segundo, Juan Luis. *The Historical Jesus and the Synoptics*. Maryknoll, NY: Orbis, 1985.

———. *The Liberation of Theology*. Maryknoll, NY: Orbis, 1976.

Sharp, Gene. *The Politics of Nonviolent Action*. Boston: Porter Sargent, 1973.

Sibley, Mulford Q. and Philip E. Jacob. *Conscription of Conscience: The American State and the Conscientious Objector, 1940–1947*. Ithaca, NY: Cornell University, 1952.

Skillen, James W. and Keith J. Pavlischek. "Political Responsibility and the Use of Force: A Critique of Richard Hays." *Philosophia Christi* 3 (2001) 421–45.

Snyder, C. Arnold. *Anabaptist History and Theology: An Introduction*. Kitchener, Ont.: Pandora, 1995.

———. "*Anabaptist History and Theology*: History or Heresy? A reply to J. Denny Weaver," *Conrad Grebel Review* 16 (1998) 53–9.

———. *Following in the Footsteps of Christ: The Anabaptist Tradition*. Maryknoll, NY: Orbis, 2004.

———. *From Anabaptist Seed*. Kitchener, Ont.: Pandora, 1999.

———. *The Life and Thought of Michael Sattler*. Scottdale, PA: Herald, 1984.

Sobrino, Jon. *The True Church and the Poor*. Maryknoll, NY: Orbis, 1984.

Stayer, James M. *Anabaptists and the Sword*. Lawrence, KS: Coronado, 1972.

———. *The German Peasants' War and Anabaptist Community of Goods*. Buffalo, NY: McGill-Queen's University, 1991.

Stayer, James M., et al. "From Monogenesis to Polygenesis: The Historical Discussion of Anabaptist Origins." *Mennonite Quarterly Review* 49 (1975) 83–121.

Stout, Jeffrey. *Democracy and Tradition*. Princeton, NJ: Princeton University, 2004.

Swartley, Willard M. "Continuity and Change in Anabaptist-Mennonite Interpretations." In *Essays on Biblical Interpretation: Anabaptist-Mennonite Perspectives,* edited by Willard M. Swartley, 326–30. Elkhart, IN: Institute of Mennonite Studies, 1984.

Toews, John B. *Czars, Soviets, and Mennonites*. Newton, KS: Faith and Life, 1982.

Toews, Paul B. *Mennonites in American Society, 1930–1970: Modernity and the Persistence of Religious Community*. Scottdale, PA: Herald, 1996.

Toulmin. Stephen. *Cosmopolis: The Hidden Agenda of Modernity*. New York: Free, 1990.

Troeltsch, Ernst. *The Social Teaching of the Christian Churches,* translated by Olive Wyon. 1930. Reprinted, New York: Harper, 1960.

Bibliography

Urry, James. *None But Saints: The Transformation of Mennonite Life in Russia, 1789–1889.* Winnipeg, Man.: Hyperion, 1988.

Voran, Dallas. "CPS in Mississippi." *Box 96* 1.12 (March 1945) 2, 4.

Weaver, J. Denny. *Anabaptist Theology in Face of Postmodernity.* Telford, PA: Pandora, 2000.

———. *Becoming Anabaptist: The Origin and Significance of Sixteenth-Century Anabaptism.* Scottdale, PA: Herald, 1987; 2d ed., 2005.

———. "Mennonite Theological Self-Understanding." In *Mennonite Identity: Historical and Contemporary Perspectives,* edited by Calvin W. Redekop, 39–61. Washington, DC: University Press of America, 1988.

———. "Mennonites: Theology, Peace, and Identity." *Conrad Grebel Review* 6 (1988) 119–45.

———. "Parsing Anabaptist Theology: A Review Essay of Thomas N. Finger's *A Contemporary Anabaptist Theology.*" *Direction Journal* 34 (2005) 241–63.

———. "Perspectives on a Mennonite Theology." *Conrad Grebel Review* 2 (1984) 189–210.

———. "Response to Walter Klaassen." In *Anabaptist-Mennonite Identities in Ferment.* Edited by Leo Driedger and Leland Harder, 27–31. Elkhart: Institute of Mennonite Studies, 1990.

———. *The Nonviolent Atonement.* Grand Rapids, MI: Eerdmans, 2001.

Wherry, Neal W. *Conscientious Objection.* Washington, DC: Selective Service System, 1950.

Williams, George H. *The Radical Reformation.* 3d ed. Kirksville, MO: Sixteenth Century Journal, 1992.

Wilson, Edward O. *Consilience: The Unity of Knowledge.* New York: Knopf, 1998.

Wink, Walter. *Engaging the Powers: Discernment and Resistance in a World of Domination.* Minneapolis: Fortress, 1992.

Wittner, Lawrence S. *Rebels Against War: The American Peace Movement, 1941–1960.* New York: Columbia University, 1969.

Wright, N. T. *Jesus and the Victory of God.* Minneapolis: Fortress, 1996.

Yoder, Dwight V. "CPS at the Crossroads." *Skyliner* 1.10 (Oct. 1943) 2–3.

Yoder, John Howard. "A Summary of the Anabaptist Vision." In *An Introduction to Mennonite History*, 2d ed, edited by C. J. Dyck, 136–45. Scottdale, PA: Herald Press, 1981.

———. "Anabaptist Vision and Mennonite Reality." In *Consultation on Anabaptist-Mennonite Theology,* edited by A.J. Klassen, 1–46. Fresno, CA: Council on Mennonite Seminaries, 1970.

———. *Christian Attitudes Toward War, Peace, and Revolution: A Companion to Bainton.* Elkhart, IN: Peace Resource Center, 1983.

———. *Preface to Theology: Christology and Theological Method.* Grand Rapids, MI: Brazos, 2002.

———. *The Politics of Jesus.* 2d ed. Grand Rapids, MI: Eerdmans, 1994.

———. *The Priestly Kingdom: Social Ethics as Gospel.* Notre Dame, IN: Notre Dame University, 1983.

Zahn, Franklin. *Deserter from Violence: Experiments with Gandhi's Truth.* New York: Philosophical Library, 1984.

Zahn, Gordon. "A Descriptive Study of the Social Backgrounds of Conscientious Objectors in Civilian Public Service During World War II." Ph.D. diss, Catholic University of America, 1953.

Zehr, Howard. *Changing Lenses: A New Focus for Crime and Justice.* 3d ed. Scottdale, PA: Herald, 2004.

Modern Author Index

Alterman, Eric 21
Assman, Hugo 66–68
Bacevich, Andrew 17
Ballard, Bruce 10
Bender, Harold 11, 12, 14, 15, 18, 41, 236
Bernstein, Richard 175
Blunt, Sheryl Henderson 9
Bonhoeffer, Dietrich 1
Breech, James 172
Brock, Peter 100
Bruns, Gerald 70
Buber, Martin 43, 49, 174, 203
Bush, Perry 128, 136, 236
Carnes, Tony 9
Chomsky, Noam 17, 146, 147
Cox, Harvey 21, 32
Crowley, Michael 9
Davis, Mike 16, 32, 186
Dobson, James 9
Driedger, Leo 30, 49, 106
Driver, John 33
Durnbaugh, Donald 231
Dyck, C. J. 14, 92
Ediger, Elmer 132, 135
Eister, Allan W. 225, 226
Farley, Edward 163, 164, 171
Finger, Thomas 7, 23–29, 33–36, 110, 162, 167, 168, 170–72, 175
Forster, Walter 130
Frank, Thomas 17
Friesen, Duane 221, 222, 224, 233
Friesen, John 101
Gadamer, Hans–Georg 13, 14, 55, 58–64, 66, 67, 69
Gandhi, Mohandas 49, 147, 156, 203
Gara, Larry 134
Gara, Lenna Mae 134
Garrett, James Leo 229
Gilligan, James 52
Gingerich, Ray 6, 17, 30, 49

Gish, Arthur 10
Glock, Charles 225
Goertz, Hans–Jürgen 20
Goode, Erich 226, 227
Gorringe, Timothy 51
Grimsrud, Ted 15, 30, 32, 43, 48, 50, 73, 156, 157, 161, 175, 182
Gustafson, James 227
Gustafson, Paul 224–226
Gutierrez, Gustavo 65–68
Hammond, Phillip 225
Harnack, Adolf 222, 232
Hauerwas, Stanley 149–153, 157
Hershberger, Eugene 133
Hershberger, Guy F. 139, 238
Holland, Scott 48
Homan, Gerlof D. 128
Horst, Samuel 100
Hunsberger, Willard 130, 134
Hunter, Richard C. 135, 136
Jacob, Philip E. 129
Janzen, Waldemar 112
Jeschke, Marlin 118, 119
Johnson, Chalmers 17, 141
Juhnke, James 102, 128
Karp, Walter 146
Kaufman, Gordon 5, 37, 39, 44, 53, 161, 162, 172
Keim, Albert 12, 129, 130, 236
Kelly, Michael 21
Kenney, William 137
Kern, Kathleen 106
Klaassen, Walter 18, 20
Kniss, Fred 112
Kohn, Alfie 52, 170
Koontz, Ted 153–159
Koop, Karl 110
Kraus, C. Norman 59, 162, 168–171, 173, 175, 191
Kraybill, Donald 30, 49, 106
Lederach, John Paul 106

249

Liechty, Daniel 172
Lind, Millard C. 59
Littell, Franklin 229
Loewen, Howard John 110
Loy, David 21, 32
MacIntyre, Alasdair 151
MacMaster, Richard 99, 100
MacQuarrie, Brian 9
Marshall, Christopher 30
McClendon, James 4, 5, 13, 34, 35, 233
McNair, David 20
Miguez Bonino, Jose 66, 69
Montagu, Ashley 52
Murray, Stuart 58
Muste, A.J. 20
Nelson, Richard 147
Neufeld, Vernon 137
Niebuhr, H. Richard 225, 226, 232
Ollenberger, Ben C. 58
Olson, Roger 32
Palmer, Parker 173
Pannabecker, S. F. 137
Pavlischek, Keith 10
Peck, Jim 156
Rawls, John 152
Redekop, Calvin W. 120, 228, 229
Reimer, A. James 34, 48, 53, 162, 166, 167, 170–175
Robinson, Mitchell 129
Roth, John 18, 91
Roy, Arundati 148
Sampson, Cynthia 106
Sawatsky, Walter 102
Schell, Jonathan 146, 147, 155, 158
Schipani, Daniel 159
Schlabach, Theron 100, 102, 112
Schüssler Fiorenza, Elisabeth 69
Segundo, Juan–Luis 65, 67, 68
Sharp, Gene 155
Sibley, Mulford Q. 129
Skillen, James 10
Snyder, C. Arnold 41, 92, 94, 95
Sobrino, Jon 65, 69
Stayer, James 19, 20, 93
Stoltzfus, Grant M. 130
Stout, Jeffrey 148–153, 155, 157–159
Swartley, Willard 6, 59, 238
Toews, John B. 101
Toews, Paul B. 102, 138

Toulmin, Stephen 51
Troeltsch, Ernst 213–228, 231–233
Tutu, Demond 183
Urry, James 101
Weaver, Alain Epp 161
Weaver, J. Denny 29, 41, 92, 95, 161, 162, 169–171, 173, 175
Weber, Max 225
Westcott, James 185
Wherry, Neal W. 128
Williams, George 92, 93
Willimon, William 152
Wilson, Edward O. 51
Wilson, Robert Q. 52
Wink, Walter 5, 30, 32, 49
Wittgenstein, Ludwig 4
Wittner, Lawrence 130
Wright, N.T. 18, 142
Yoder, John Howard 2, 4, 6, 9, 10, 14, 15, 19. 28, 30, 34, 35, 53, 95, 145, 149, 151, 175, 228–231
Zahn, Gordon 134, 135
Zahn, Franklin 156
Zehr, Howard 6, 30, 32, 48, 181
Zwingli, Ulrich 55, 92, 93

Scripture Index

Genesis	74, 199		*Jeremiah*	78, 79
1	50, 73, 205		29:7	79
2	203, 206			
3	73, 193		*Daniel*	192
4–11	73			
11	73		*Hosea*	78, 194
12	73, 74, 184		11	78
12:3	73, 157		11:1	78
			11:2	78
Exodus	188		11:8–9	78
15	74			
1:13–14	188		*Amos*	78, 194, 202
2:23–25	74		2:6–7	78
19:6	75		5:2	78
Deuteronomy			*Micah*	183
17:1–7	77		6:8	183
Joshua			*Matthew*	
8:18–29	75		18	119
			28:18–20	184
Judges	76			
8:23	76		*Mark*	80, 194
			1:15	194
1 Samuel			2:23–28	182
8:1–3	76		8:3–5	81
8:5	76		8:27–38	81
8:11–18	76		11:18	82
1 Kings			*Luke*	
9:6–8	77		7:18–23	194
11:4	77			
21	77		*John*	
			1:10	173, 208
Job	211		2:23–24	81
			3:16	159, 173, 208
Isaiah			19:13	82
40	194			
53	192		*Acts*	82, 83
			1:8	82, 208
			3:2–5	83

Acts (continued)
3:13	83
7:58	84
9:1	84
9:3–9	84

Romans 187, 188
1	188
1–3	85
1:5	83
6:1–4	117
12	120
12:1–2	119
13:8	85

1 Corinthians
2:8	114

Galatians
1:13–14	84

Revelation 43, 44, 50, 75, 85, 86, 87, 182, 184, 187, 188, 209, 210, 211
2–3	187
5	86
5:6	86
13:4	86
13:10	75
19	209
20	211
21	50
21–22	74, 87, 88, 159, 211
21:1	87
21:1–4	182
21:12	87
22:1–2	87

Subject Index

Abraham 73–74, 83, 157, 184, 195
Academic freedom 237–39
Anabaptism, definition of 3, 7, 11, 12–21, 41, 58–59, 142–44
Anabaptist assimilation; acculturation 100–105, 120, 123
Anabaptist church discipline 118–19, 208
Anabaptist Confessions of Faith 110–11
Anabaptist distinctiveness 23, 29, 41, 58–59, 94–95, 109, 111, 122, 124, 143–44, 157–59, 175, 218–19
Anabaptist ethnicity 42, 97, 102, 105
Anabaptist higher education 235–39
Anabaptist migrations; search for tolerance 96–103, 145
Anabaptist origins 92–94
Anabaptist priesthood of believers 95, 98, 105, 118
Anabaptist separation; non–conformity 17, 95, 98, 102, 105–06, 119–22, 159
Anabaptist theology 2, 5, 7, 9, 23–36, 38, 70–71, 87–88, 96, 109–24, 139–40, 154, 159, 161–76, 191–211, 235–39
Anabaptist tradition 1–3, 10–13, 16, 21, 22, 2527, 33, 41–42, 44, 55, 58–59, 88, 91–107, 142–45, 179, 215, 236
Anabaptist witness; outreach; evangelism 17, 22, 42, 97, 122–24, 144–45, 229–30
Anabaptists and economic sharing 20, 21, 23, 144
Anabaptists as troublesome 17–21, 27
Anabaptists, persecution of 41–42, 94–96, 102, 122, 141, 230
Baptism 3, 4, 12, 18, 32, 41–42, 92, 95–98, 106, 114–17, 122, 175
Believers churches; minority traditions 227–33
Bias in interpretation 61–63, 67–71
Bible; scripture 10, 28, 31, 32, 39–40, 49–50, 53, 55, 57–71, 73–88, 93, 95,

Bible; scripture (*continued*)
98, 105, 111–13, 158, 164, 167–70, 172–73, 175–76, 179–81, 183, 195–99
Biblical apocalyptic 186–88
Biblical law 75, 85, 182, 188
Christian community; faith community 1, 2, 5, 10, 14, 21, 22, 47, 55, 74, 79, 82, 87–88, 106, 113, 117–19, 133–36, 138, 142, 144, 151–52, 162, 173, 189, 207–08, 213, 228, 235–39
Christology 25, 53, 110–11, 113–14, 154, 191–95
Citizenship 141–59, 183–84
Civilian Public Service 127–40
Compromise 222–24
Congregational theology 38, 39, 41, 44–45, 176
Conscientious objection 101, 103–05, 125, 127–40, 145, 156
Constructive theology 39, 171–72, 174–75
Convictions 4, 5, 7–11, 21, 23, 27, 35, 36, 47, 87–88, 96, 102, 105, 109–10, 144–45, 152–53, 157, 179
Creation 73, 174, 182, 201, 203, 205
Cross; crucifixion 81–82, 194–95
Democracy 141–42, 144, 146–59
Discipleship; following Jesus 1, 12, 38, 41, 58, 70, 86, 87, 93, 95, 98, 113–14, 116, 123, 179, 220
Ecclesiology; doctrine of the church 169, 207–08, 239
Economics 16, 20, 32, 80, 144, 159, 183, 185–86, 229
Empire; militarism 16, 17, 19, 21, 22, 71, 76–77, 79, 85, 88, 141–42, 146–48, 154–55, 158, 187
Eschatology; vision 25, 32, 43–44, 52–53, 171, 177, 179–89, 209–11
Ethics 34, 37–38, 44, 47, 49, 70–71, 164–65, 231

Subject Index

Free church 19, 115, 143, 157–58, 231, 233
Globalization 185–88
God, Doctrine of 30, 47–53, 74–75, 84–86, 88, 93–95, 112, 147, 155, 158–59, 165, 180–81, 229
God's healing strategy 73–88, 184–85
Heaven 180–81, 210–11
Hermeneutics; reading strategies 13–16, 28, 39, 40, 55, 57–71, 111–13, 164, 171–72, 175, 197–99
Historical consciousness 60, 66, 163–65, 171–73
Holy Spirit 32, 82, 111–12, 115, 176, 196, 202–04
Hope 43–44, 87
Humanity, theology of 43, 115, 170, 174, 193, 204–07
Jesus, story of; message of 4, 9–11, 13, 15, 16, 18, 21, 23–25, 28, 30, 31, 35, 36, 47, 48, 50, 53, 58, 70, 79–82, 112–14, 154–55, 169, 176, 182, 184–85, 187, 191–95, 197–202, 204–06, 208–11, 216, 228
Justice 10, 20, 22, 25, 30, 34, 47, 48, 51, 65, 69, 75–80, 85, 88, 119, 151–52, 183, 193–94, 200, 202–03, 210, 217
Kingship 75–79, 184, 205
Liberalism 150–52
Liberation theology 57–58, 64–71, 159
Mainstream Christian theology 1, 29–36, 50–51, 164
Mennonites 1–3, 11, 12, 15, 22, 24, 91–92, 96–107, 109–24, 128–40, 145, 238
Mental health work 137–38
Moses 74–75, 77
Mutual aid 41, 103, 123–24, 230
Neo-Mennonites 161–79
Objectivity 61–63, 65
Pacifism; nonviolence 1, 2, 4, 7, 9, 11, 12, 14–20, 22, 23, 25, 28, 30, 35, 36, 41, 47–53, 86, 88, 95, 98, 101, 103, 105–06, 127–40, 143, 147, 152–58, 165, 175, 192
Pastoral ministry 37, 38, 163
Paul 83–85, 176, 216
Philosophical hermeneutics 57–71
Practice-oriented theology 31–33, 35–37, 109–24, 191

Religious "idea" 215–16, 220–22, 232
Resurrection 82, 188, 192, 194–95
Salvation 25, 32–33, 41, 50, 73, 75, 83, 111, 115, 154, 181, 187, 193–95, 203, 206–07
Sectarianism; church–sect typology 215–33
Sin 69, 85, 110–11, 114, 116, 132, 195, 200, 206–07
Suspicion 68–69, 94, 164, 228
Theological language 5, 153–57, 165
Theological method 7, 28–33, 37–45, 49–53, 69–70, 166–76
Tradition 50–51, 60, 89, 164
Violence 19, 31–32, 47–53, 74–75, 84–86, 88, 93–95, 112, 147, 155, 158–59, 165, 180–81, 229
Worldviews 5, 180, 181, 186, 188

www.ingramcontent.com/pod-product-compliance
Lightning Source LLC
Chambersburg PA
CBHW062011220426
43662CB00010B/1289